AUGUSTUS JOHN

JACOB EPSTEIN

JAMES DICKSON INNES

GWEN JOHN

HENRY LAMB

DERWENT LEES

WYNDHAM LEWIS

WILLIAM ORPEN

WILLIAM ROTHENSTEIN

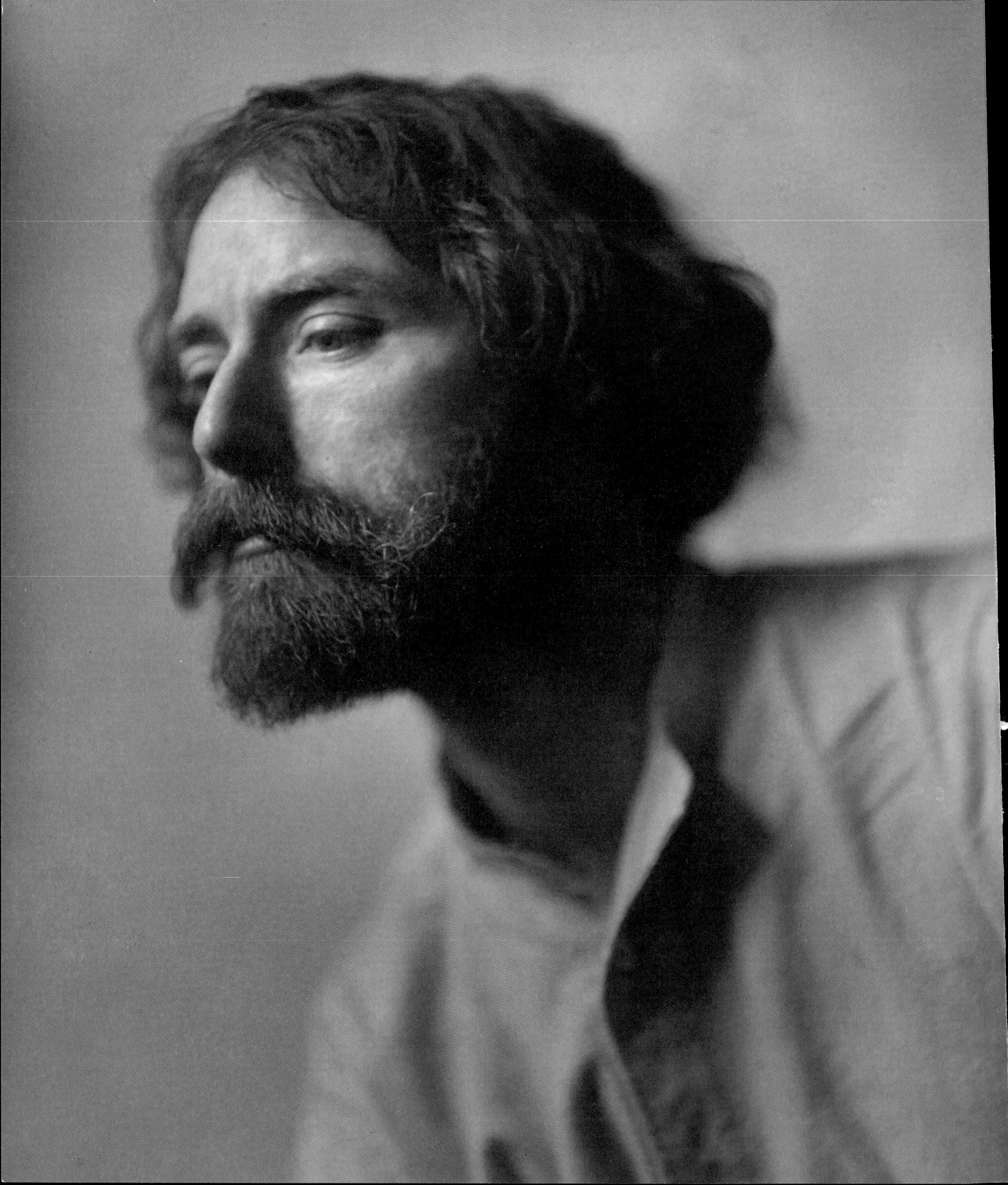

AUGUSTUS JOHN
& the First Crisis of Brilliance

David Boyd Haycock

96 / 129 Portland Road
London W11 4LW
+44 (0)20 7229 1099
piano-nobile.com

PIANO
NOBILE

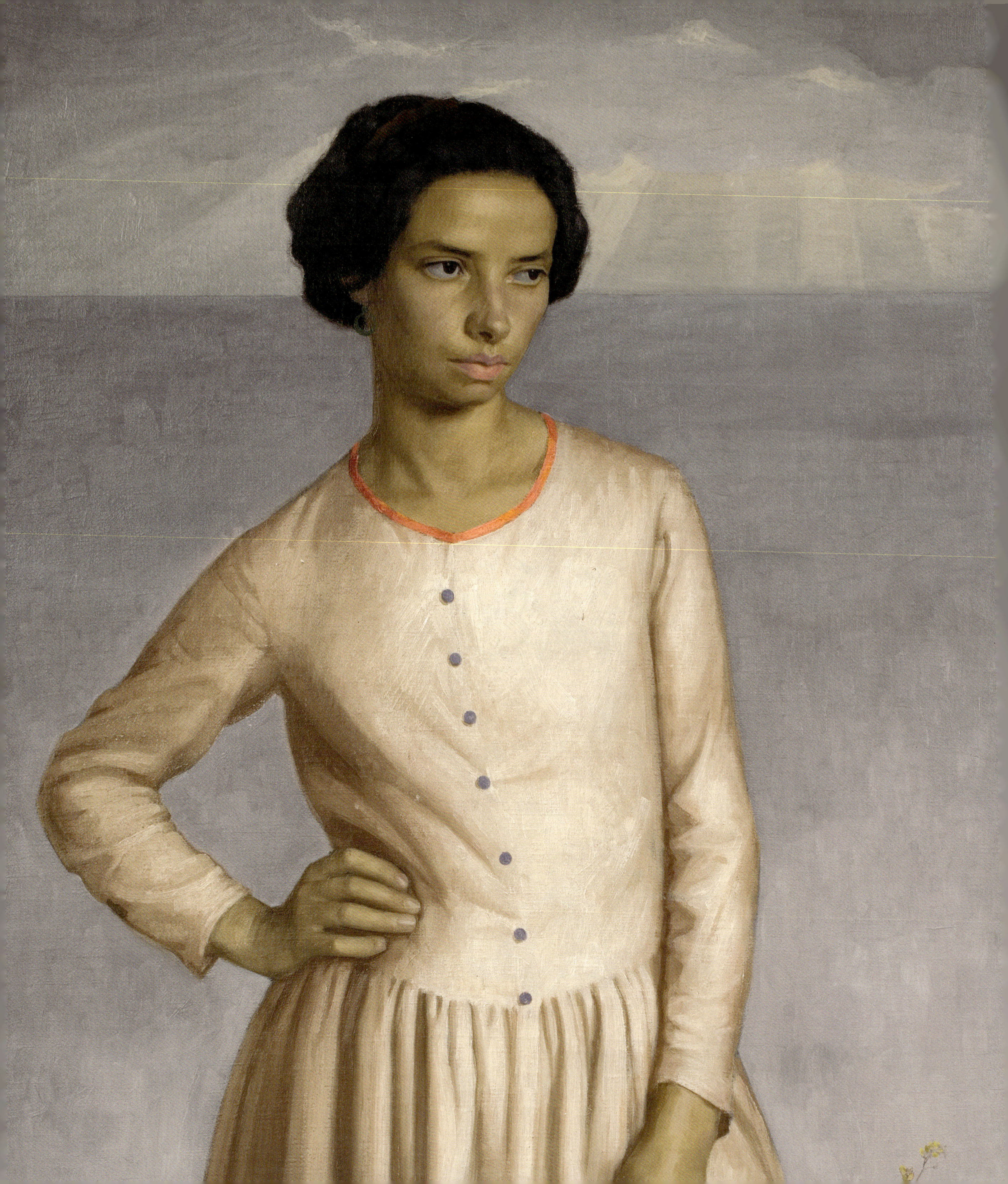

CONTENTS

PIANO NOBILE

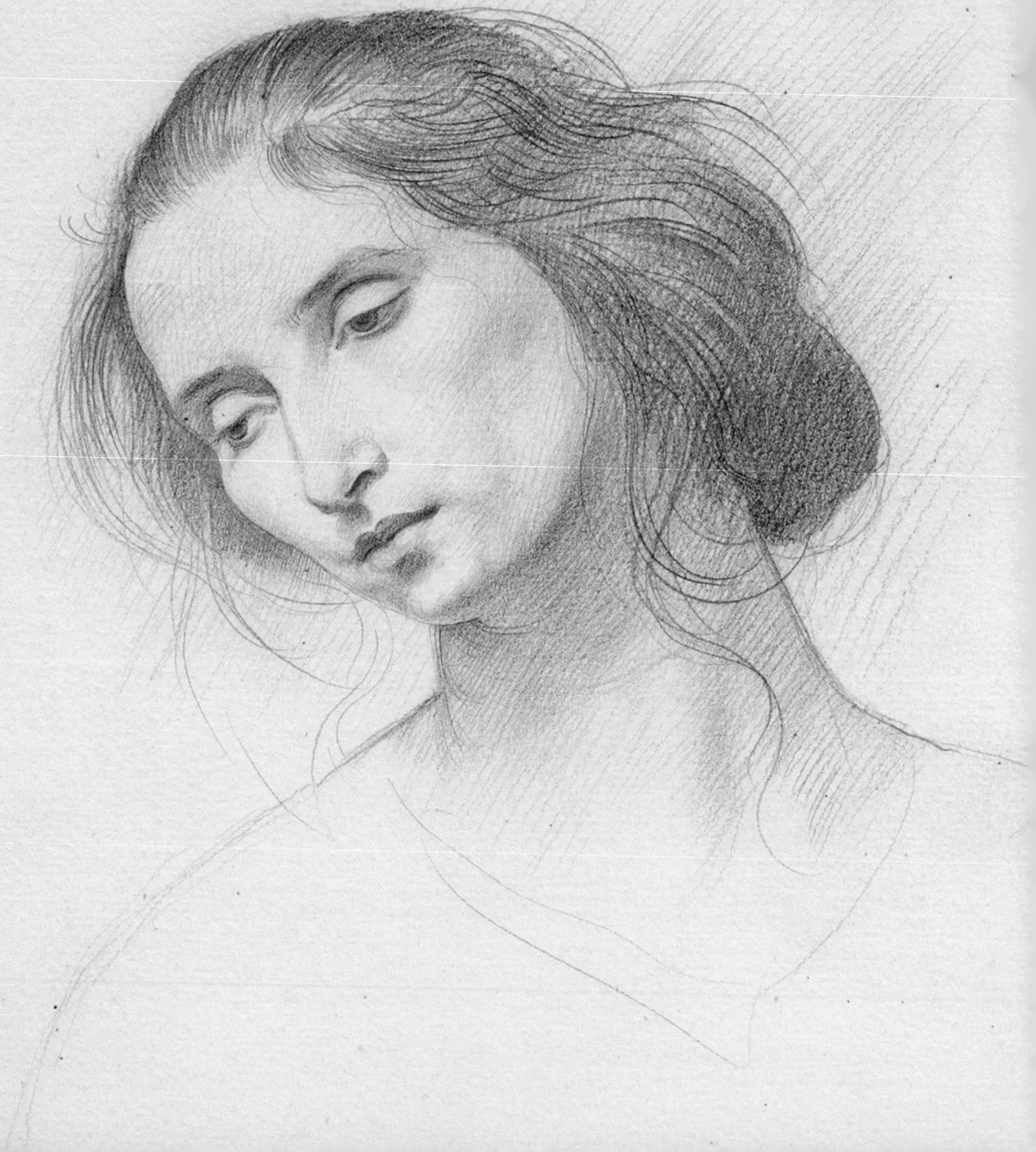

PREFACE

Robert and Matthew Travers

Augustus John and the First Crisis of Brilliance tells the story of not one but several highly talented artists. Although Augustus John was the leading light of his generation, a bohemian with strong instincts, his wide circle of friends included many other brilliant pictorial artists. Many of them studied at the Slade School of Art in the 1890s and contributed to what their tutor, Henry Tonks, described as the school's first 'crisis of brilliance'. Augustus's older sister Gwen John began her studies there a year later than he did in 1895, while William Orpen was there between 1897 and 1899.

Others encountered John as fresh-faced admirers. Wyndham Lewis was a Slade student between 1898 and 1901, and first sighted the great man when John returned one day to work in the life room. Henry Lamb studied under him and Orpen in 1906 at the short-lived Chelsea Art School. Under John's auspices his young friends Lewis, Lamb and James Dickson Innes joined him in 1911 as members of the Camden Town Group, a project overseen in part by John's direct contemporary Spencer Gore (himself another Slade alumnus). And it was together with Innes and another Slade artist, Derwent Lees, that John took inspiration from Snowdonia in 1911–13.

Much as British art was set alight in the 1910s by the milieu of artists and writers centred on Vanessa Bell, Roger Fry and Duncan Grant, just a few years earlier Augustus John and his peers likewise were living and working in the vanguard of creativity. These circles intersected for a time: Clive and Vanessa Bell purchased John's work, the Omega Workshops recruited Wyndham Lewis, they all frequented the Café Royal, and there were many mutual friends and acquaintances. The 'art world' they shared was a very small and tangled one.

We are delighted to have had curatorial assistance from Dr David Boyd Haycock who we worked with previously in relation to Mark Gertler and Paul Nash, two artists who featured in David's earlier book *A Crisis of Brilliance* (2009), which told the story of a later, equally gifted generation of Slade students. His new book *Brilliant Destiny: The Age of Augustus John* (2023) provided the inspiration for this exhibition, which follows a similar chronology beginning with John's student days and continuing until the outbreak of war in 1914. We are grateful to him for his insightful contributions that follow here.

This exhibition and publication would not have been possible without loans from private collectors, and we are hugely grateful to them for generously lending their precious possessions. The exhibition has also been significantly enhanced by loans from Ben Uri Gallery & Museum and Southampton City Art Gallery. It is an honour to work with these institutions and we are very grateful to them and their staff.

Cat.8 (detail)

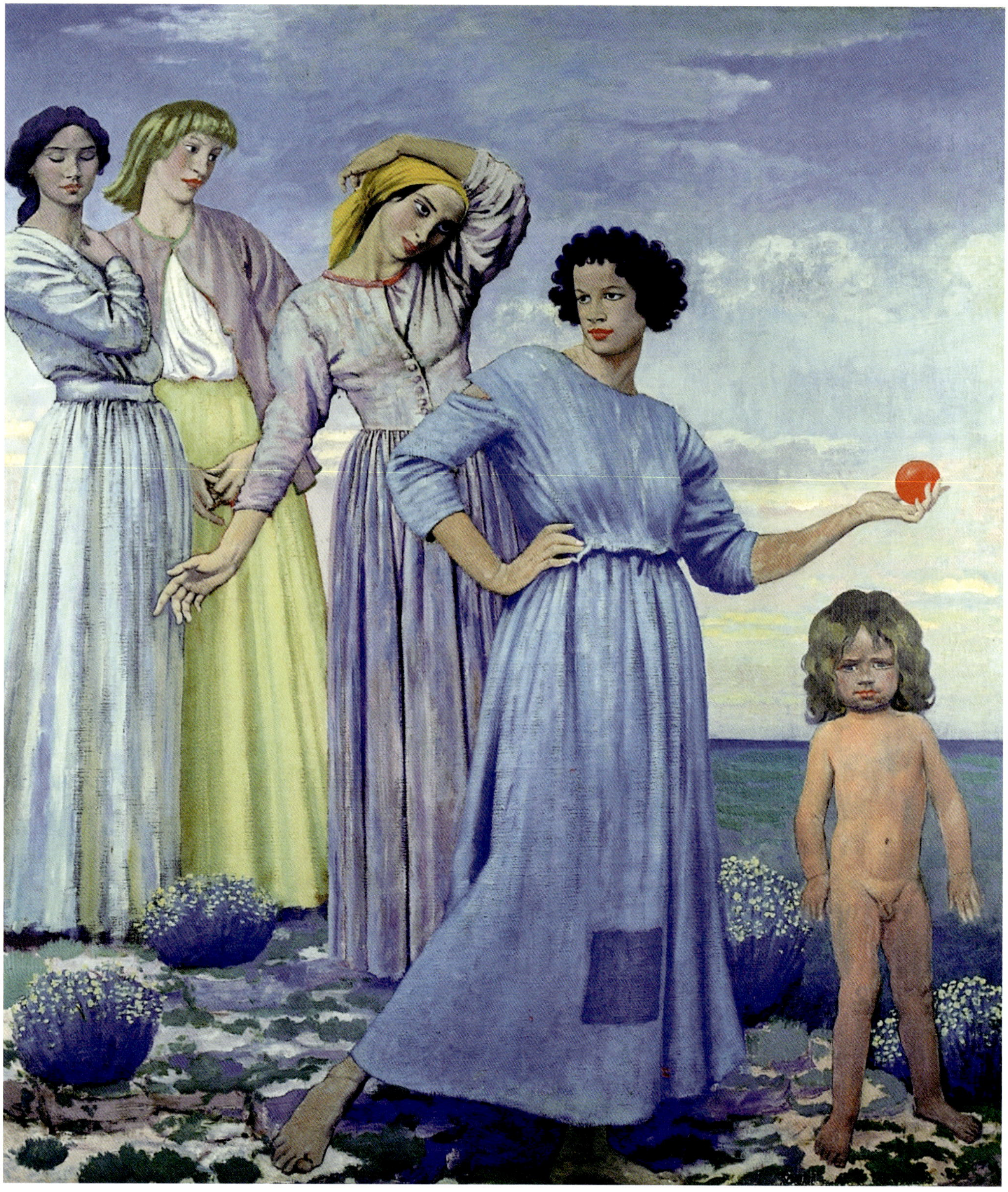

Fig. 1. Augustus John, *The Way Down to the Sea*, 1909–11, Private Collection

'THE PROMISE OF ASTONISHING GENIUS'

David Boyd Haycock

> *Talent* and *genius* [...] are not merely different, they are in polar opposition to each other. *Talent* is intellectual power of every kind, which acts and manifests itself [...] through the *will* and the *active* forces. *Genius* [...] is that much rarer species of intellectual power which is derived from the *genial* nature—from the spirit of suffering and enjoying—from the spirit of pleasure and pain.[1]
>
> —Thomas de Quincey (1834)

It was Henry Tonks, Master of Drawing and then Slade Professor at the Slade School of Art in London, who coined the paradoxical phrase 'a crisis of brilliance.' I believe that by this incongruous phrase he was suggesting that technical skill is not sufficient to guarantee artistic success. Even the most gifted student has to pass through numerous challenges—or crises—before achieving mastery and reputation. In the era of Augustus John, who attended the Slade between 1894 and 1898, these were, potentially, many. The most serious, perhaps, was the crisis of influence—which, in part, is what this exhibition is about: the relationships between a group of artist friends, how they influenced each other, learnt from each other, helped and even sometimes hindered one another.

Just as important though was the influence of history. Tonks encouraged his students to study the old masters first hand, to look at the work of Ingres, Van Dyck, Raphael, Michelangelo and Titian in the British Museum and the National Gallery. The deeper John dived into the history of art, however, the more complicated things seemed to become. As a young teenager growing up in south-west Wales he had fallen in love with the Pre-Raphaelites; arriving at the Slade he fell under the spell of James McNeill Whistler, Aubrey Beardsley and (following a trip to Amsterdam) Rembrandt, who became his greatest idol. Later, in Paris in the early 1900s, he encountered the work of the the French Symbolist painter Pierre Puvis de Chavannes (1824–1898), and then that of Paul Cezanne; in 1907 he met no less a figure than Picasso, quickly coming to admire the young Spaniard's 'Blue Period.' Not long afterwards he made a trip through northern Italy. There he extended his knowledge of the Renaissance, and in Florence he particularly admired Botticelli's *Primavera*.

Each encounter influenced John's work. 'Such [artistic] progress as is possible,' he reflected in 1941,

> seems [...] to necessitate a backward route. As by way of the eighteenth we arrive at the seventeenth century, so by another stage we reach the Renaissance and from there overtake the 'Primitives' to linger at Byzantium

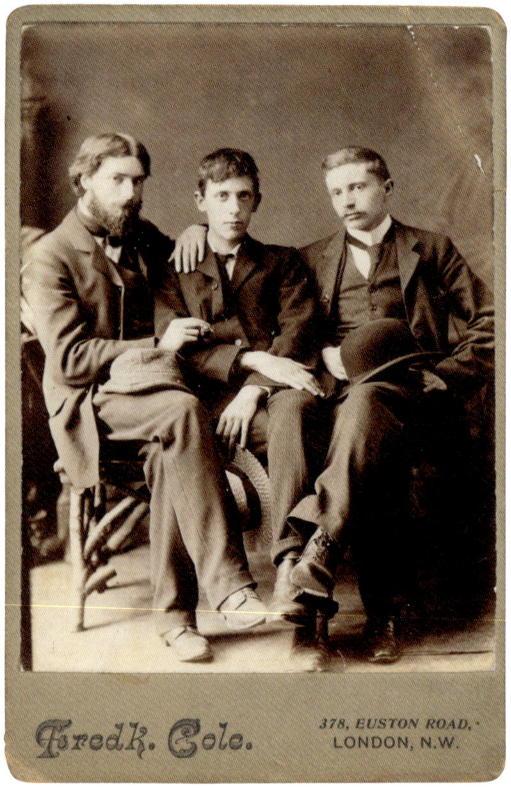

Fig. 2. Augustus John, Ambrose McEvoy and Philip Wilson Steer, c. 1900, photographed by Frederick Cole, National Portrait Gallery, London

> before plunging into Antiquity. This of course leads us to the East and Pre-History where at last crawling into the caverns of Paleolithic man we think we have come to the end of the journey.[2]

The weight of history on John was clear to contemporaries. In 1914 the eminent critic Sir Claude Phillips wrote that though, in 'his best moments,' John was 'a magnificent painter,' he was yet nothing more than 'a compound of Puvis de Chavannes and Piero della Francesca, with certain minor and more modern influence.'[3] John's friend and antagonist, Percy Wyndham Lewis, agreed. In 1915 he claimed that John had 'tried his hand at the whole of European art, from Giotto to Watteau and Constantin Guys. Rodin and Degas marked the limit of his scholastic appetite, I think.'[4] Or, as another (more admiring) critic put it in 1917, 'the whole character of the art of Augustus John [...] combines the most reckless allusions to the work of past painters with the strongest expression of personal identity.'[5]

If history posed its problems, the present could be no less intimidating. Another potential crisis for John and his young contemporaries was the challenge of finding an artistic direction and identity in a time of revolution in art. The period from the 1880s to the 1910s was an anarchic one, when various movements—from Realism and Symbolism to Post-Impressionism and Cubism—vied noisily for attention. Added to this there were the potential (perhaps unavoidable) crises involved in one's personal life, never easy for youth. Early adolescent friendships and relationships can often be followed by conflict, heartbreak, or—at the very worst—death. By 1914 John had lost his mother, his wife ('I am not going to set down a catalogue of my sensations during this long-drawn-out crisis,' he recorded in his last autobiography), as well as his favourite son and two good friends, Spencer Gore and James Dickson Innes.[6] And if the personal crises of grief, or boredom, or the occasional loss of confidence were to be tempered by the delights of alcohol, or sex, then this could easily lead one off the path of hard work (which was ever a danger for John). These, then, were just some of the challenges he and his young contemporaries had to face—not to mention the great crisis that overwhelmed everyone in the summer of 1914, with the devastating outbreak of war.

According to Tonks, whose long career at the Slade spanned the years 1892 to 1930, there were just two 'crises of brilliance' at the school. The second was the group of artists who gathered in the period immediately prior to the outbreak of the First World War. They included David Bomberg, Dora Carrington, John Currie, Mark Gertler, Paul Nash, C.R.W. Nevinson, William Roberts, Stanley Spencer and Edward Wadsworth. The School's 'first crisis of brilliance,' though, had been in the 1890s, when its students had included not just Augustus John and his sister Gwen, but also Edna Clarke-Hall, Spencer Gore, Percy Wyndham Lewis, Ambrose McEvoy (fig. 2), Ida Nettleship and William Orpen.

Despite the reservations of critics and friends, for much of the first half of the twentieth century Augustus John was in the front rank of living British artists. At the time of his death he was widely (if not universally) hailed as one of the greatest of all British painters. According to *The Times* in its obituary published on 1 November 1961, in his latter years John's work had been bought 'eagerly [...] by a public which had learnt to think of him as the great genius who could do nothing wrong.'[7] It was even before he had left the Slade in 1898 that John was being spoken of as something more than simply a master draughtsman—he was a 'genius'. One of John's earliest admirers, the artist William Rothenstein, recorded that Tonks liked to relate 'a story that John was quiet, methodical and by no means remarkable when he first came to the Slade.' Then, while home in Tenby one summer vacation from the Slade, he dived into the sea, 'struck his head on a rock, and came out of the water—a genius!'[8]

Whilst John acknowledged the truth of his diving accident, he denied any sudden transformation. Nevertheless, Rothenstein would bow to what was certainly the extraordinary gift of the young student. He later wrote that even before John left the Slade at the age of twenty, 'he gave promise of astonishing genius,' already possessing 'the copiousness which goes with genius,' together with 'the eager understanding, the imagination, the readiness for intellectual and physical adventure one associates with genius.' Just a year later, as they holidayed together in Normandy, painting and drawing, 'everything John did bore the mark of genius.'[9] This then, would be a particular crisis of John's own: the burden of expectation, the weight associated with carrying the mantle of genius.

'Genius' was a word that recurred throughout John's life. This was sometimes to his detriment, for his work certainly did not please—or impress—everyone. 'Mr. John is evidently a genius,' a review in *The Athenaeum* conceded in 1902, 'if by that we understand the power of seeing things in a new and personal manner; but his work shows a perverse disregard of beauty which is to be regretted. Since his originality is assured he might the more safely aim at academic excellences [*sic*], and emulate that more persuasive style which tradition and authority command.'[10] In the years that followed this review, claims for John's 'academic excellences' rose and fell. In 1938, by which time John was approaching his sixtieth birthday, Anthony Blunt would write possibly the best known critical response of the artist's whole career: 'Everyone is agreed on the fact that Augustus John was born with a quite exceptional talent—some even use the word genius—and almost everyone is agreed that he has in some way wasted it.' It was perhaps little compensation that in this *Spectator* article Blunt went on to add, 'John is almost as gifted as a painter can be. It is only because his gifts are so great that one is forced to judge him by the very highest standards, and it is only by such standards that he seems to fail.'[11]

This word 'genius' is a complicated one. It originates from the eponymous Latin word, which itself derives from the verb *gignere*, to beget (an etymological root that, appropriately enough, also gives us the English word 'genitals'). The *genius* was the pagan Roman (male) 'guardian spirit,' allotted to a man at birth, and which governed his fortunes, determined his character, and in due course guided him to the next world. The concept of the artistic 'genius' had its origins in the Renaissance, and the wonder expressed by writers such as Giorgio Vasari at the extraordinary creative achievements of artists such as Michelangelo, Leonardo da Vinci and Raphael. By the mid-eighteenth century it had achieved the meaning by which we best understand it in our current context: 'Innate intellectual or creative power of an exceptional or exalted type,' as the *Oxford English Dictionary* defines it, 'instinctive and extraordinary capacity for imaginative creation, original thought, invention, or discovery.'[12] The German philosopher Immanuel Kant made a lengthy investigation of genius in *The Critique of Judgement* (1790). For Kant, the primary definition of genius was 'a *talent* for producing that for which no definite rule can be given: and not an aptitude in the way of cleverness for what can be learned according to some rule; and that consequently *originality* must be its primary property.'[13]

It was not an easy mantle to carry. In his 1864 essay on William Shakespeare, the French writer Victor Hugo—who aspired to the title himself—declared: 'A genius is a man accused.' Men of genius like Shakespeare, Dante, Michelangelo, Rembrandt and Beethoven were, Hugo explained, 'imperious, tumultuous, violent, passionate beings, hard riders of winged steeds, [and] transgressors of limits [...].' Another French writer, Balzac, saw genius as (perhaps) a form of illness. The artist, he wrote, works 'under the sway of certain circumstances whose combination is a mystery. He is not master of himself.'[14] In cultural as well as medical terms, the notion of genius enjoyed its heyday in Hugo and Balzac's era, the nineteenth century. Its nature was explored in books such as *Hereditary Genius: An Inquiry into its Laws and Consequences* (1869), written by Charles Darwin's cousin, Francis Galton. In her recent study, *Genius in France: An Idea and its Uses*, Ann Jefferson argues that since the word lacked clear definition, it possessed an elasticity of meaning that allowed it to be widely applied, yet broadly understood, with clear associations to notions of originality and uniqueness.[15] A consensus also existed that genius was generally a masculine trait. Exceptions to this interpretation tended either to reject their femininity (in the case of the painter Rosa Bonheur), or ran the risk of mental collapse (as in the case of Rodin's great protégée, the sculptor Camille Claudel: 'A genius such as yours is rare,' Rodin told her in 1897.[16] But she would spend the last thirty years of her life locked away in an asylum).

The idea of the artistic 'genius' has now largely fallen out of critical use—partly because it has accrued certain negative associations, particularly those of masculinity and reckless indifference to others, that have become unfashionable, or outdated. In her influential 1971 essay, 'Why Have There Been No Great Women Artists?', Linda Nochlin argued that scholars would have

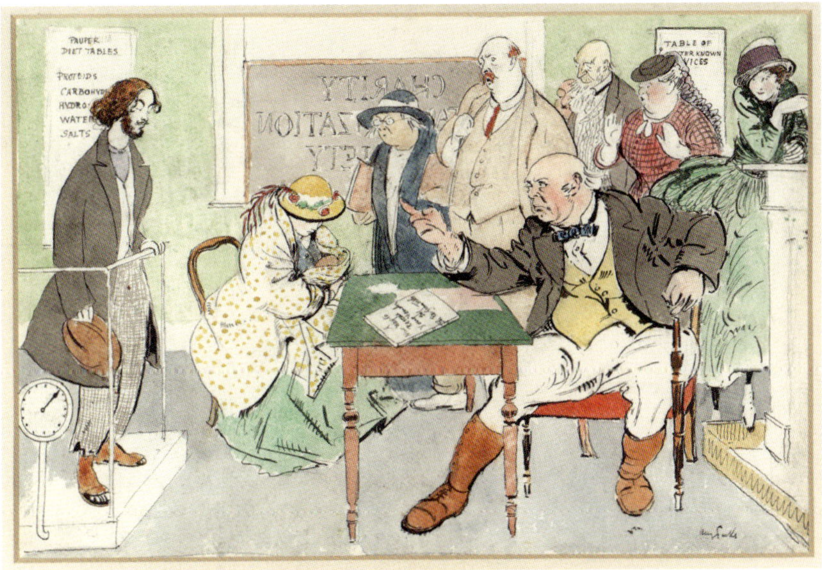

Fig. 3. Henry Tonks, *Charity Organization Society*, n.d., Tate

to 'abandon the notion, consciously articulated or not, of individual genius as innate, and as primary to the creation of art.'[17] In the 1990s the Guerrilla Girls featured it as one of the ten commandments in their poster, *Code of Ethics for Art Museums*: 'Thou shalt admit to the Public that words such as genius, masterpiece, seminal, potent, tough, gritty and powerful are used solely to prop up the Myth and inflate the Market Value of White Male Artists.'[18] This is not entirely true (these words might equally well describe a black artist such as Jean-Michel Basquiat, and museums have other interests beside market value) but it is forcefully put. More recently, art historian Ruth Millington has similarly described the artist 'genius' as a 'myth,' one that 'perpetuates the idea that the success of the world's greatest artists rest on their natural creative talent, above all else. A gendered term, genius is also the preserve of men, with the likes of Michelangelo and Manet, Rossetti and Picasso meeting its masculine criteria. Dreaming up ideas in isolation and driven by unstoppable originality, these individuals made "masterpieces" alone in their studios, or so the story goes.'[19]

In a 2020 article in *The Paris Review* the American cultural critic Cody Delistraty argued in a similar vein. 'The Artistic Genius is certain of his talents', Delistraty suggests: 'he is certain of his project. These men were emotionally brutal, sure in their vision, often blustering and quick to anger.'[20] Whilst John (though sometimes too uncertain of his direction) might appear to fit this latter pattern, I do not consider the word 'genius' without use or meaning. Many students attend art school; few prosper. Hard work is not enough; something more than mere talent, too, is required. What is that magic, mysterious, inspiring ingredient if not, in some measure or another, that which is best described as 'genius'? If this is the case, what is it that John achieves in his work that might make one consider him 'a genius'? For many admirers of his early work it lies in

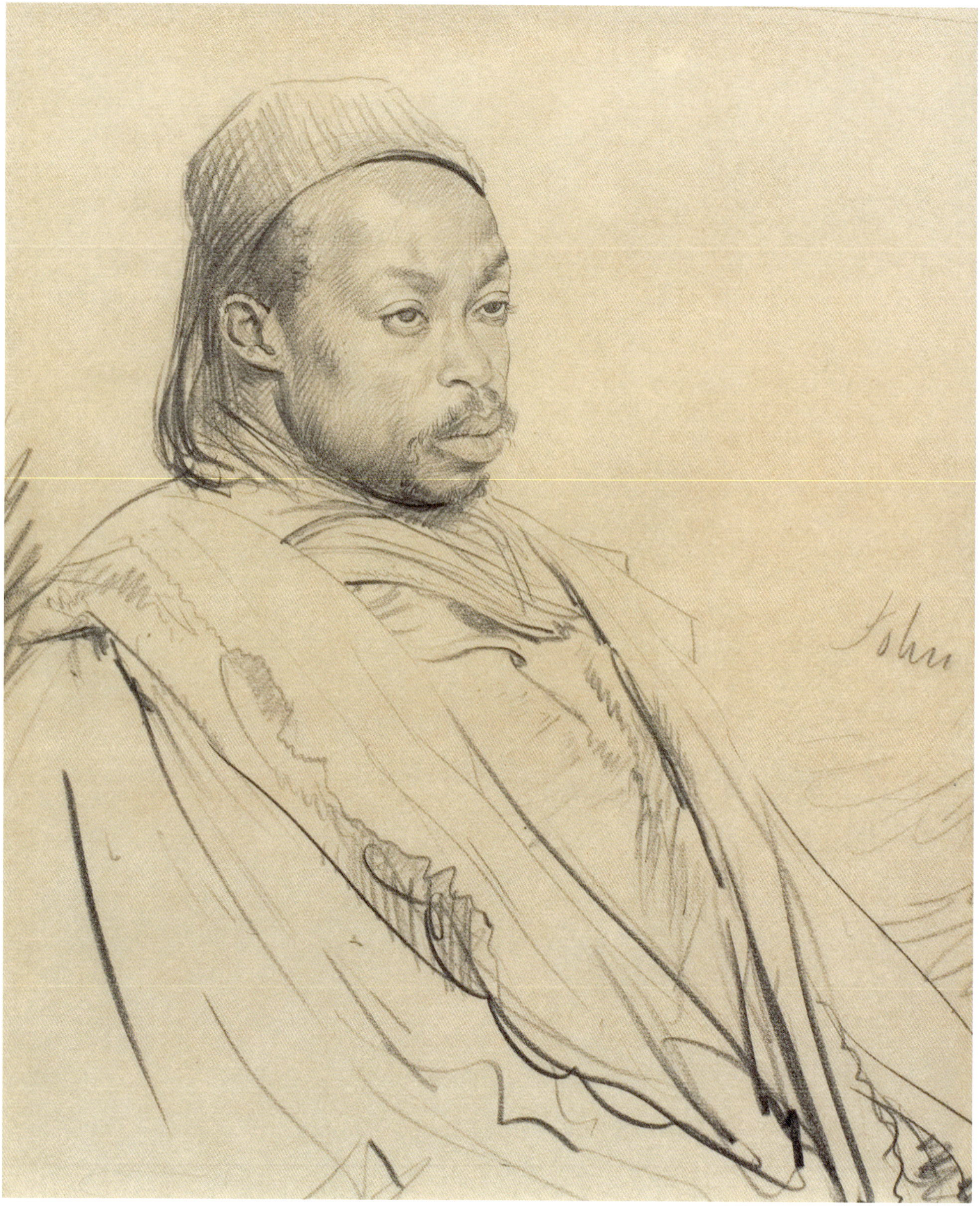

Fig. 4. Augustus John, *The Moor*, c. 1900–05, Private Collection

his drawings (fig. 4). The very best have an intensity and beauty to them that is almost unrivalled. Yet his drawings can often be surprisingly clumsy. It was here, perhaps, that he ultimately failed: he was inconsistent, unpredictable, often disappointing.

That 'genius' can exist without any inherent specification of gender is clear—and becoming clearer all the time. Augustus John's prediction that he would one day (deservedly) be best remembered not for his own achievements, but as the brother of Gwen John, is coming true.[21] Still, whilst it has to be accepted that 'genius' is a friable, amorphous (and at least historically, a gendered) term, nonetheless the idea of the artistic genius cannot be ignored. For it was in a milieu in which the notion of 'genius' existed as a reality that the young Augustus John first emerged as an artist. Even if he himself demurred, contemporaries such as Henry Tonks and William Rothenstein saw him as—and called him, no doubt sometimes to his face—a genius. On the London art scene in the first years of the twentieth century he was the young man of the moment. Virginia Woolf asserted that by 1908 the era of the popular Edwardian painters John Singer Sargent and Charles Wellington Furse 'was over. The age of Augustus John was dawning.'[22]

This was not mere retrospective dreaming. In 1908 Woolf's sister and brother-in-law, Vanessa and Clive Bell, bought John's painting, *The Childhood of Pyramus* (fig. 5). It was a large canvas of some twenty feet square, clearly influenced by Puvis de Chavannes. John's new lover, Lady Ottoline Morrell, would describe seeing the Bells admiring the painting in John's studio, Clive 'gesticulating in an excited way, showering speechless admiration, Vanessa, head bent, approving.'[23] The Bells' admiration for John's work would be short-lived, but for a while the painting hung in their Bloomsbury home. Four years later another of John's big pictures, *The Mumpers*, caused a sensation when exhibited at the New English Art Club, then the leading place for exhibiting contemporary art outside of the Royal Academy. 'Have you seen John's pictures at the New English?' Lytton Strachey wrote to Virginia Woolf excitedly from his writer's retreat in Berkshire. 'Are they as colossal as the *Times* says? It's all I can do to prevent myself tearing up to the Metropolis to see them.'[24] In its review of the exhibition, *The Observer* described *The Mumpers* as 'the first mature masterpiece of Post-Impressionism, which has hitherto been either tentative and experimental or extravagant and sensational.' Elsewhere in the same exhibition, the *Observer*'s critic saw 'the powerful influence exercised by this man of genius [John] over the younger generation, though too many of them follow the letter rather than the spirit' of their master.[25]

Walter Sickert would concur with this judgement. As he wrote in a review of another exhibition, published in *The New Age* in May 1914,

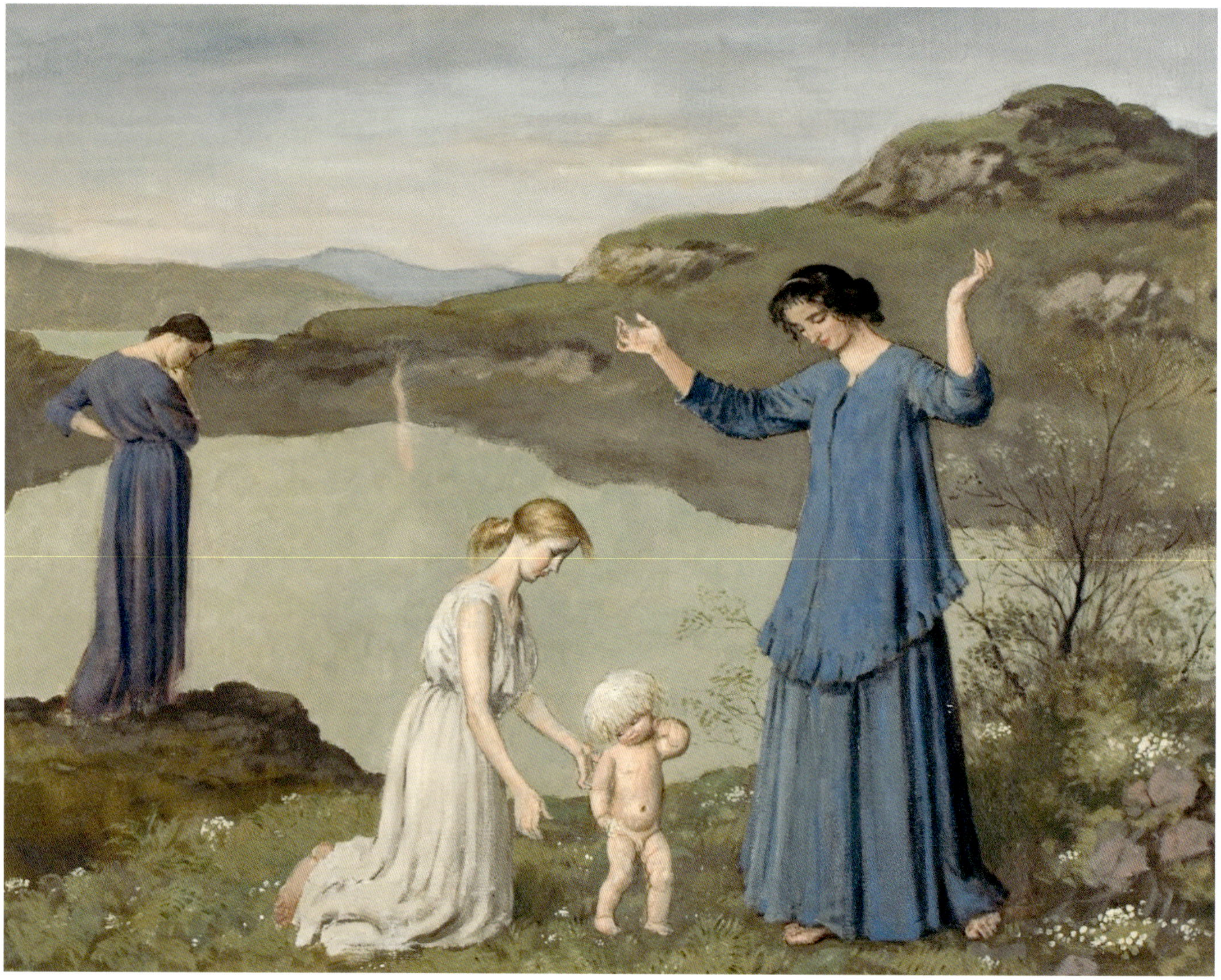

Fig. 5. Augustus John, *The Childhood of Pyramus,* 1907, Johannesburg Art Gallery, Johannesburg

> A certain number of Slade students and others appear to have come, quite justly, to the conclusion that to go on trying to learn to draw as well as John would be not only a long and arduous, but probably an impossible task. The Cubists may perhaps best be described as the group who have thrown up the sponge of Augustus John.[26]

This was almost certainly a reference to Wyndham Lewis, who had exhibited his Cubo-Futurist paintings alongside works by Sickert and John at the Camden Town Group's first exhibition, in 1911. Lewis had arrived at the Slade the term after John's glorious, prize-winning departure. He greatly admired John's work, and took around with him what he called a 'book of John's torn-up drawings,' an album of discarded work which he had found and pieced back together.[27] But when Lewis accompanied the Johns on a holiday to Normandy in 1906 he wrote to his mother that he 'very badly' wanted to do some painting.

However, like Rothenstein before him, Lewis found it hard to work in John's presence. 'I feel that if I were left alone,' he explained to his mother, 'I could both write and paint just now: but near John I can never paint, since his artistic personality is just too strong, and he is much more developed, naturally, and this frustrates any effort.'[28] It seems very likely that Lewis saw in Cubism, Futurism and Vorticism a way of escaping the fact that he would never be as a good a traditional painter as John. With this new freedom, Lewis would launch his own attack on John in the pages of the second volume of the Vorticist magazine, *BLAST*, in 1915. There he would write that, despite John's 'incomparable power, he had not very great control of his moyens [ability], and his genius seemed to prematurely exhaust him.'[29] Nonetheless, decades later Lewis would write that John's 'gifts [...] were so great that he, quite literally, had he lived in the seventeenth century, could have stood beside Rubens as an equal.'[30]

Lewis was not the only young artist disturbed by John's great artistic gift. At the same time as Rothenstein championed his young friend's brilliance, he saw his own achievements decline. He later wrote that on first seeing John's drawings in 1899, he knew that they 'were truly remarkable; so remarkable that they put mine [...] into the shade. Here was someone likely to do great work; for not only were his drawings of heads and of the nude masterly; he poured out compositions with extraordinary ease.'[31] Rothenstein would invite John and Orpen to visit him in Normandy in the summer of 1899, where he was honeymooning with his new wife, Alice. It was there that he painted one of his best-known works, *The Doll's House* (fig. 6), which featured John standing alongside Alice. The painting would win a silver medal when exhibited in the British Section of the Exposition Universelle at the Grand Palais in Paris the following year, but it was also one of his last that might be claimed as a masterpiece. 'Why couldn't I, like Orpen,' he asked himself, 'discover a method which suited my gifts, and adopt it? But

I couldn't control my nerves.'[32] It was almost as if, intimidated by John and Orpen's superior talent, his self-confidence withered.

Rothenstein later admitted that he drew less as the century ended, and wondered if 'perhaps the excellence of John's drawings put me off'.[33] In 1923 he would write in a short essay on John, 'It may be suspected that his closest intimates remain a little in awe of him.' This was almost certainly true of Rothenstein. As he went on to acknowledge, John's output of work was

> enormous, produced like a natural force, with a special instinctive quality, a feeling for life itself, which is beyond the reach of any imitator. Many traditions meet in him, but he belongs to no school, and will leave no considerable one, though his influence on his contemporaries has been manifest.[34]

This influence also exerted itself on Gwen John, to the extent that she was overwhelmed to some degree by her brother's fame and personality. This had not been immediate. As students at the Slade they lived for a time together in London, and their flat was often a hub of activity, with fellow students meeting there to draw together.

But as she grew older, Gwen increasingly distanced herself from Augustus, and from others. Her walking trip through the south of France with Dorelia in 1903 was surely an attempt (on both their parts) to escape him. And after Gwen settled permanently in Paris, she never lived with another person again. She would find her brother's more frequent presence in Paris after Ida and Dorelia moved there in 1906 unsettling. 'I was very troubled,' she would tell Rodin around this time: 'I was thinking before I went to sleep of my brother, and how he made me miserable in England and how I was miserable in England.' Another night she had a nightmare that she was beating Augustus with her fists, whilst he just smiled at her.[35]

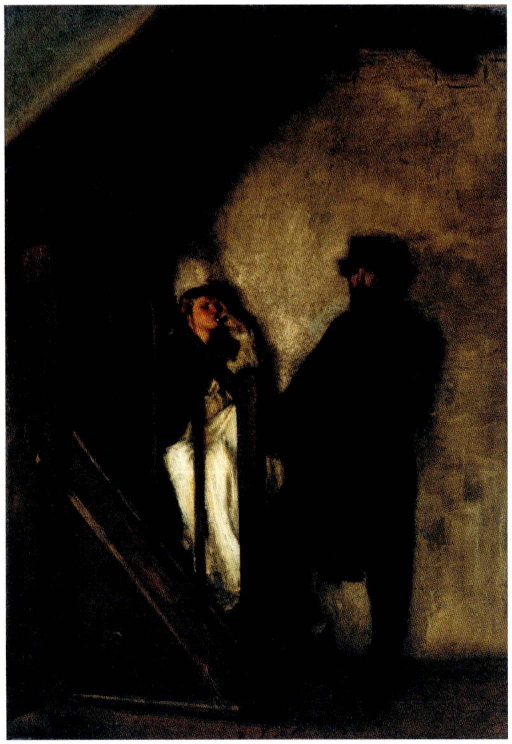

Fig. 6. William Rothenstein, *The Doll's House*, 1899–1900, Tate

It appears that many artists who knew John in his youth had to find some way of escaping his influence. It was on account of seeing John's drawings that C.R.W. Nevinson decided to go to the Slade to study in 1908. But in his *Futurist Manifesto: English Art*, written with Filippo Marinetti, Nevinson would decry what he called the 'old grotesque idea of genius' that an unnamed but clearly recognizable John (see fig. 3) represented: 'drunken, filthy, ragged, outcast; drunkenness the synonym of Art, Chelsea the Montmartre of London; the post Rossettis with long hair under the sombrero and the other passéist filth.'[36] Similarly aware of what had been John's significance, in 1915 in the second volume of *BLAST,* Wyndham Lewis dubbed the years leading up to the Great War 'the Augustan decade.' But by 1915, Lewis argued, that his moment had passed. 'That you will enter the history books, you know, of course,' he told John that same year. 'You will not be a legendary and immaculate hero, but a figure of controversy, nevertheless.'[37]

This collection of paintings and drawings by John and various of his young contemporaries aims to address some of the questions posed here. Can we accept the notion of artistic 'genius,' and if we do, can we accept John as such? As many contemporaries noted, his output was mixed, and his choice of subjects and even his execution could be 'ugly'. Furthermore, John divided opinion, just as he does today. But that he was an influential figure on the contemporary art scene cannot be denied. As the works here testify, talent surrounded him. He intimidated many; others (which was really ultimately his wish) he inspired. He taught, and with the proceeds from the sale of his work, he bought. A number of young, struggling modern artists—David Bomberg, Jacob Epstein, James Dickson Innes, Wyndham Lewis and Amedeo Modigliani among them—owed something to John's financial largesse.

That there is not more work by some of their talented female contemporaries is regrettable. This is in part is due to the nature of the times. Not all possessed Gwen John's resilience or her determination. (Even she, however, experienced an artistic crisis, and largely stopped painting or drawing in the final decade of her life.) Though some female artists, including Elizabeth, Lady Butler, and Dame Laura Knight, were able to marry and enjoy considerable success and recognition, it was not easy for a late nineteenth- or early twentieth-century woman to combine matrimony with an artistic career. The life of Ida John was the clearest example of this. It was not easy even if they did not marry. Perhaps a little unfairly, Duncan Grant blamed Henry Tonks for the ultimate obscurity of the Slade's brilliant female students. As Tonks's biographer wrote in 1939, his belief 'that woman's is the harder lot in life, did not suffice to turn him into a feminist.' Grant felt that his friend Constance Lloyd, 'a gifted painter' who studied at the Slade at the same time as Gwen John, 'suffered as did so many talented students from [Tonks's] total misconception of their gifts.'[38] This, though, is a subject to be examined elsewhere, in its own deserved depth and detail.

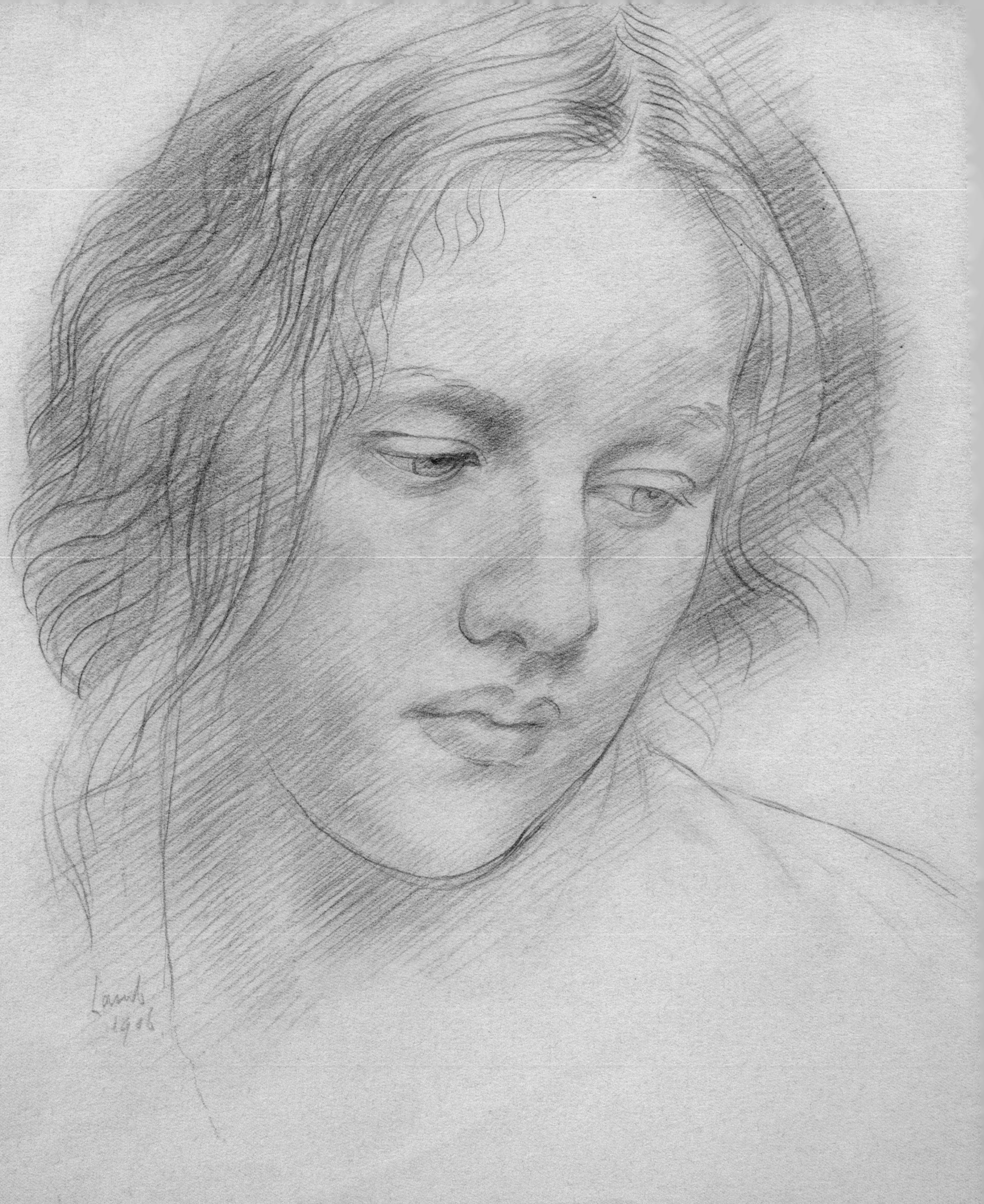

WORKS

David Boyd Haycock

1

AUGUSTUS JOHN

Portrait of Miss Spencer-Edwards, c. 1899
Red chalk on paper
30.5 × 24.1 cm | 12 × 9½ in

Provenance

P. & D. Colnaghi & Co., London
C.N. Barlow
Private Collection

Exhibitions

London, Arts Council, *Exhibition of Drawings and Paintings by Augustus John*, 1949, cat. no. 103 (listed as 'Portrait of Mrs Spencer Edwards')

Fine drawing was the *raison d'etre* of the Slade, and it was hammered home in the Life Class under the discerning eye and critical tongue of Henry Tonks. As one of John's fellow students, Edna Clarke-Hall, later recalled, 'Tonks very much disliked fussy drawings, he wanted clean, straightforward drawings with beautiful lines. "Choose your line and draw it," he used to say.' He forbade rubbing out, and had no time for smudging—'you just had to be very good at lines.'[1] Drawing was where John's greatest strength lay, and he learnt by extensive practice, combined with disciplined study of past masters—a further practice Tonks keenly encouraged. As another contemporary student recorded, Tonks 'advised us to go every day for ten or fifteen minutes to the National Gallery, the South Kensington Museum, or the Print Room of the British Museum, to study one picture, make a sketch of its pattern and rhythm, and buy a postcard reproduction and pin it up at home.'[2] Serious study was thus the foundation of John's technique. As the artist John Piper observed in 1940, 'John's distinction as a draughtsman and his sense of proportion are the result of intensive museum study.'[3]

The year this drawing was made was an important one for the young artist: he was invited to join the New English Art Club (NEAC), exhibiting with them for the first time that April. He also showed at the Carfax Gallery, which William Rothenstein and John Fothergill had established that same year. And in the summer of 1899 he was invited to Normandy to join Rothenstein and his new wife, Alice, on holiday there along with a number of other friends, including Charles Conder and William Orpen. It was on this trip that Rothenstein painted John as one of the characters in *The Doll's House* (fig. 6). Travelling on to Paris, Rothenstein introduced John to the work of Pierre Puvis de Chavannes. Another artist John admired there was Honoré Daumier.

John was very poor at this period of his life, though any money he earned from a sale was quickly spent. Spencer Gore later remarked how admirers took advantage of John's frequent changes of address to collect the torn-up scraps that littered the floor after he left. 'I know people who got many wonderful drawings that way', Gore recalled, by piecing them back together again. One such was Wyndham Lewis, who treasured what he called his 'book of John's torn-up drawings'.[4]

His poverty meant that John often used friends, like Mary Spencer-Edwards (a former Slade student and the future wife of his friend Ambrose McEvoy), as models. He would find sitters wherever he could, later recalling how a young woman he befriended one night on the Tottenham Court Road and employed as a model, though 'poor enough herself [...] would sometimes offer me a pound or two if she thought I needed it.' If he required smart clothes for a special occasion he borrowed them from Charles Conder. One night Orpen ran into him, 'drunk as a lord' and dressed in Conder's curious, old-fashioned clothes that he had bought in Paris flea markets—'checked waistcoat, high collar, tail-coat, striped trousers.'[5]

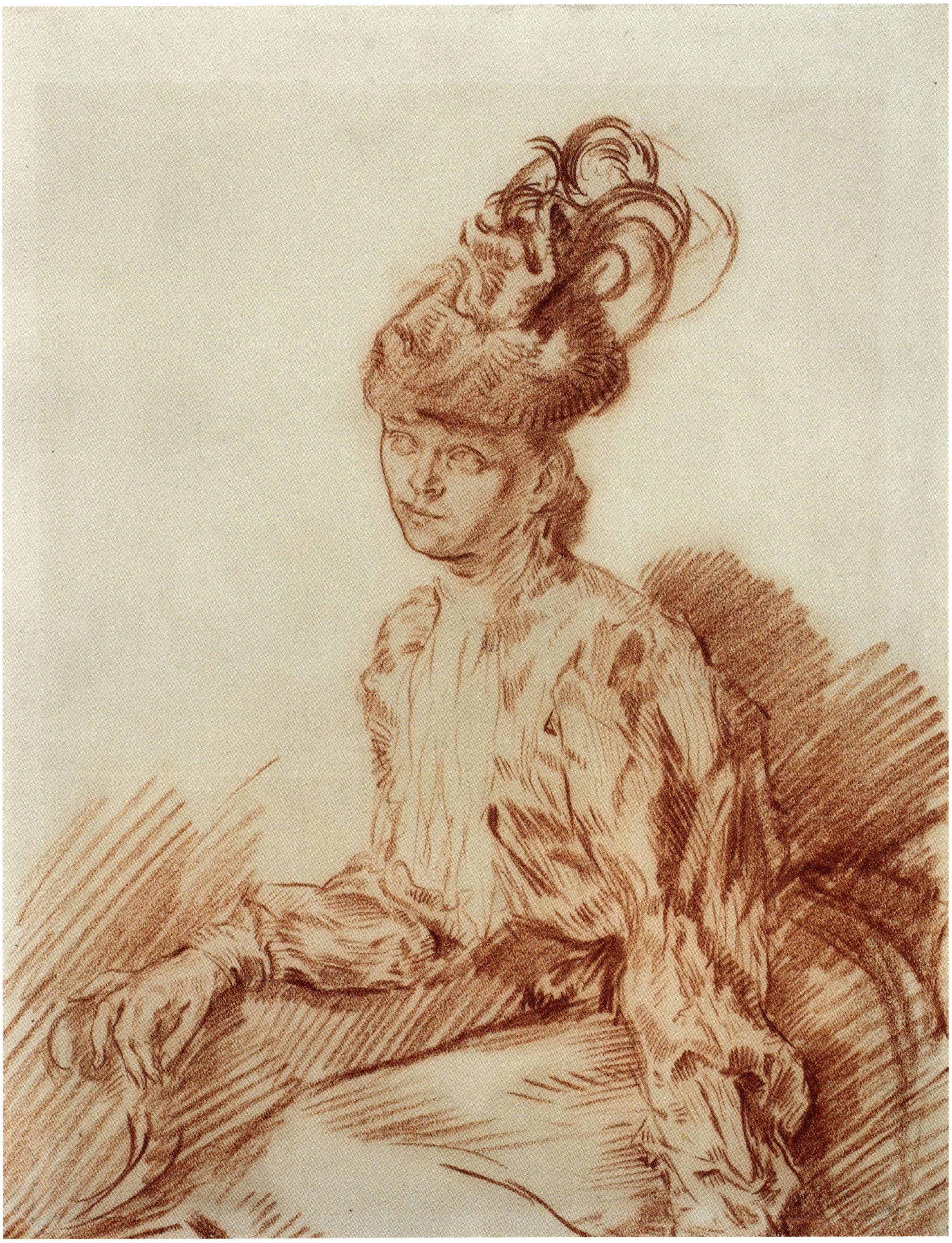

2

WILLIAM ORPEN

Portrait of Ida Nettleship, 1898
Signed and dated lower left 'Orpen 1898.'
Red chalk on paper
29 × 20.5 cm | 11⅜ × 8⅛ in

Provenance

J.L.W. Bird, London
Private Collection
At Dreweatts, Newbury, 25 Oct. 2023, lot 28
Private Collection

Exhibitions

London, J.L.W. Bird, *Spring Exhibition*, March – April 1981, unnumbered

Ida Nettleship was the daughter of the artist John Nettleship and his wife Ada, a successful society dressmaker. Ida was a talented, ambitious artist, and in 1895 she was awarded one of the two annual Slade scholarships. As she told her friend and fellow student Edna Waugh later that same year, 'I desire a studio and ability to paint for myself, and I want to paint people—portraits. Oh I want real things—I know I can get them and I will.'[6] The ability and ambition of the students was one of the Slade's great strengths. As one former student observed in 1907, '[g]ood pupils in a school come by batches; contagion and emulation spur the leader on and pull others in his train'.[7]

In March 1897, not long after her twentieth birthday, Ida Nettleship went to Italy to study in Florence. The following summer—the year Orpen made this portrait of her—she joined Gwen John and Gwen Salmond for three months in Paris, where they furthered their studies at an atelier run (albeit briefly) by James McNeill Whistler. That same summer Augustus John would win the Slade's annual Summer Composition competition with his epic canvas, *Moses and the Brazen Serpent*. Orpen would equal John's achievement a year later with *The Play Scene from 'Hamlet'*, which featured John in the foreground, embracing Ida Nettleship.

By 1901 Orpen would be making a considerable stir in the press with his submissions to the twice-yearly NEAC exhibitions. Co-founded in 1885 by the Slade Professor, Fred Brown, the NEAC was the chief group outside of the Royal Academy for showing contemporary art in London. Its members included Henry Tonks and Philip Wilson Steer (see fig. 2), who taught oil painting at the Slade. Along with the Carfax Gallery, which was founded by William Rothenstein and John Fothergill in 1899, the NEAC (which hired various locations for its shows) was the most important exhibition venue for the best of the former Slade students.

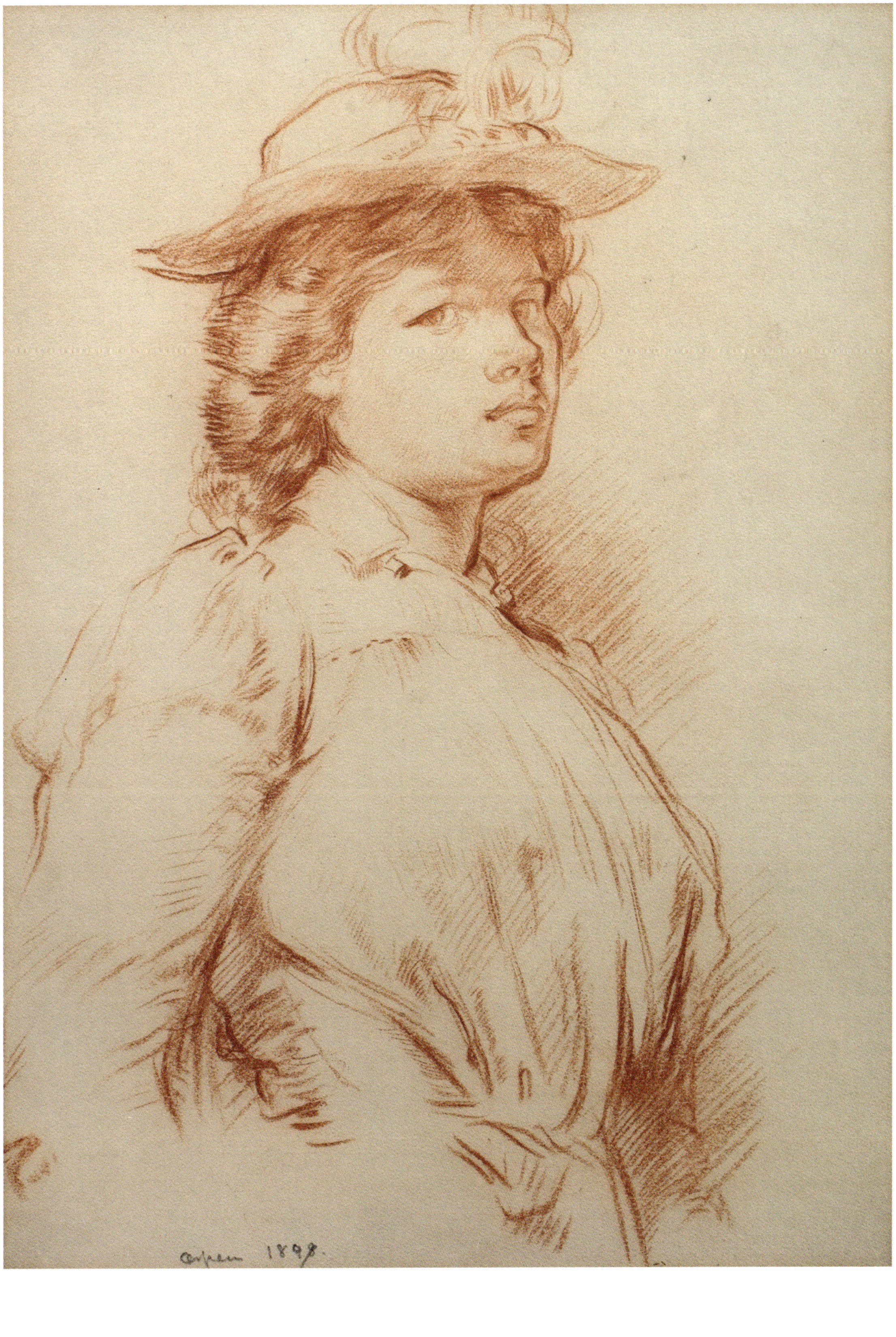
Orpen 1898.

3

AUGUSTUS JOHN

Portrait of Ida, c. 1901
Red chalk on paper
20.3 × 15.2 cm | 8 × 6 in

Provenance

The Artist
Sir Allen Clark, acquired directly from the artist
Private Collection

Exhibitions

Poole, Poole Museum and Salisbury, Salisbury Museum, *Augustus John: Drawn from Life*, 26 May – 30 Sept. 2018 and 18 May – 29 Sept. 2019, cat. no. 4

'The only way to know if you love a person,' Ida had advised Edna Waugh in 1896, 'is to forget all about it until one day you will laugh to think you ever doubted.'[8] By 1899 Ida and John were clearly in love, but their relationship did not run smoothly. John possessed a roving eye, and whilst on a painting holiday with Charles Conder in Swanage in the summer of 1900 he proposed to a young Austrian woman he met at their boarding house. This, however, came to nothing. Instead, and to many people's surprise, on Saturday 12 January 1901—only a few day's after John's twenty-third birthday, and a few weeks before Ida's twenty-fourth—they married. They would, for a while, be very poor. Conder later recalled visiting their flat and finding John in bed because he had only one set of clothes to wear, which Ida was busily repairing. Conder was so moved by this sight that he bought a bundle of John's drawings.[9]

Ida would never fulfill her ambition to become an artist. Following her marriage to John she was soon pregnant, and their first son was born in January 1902. Ida went on to have four more children before dying of puerperal fever in Paris in 1907. John would be devastated at her death, and sought to capture her character—and her importance to him—in numerous paintings he made after her death, including such major works as *The Way Down to the Sea* (fig. 1) and *Lyric Fantasy*.

By 1901 both John and Orpen were beginning to appear in the press. Orpen enjoyed such 'enormous success' with the NEAC in April 1901 that the London correspondent for the American edition of *The Artist* reported that his name 'has been on everybody's lips during the past month,' and he was now 'in the very front rank of British painters [...].' But as *The Artist's* anonymous correspondent added in the same review, he had 'been given to understand that Mr. Orpen owes much of his artistic knowledge to Mr. A.E. John'. Given the quality of John's recent work, however, *The Artist* felt that 'it would be difficult to give credence to this assertion.' Although John could produce works worth lingering over, *The Artist* complained that his greatest fault was 'ugly *pastiche*'. At the NEAC's 1902 spring exhibition, it was Orpen, according to *The Athenaeum*, who 'as usual attracts most attention among the younger members.'[10]

In the summer of 1902 Orpen and John had their work included in the 'Art and Industrial Exhibition' held in Wolverhampton. Frank Rutter, who was soon to emerge as a leading critic and curator, later recalled that the gallery with work by John, Orpen and Steer was 'sensational', and it was this that first alerted him to the fact that 'a really great school of British painters' was emerging.[11] But even by March 1903 *The Manchester Guardian* noted that '[o]utside of a certain circle [John's] art is hardly known'. Orpen was the more conventional talent, and his work suited contemporary taste. As the Carfax Gallery's manager joked, whilst people came to look at the Johns, they left with an Orpen.[12]

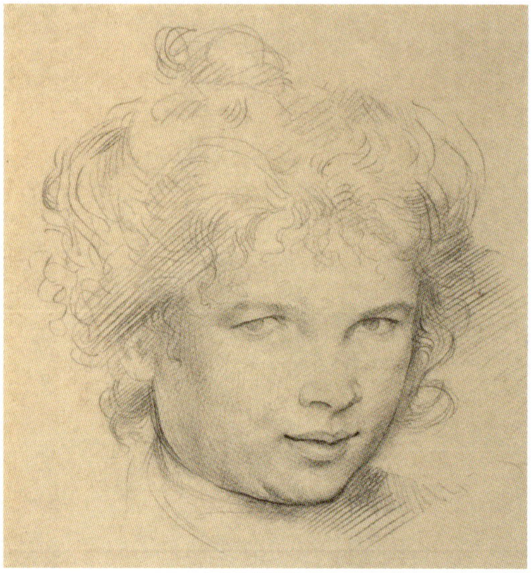

Fig. 7. Augustus John, *Portrait of Ida Nettleship*, n.d., Private Collection

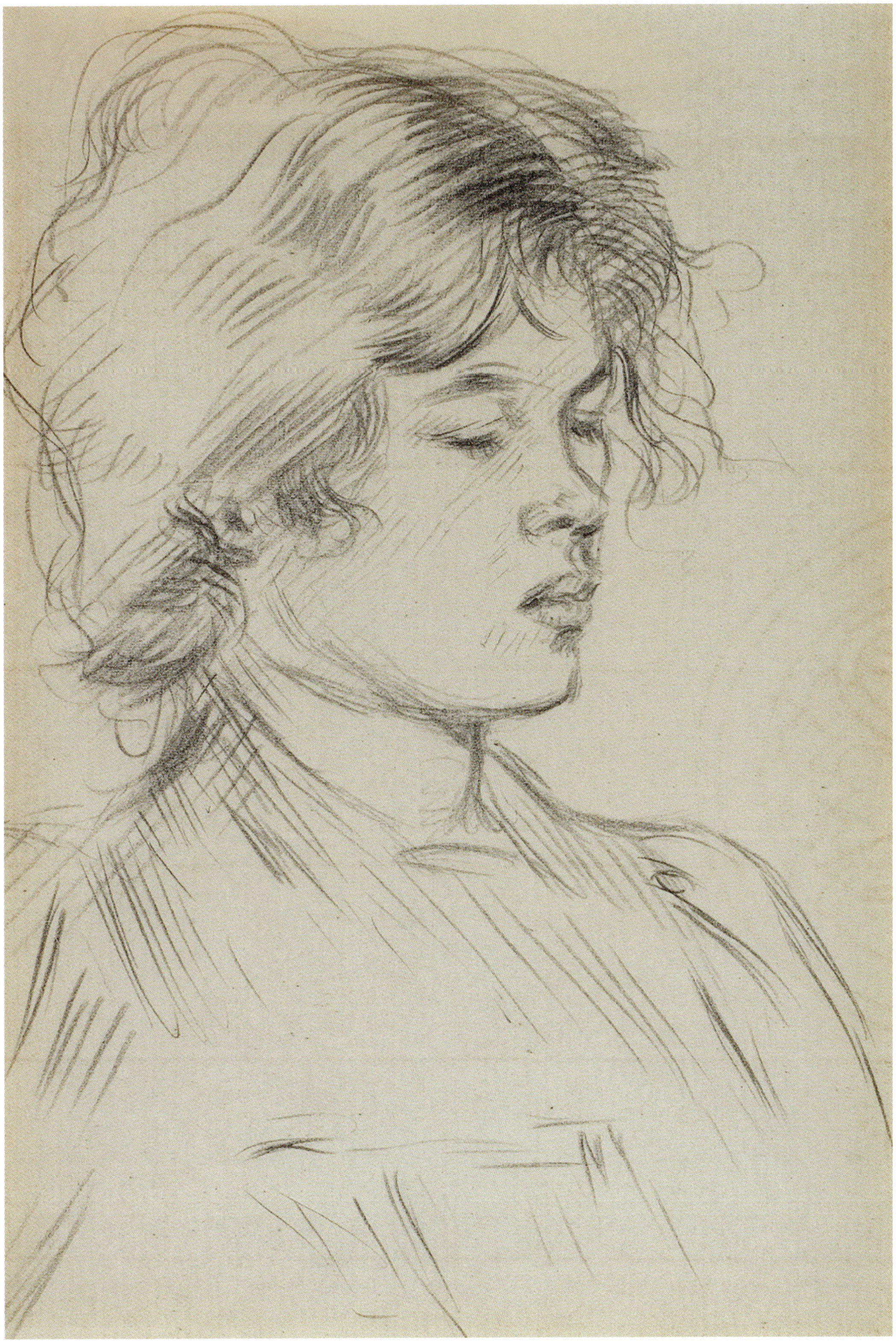

4

AUGUSTUS JOHN

Portrait of Percy Wyndham Lewis, c. 1905
Red chalk on paper
18.5 × 12.5 cm | 7¼ × 4¾ in

Provenance

Private Collection, Bradford
At Hartleys Auctioneers, Ilkley, 20 March 2019, lot 529
Private Collection
Piano Nobile, London, 2023

Having been expelled from Rugby School, Percy Wyndham Lewis (1882–1957) enrolled at the Slade in autumn 1898, the term after John's departure. He was sixteen, and soon proved himself an able—if often idle and rebellious—student. Lewis and John met in London some four years later, beginning a life-long (though never easy) friendship. John soon dubbed Lewis 'the poet,' and as Lewis's biographer, Paul O'Keeffe, has observed, Lewis

> invariably wrote to John about his literary projects, never on the subject of painting or drawing. In truth he seemed far too daunted by [John] even to discuss art with him, let alone lay brush to canvas or charcoal to paper in his vicinity. He could feel equal or superior to John only in the realm of literature.[13]

Lewis did not find his artistic confidence and direction until around 1910, when he discovered Cubism—a path John would never pursue.

In the second volume of his Vorticist magazine, *BLAST*, published in 1915, Lewis wrote that John had 'carried academic drawing farther than it has ever been carried in England [...] I consider John, in the matter of his good gifts, and much of his accomplishment, a great artist. He is one of the most imaginative men I have met, and the one who suggested the greatest personal horizons.' Lewis then dubbed the years up to the outbreak of the First World War 'the Augustan decade.' But, he argued, John's more recent work had failed to live up to earlier promise.[14]

In a subsequent letter to John in which he elaborated on this claim, Lewis reiterated his belief that John 'had, *pour commencer*, as much talent as a man may comfortably possess.' But, as Lewis explained, it was his belief that John (who was almost five years his senior) had been hampered from the very start of his career. This was because the age he had been born into

> was a rather stagnant time just after the full blast of Victorianism—surely one of the most hideous periods ever recorded. You began by shipwrecking yourself on all sorts of romantic reefs. Among other things you consumed a good deal of Verlainesque [i.e. Symbolist] liquor. Whether a craft is still sea-worthy after such buccaneering I don't know. But lately you have not, to put it mildly, advanced in your work. That you will enter the history books, you know, of course! Blast is a history book, too. You will not be a legendary and immaculate hero, but a figure of controversy, nevertheless.
>
> When I think of you, the work I look to is the magnificent series of paintings, drawings, etchings you led off with, and the equals of which you latterly have not exhibited.[15]

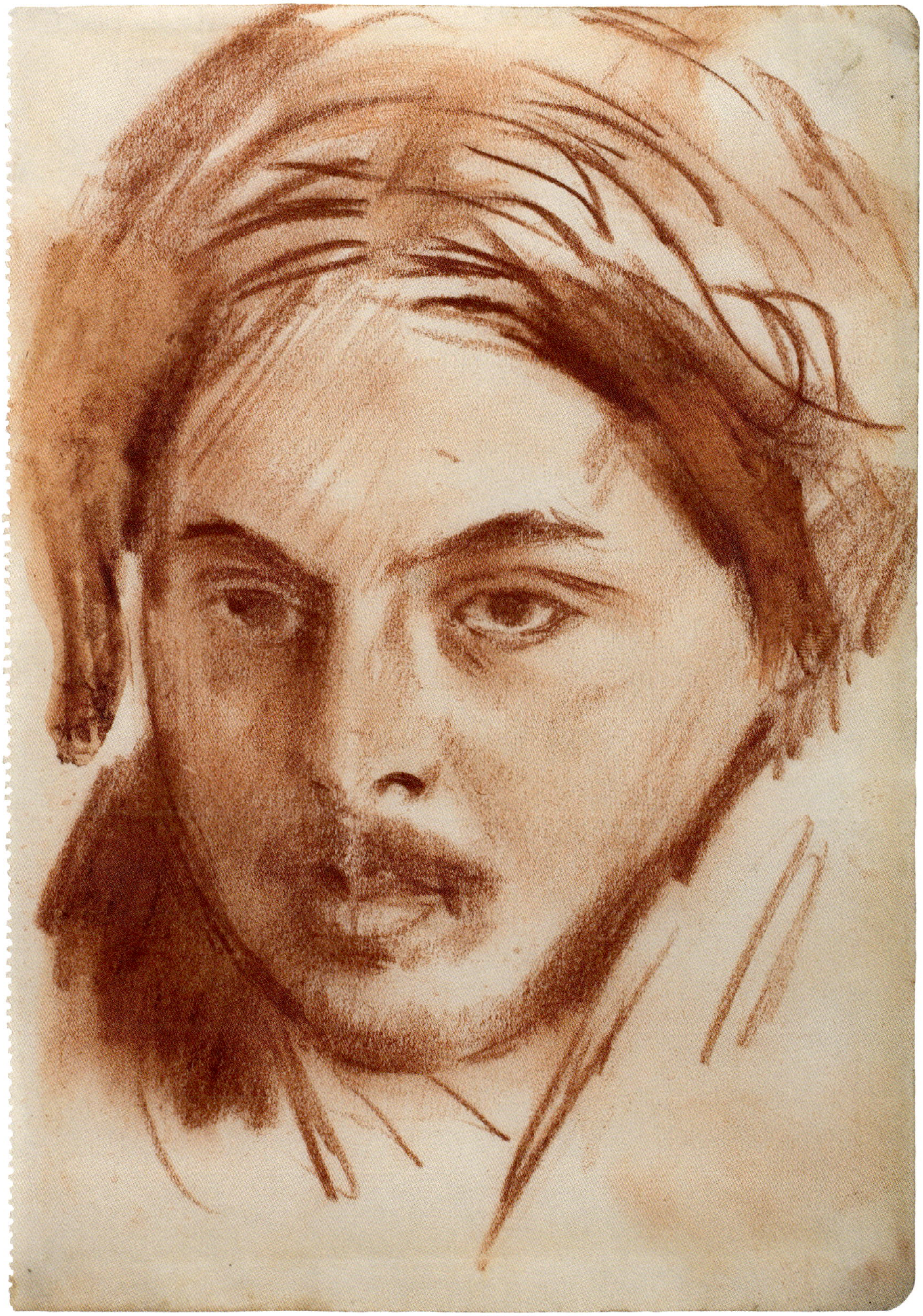

5

AUGUSTUS JOHN

Alick Schepeler, 1906–07
Graphite pencil on paper
18 × 14 cm | 7⅛ × 5½ in

Provenance

Alick Schepeler
Sylvia Mason, given by the above
Private Collection, by descent
Tamlyn & Son, Bridgwater, 7 April 2009, lot 239
The Maas Gallery, London
Private Collection, 2009

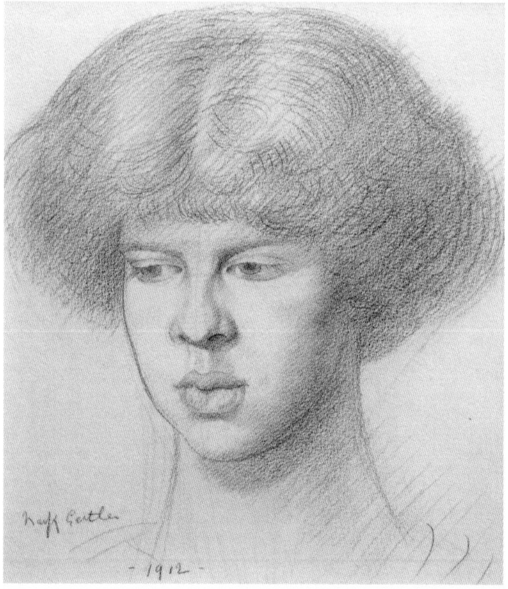

Fig. 8. Mark Gertler, *Study for 'The Violinist'*, 1912, Private Collection

In London sometime in late 1902 or early 1903 John met a beautiful, rather enigmatic young woman, Dorothy McNeill (see cats. 7 and 8). He renamed her Dorelia, and she became his mistress and muse, and for a while she lived with John and Ida in a *ménage à trois*. Following the birth of John and Dorelia's son Pyramus in the summer of 1905, Dorelia and Ida moved to Paris together. They left John in London to focus on his work (though he made regular trips to France to visit them and their children). Unsurprisingly, back at home he took another lover, Alick Schepeler, of whom he made many impressive drawings, including this one. This drawing shows John developing a more fluid style of draughtsmanship, perhaps inspired in part by the periods he had spent teaching first at Liverpool School of Art and then Chelsea Art School. It was drawings of this type that would inspire many of the later students at the Slade, in particular Mark Gertler, who exhibited alongside John in London in around 1910 and whose drawings bear a great similarity to his (fig. 8).

John's multiple relationships (and others that followed) gave rise to his reputation as the man with three wives: 'He was no fit man for a young girl to know', the unmarried Dora Carrington was warned in 1917. 'Had three wives, etc. etc.' But, as she responded, 'just because he has a reputation for being wild with women, and wine, it's absurd to think he's a savage beast.'[16]

John's wayward relationship with women and drink enhanced his almost mythical status, and in time came to eclipse, to some degree, his many artistic merits. But his early reputation was almost entirely founded upon his extraordinary ability as a draughtsman. In Britain at least, this was a medium that did not receive the same critical attention or acclaim as oil painting. In 1904 Laurence Binyon, Assistant Keeper of Prints and Drawings at the British Museum, complained that drawing 'has always been more or less neglected in England. We have never had a living school of draughtsmanship, handing down a tradition of vigorous boldness or scrupulous and searching severity; only, as so often in things English, sporadic examples.' The critic D.S. MacColl concurred. 'First-rate drawing, rare everywhere, has been very rare in England,' he suggested in 1907.[17]

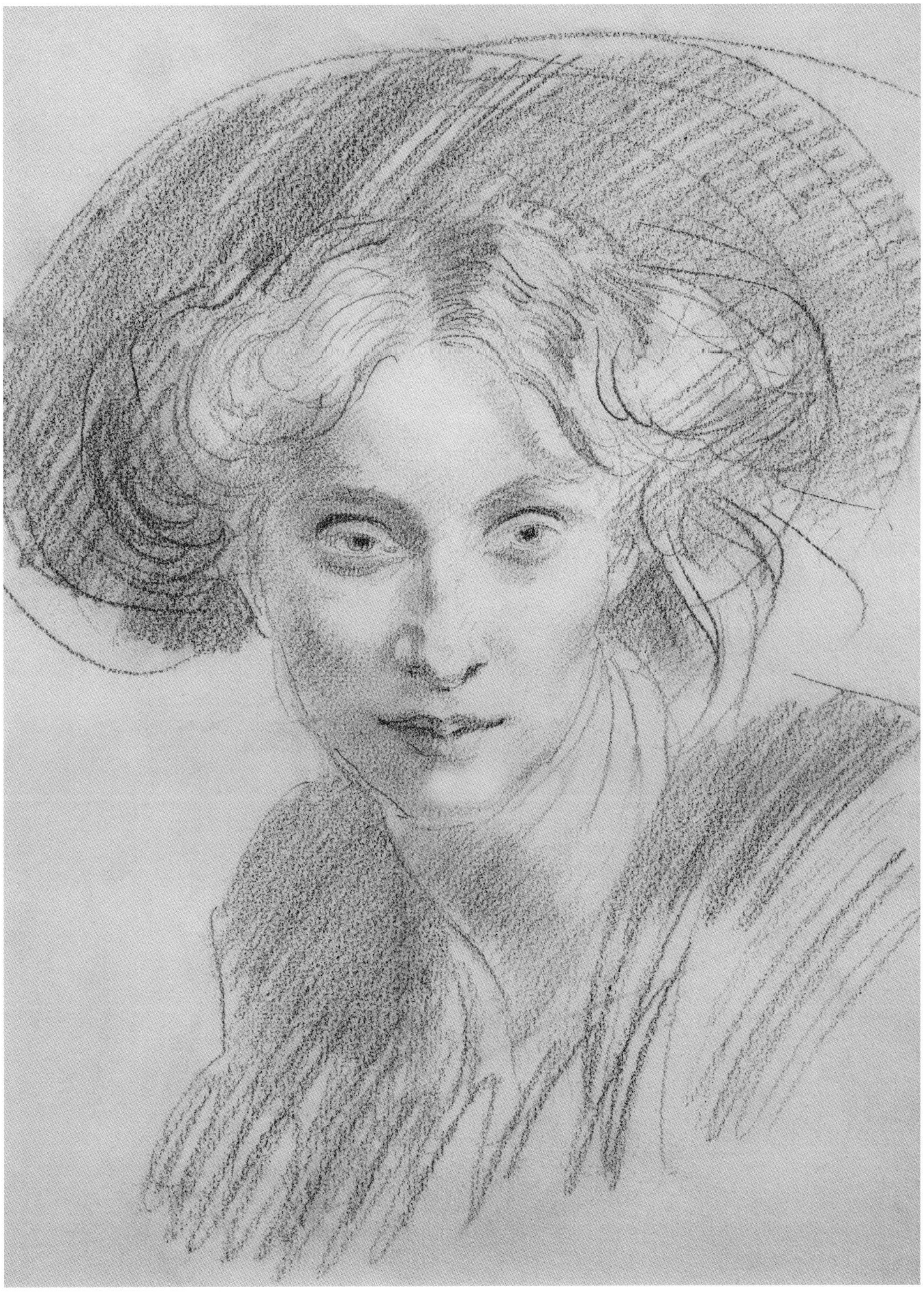

6

AUGUSTUS JOHN

Portrait of Mary McEvoy, 1907

Signed, dated and inscribed lower right 'John. 07/ to Ambrose/ McEvoy'
Graphite pencil on paper
30.8 × 22.6 cm | 12⅛ × 8⅞ in

Provenance

Ambrose and Mary McEvoy, given by the artist, 1907
With Arthur Tooth & Sons, London
Miss E. Doucet, by 1954
Dudley Tooth, by 1965
Private Collection, by descent
At Sotheby's, London, 10 June 2014, lot 11 (listed as 'Mrs Ambrose McEvoy')
Offer Waterman, London
At Sotheby's, London, 19 Oct. 2023, lot 168
Private Collection

Exhibitions

Leeds, Temple Newsam, *Paintings and Drawings by Augustus John*, July – Aug. 1946, cat. no. 83 (listed as 'Portrait of Mrs. Ambrose McEvoy')
London, Royal Academy of Arts, *Exhibition of Works by Augustus John*, March – June 1954, cat. no. 59 (listed as 'Mrs Ambrose McEvoy')
Sheffield, Graves Art Gallery, *Augustus John: An Exhibition of Paintings, Drawings and Prints*, Aug. – Oct. 1956, cat. no. 66 (listed as 'Mrs Ambrose McEvoy')
London, Upper Grosvenor Galleries, *A Loan Exhibition of Drawings and Murals by Augustus John*, April 1965, cat. no. 56 (listed as 'Mrs Ambrose McEvoy')
London, Olympia, *Augustus John*, Feb. 1999, cat. no. 66
London, Hazlitt Holland-Hibbert, *Augustus John: Masterworks from Private Collections 1900–1920*, Sept. – Oct. 2004, unnumbered

Literature

Exhibition of Works by Augustus John, exh. cat., Royal Academy of Arts, 1954, cat. no. 59, p. 17 (illus.) (listed as 'Mrs Ambrose McEvoy')
Augustus John: Masterworks from Private Collections 1900–1920, exh. cat., Hazlitt Holland-Hibbert, 2004, p. 51 (illus.)

Mary Spencer-Edwards, the subject of an earlier drawing by John (cat. 1), was born in Somerset and had been a student at the Slade before McEvoy and John's arrival. She exhibited with the NEAC between 1900 and 1906, and her works received occasional positive mention in the press. An early painting, *Interior: Girl Reading* (1901), was shown at the NEAC in 1902, and was purchased by the Tate in 1927. The painting shows the influence of the Dutch old masters, which was unsurprising from a young graduate of the Slade. Tonks encouraged all his students to study Michelangelo, Holbein, Rubens, Rembrandt, Ingres and Watteau, and when not in the Life Class they would spend time studying and copying original works in the National Gallery and the British Museum's Prints and Drawings Room.

It was John who introduced Mary to Ambrose McEvoy, whilst he was at work making a copy of a painting in the National Gallery, and they married in 1902.[18] All the young Slade artists and their friends frequently sat for each other, and there is another portrait of Mary by John in the Fitzwilliam Museum's collection, from around 1902, and a watercolour portrait of Mary by Ambrose McEvoy, *The Artist's Wife* (c.1913), in the Tate collection. The students frequently used each other as models; Edna Clarke-Hall would write of how she sometimes felt 'very lonely' after her marriage, and how she would 'long for the old Slade days when we were all drawing together; these happy times seemed gone forever.'[19]

Ambrose and Mary McEvoy both regularly exhibited with the NEAC. A review in *The Athenaeum* in April 1901 picked out John, Orpen and Ambrose McEvoy for particular attention, noting that 'the work of these painters affords considerable promise for the future; it is uncompromisingly scholarly and sincere [...] Their work is often student-like, but it is never amateurish or incompetent.'[20]

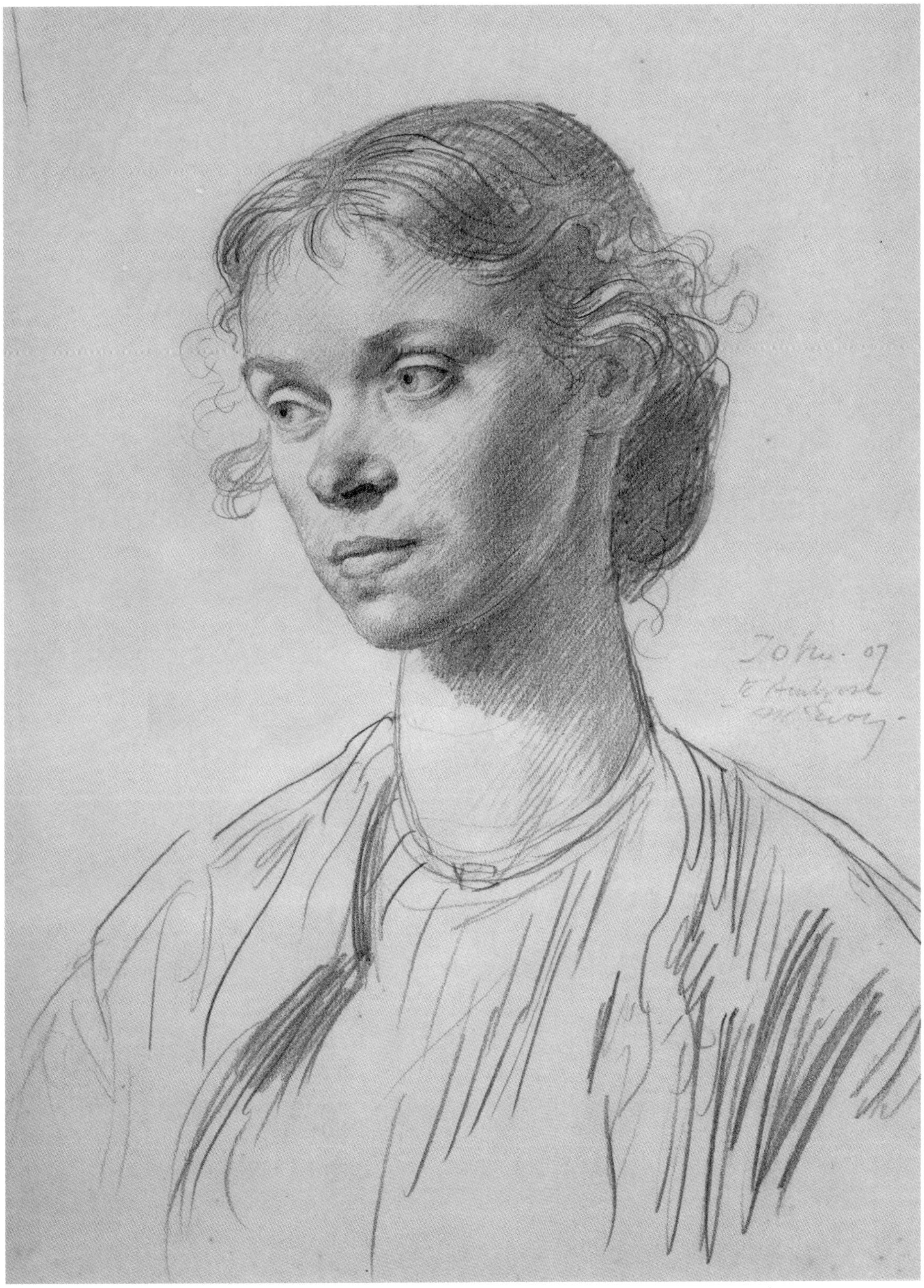
John. 07

7

AUGUSTUS JOHN

Dorelia standing with right arm above, 1907
Graphite pencil on paper
38.1 × 22.3 cm | 15 × 8¾ in

Provenance

Thomas Agnew & Sons, London
Private Collection

Exhibitions

Cardiff, National Museum & Gallery, Cardiff; London, Spink & Co.; and Conwy, Royal Cambrian Academy, *Theme and Variations: The Drawings of Augustus John 1901–1931*, 20 July – 1 Sept. 1996; 9 Sept. – 4 Oct. 1996; and 2 Nov. – 1 Dec. 1996, cat. no. 46
Poole, Poole Museum and Salisbury, Salisbury Museum, *Augustus John: Drawn from Life*, 26 May – 30 Sept. 2018 and 18 May – 29 Sept. 2019, cat. no. 23

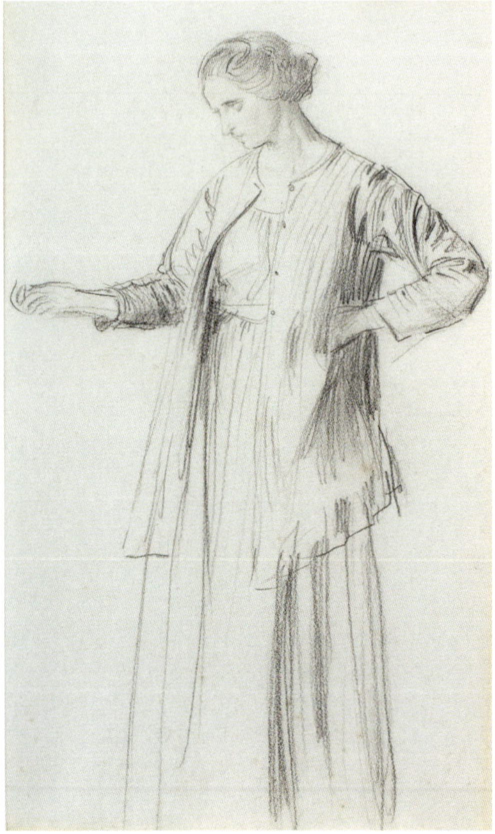

Fig. 9. Augustus John, *Dorelia*, c. 1907–09, Private Collection

Through intensive study, combined with the careful guidance of Henry Tonks, John had already achieved a remarkable technical ability by the late 1890s. William Rothenstein, who became his earliest and most enthusiastic patron, was one of the first to recognise this. Rothenstein was a few years older than John, and had been at the Slade briefly in the late 1880s, before the arrival of Brown, Tonks and Steer had raised the dynamic of the school.

Having spent time studying in Paris, Rothenstein returned to London in 1893, which is when he first met John. As he recorded many years later,

> [John] brought me his drawings, which were truly remarkable; so remarkable that they put mine [...] into the shade. Here was someone likely to do great work; for not only were his drawings of heads and of the nude masterly; he poured out compositions with extraordinary ease; he had the copiousness which goes with genius, and he himself had the eager understanding, the imagination, the readiness for intellectual and physical adventure one associates with genius.[21]

To Rothenstein's surprise, John found it hard in his early years to sell his work, and he was frequently very poor, changing his lodgings around London frequently as his money ran out.

For a while in the 1900s Rothenstein was effectively John's dealer. He showed his drawings to more established artists such as John Singer Sargent, Charles Conder and Charles Wellington Furse. The last, who had been a scholarship student at the Slade in the 1880s, selected a number to buy, though was taken aback when John asked £2 for each of his nudes. Rothenstein considered this price 'modest ... but Furse hadn't expected a student to ask so much.'[22] In fact, and to his surprise, Rothenstein often initially found it hard to persuade collectors to buy any of John's drawings. 'It was not so much the indifference of the critics, of artists and collectors that angered me,' he later recalled, 'as their constant assertion that John couldn't draw, that his work was "ugly." These lovely things badly drawn and ugly! Were people blind? So John often needed his friends' help'.[23]

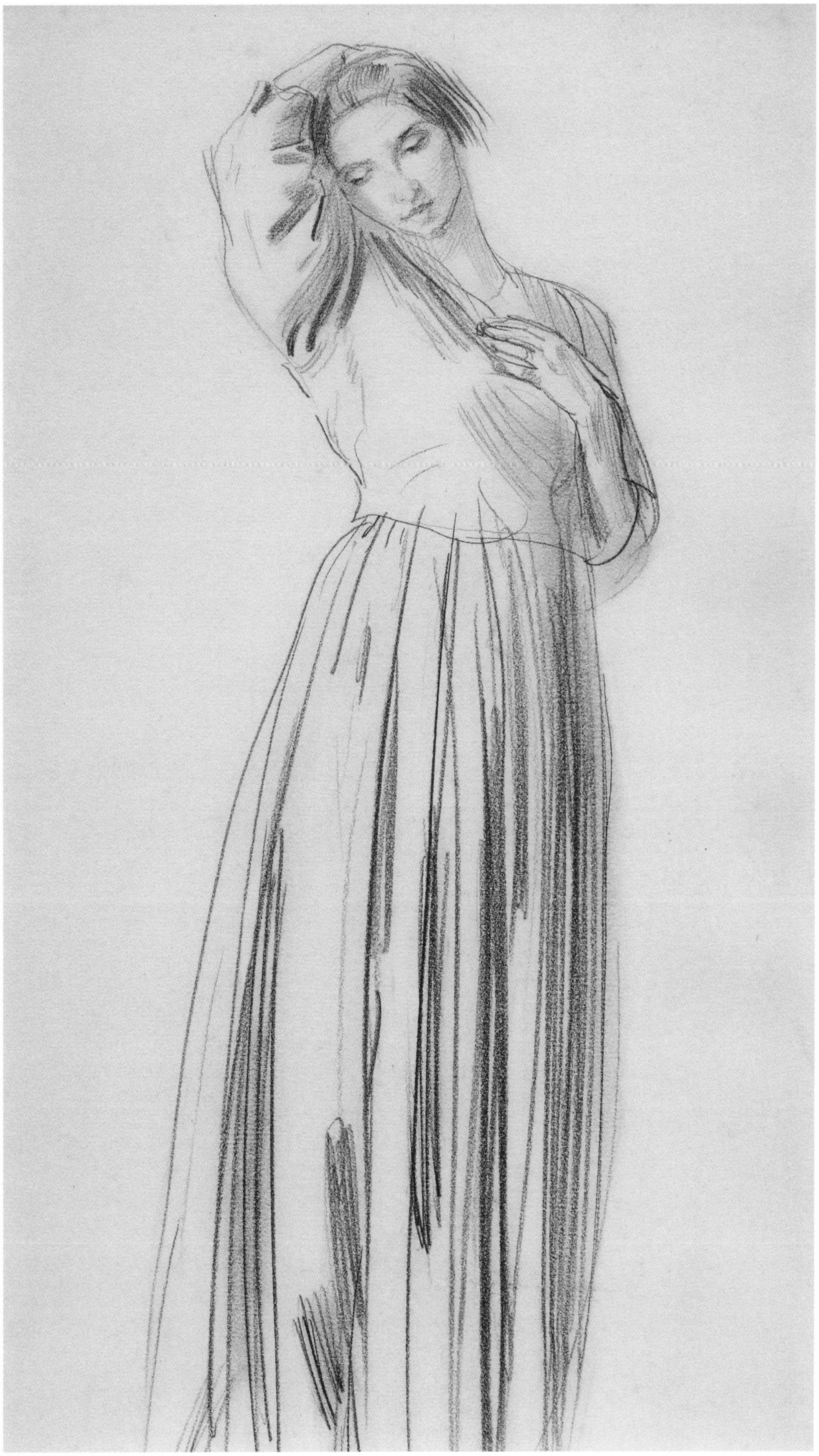

8

AUGUSTUS JOHN

Dorelia, 1909
Signed and dated lower right 'John/ 09'
Graphite pencil on paper
25.4 × 16.5 cm | 10 × 6½ in

Provenance

Vernon Wethered
J.L.W. Bird Fine Art
Private Collection

Exhibitions

Cardiff, National Museum & Gallery, Cardiff; London, Spink & Co.; and Conwy, Royal Cambrian Academy, *Theme and Variations: The Drawings of Augustus John 1901–1931*, 20 July – 1 Sept. 1996; 9 Sept. – 4 Oct. 1996; and 2 Nov. – 1 Dec. 1996, cat. no. 54
Poole, Poole Museum and Salisbury, Salisbury Museum, *Augustus John: Drawn from Life*, 26 May – 30 Sept. 2018 and 18 May - 29 Sept. 2019, cat. no. 6

Literature

David Boyd Haycock, *Augustus John: Drawn from Nature*, exh. cat., Paul Holberton Publishing, 2018, cat. no. 6, pp. 17, 38, 41 (illus.)
David Boyd Haycock, *Brilliant Destiny: The Age of Augustus John*, Lund Humphries, 2023, p. 86, fig. 6 (illus.)

Drawn when John was in his early thirties, a full decade after his departure from the Slade, this pencil portrait of Dorelia McNeill is one of his finest, and an exemplar of what Stanley Spencer would later call 'the Slade Way'. Wyndham Lewis would later write that when he was a student at the Slade there hung on a prominent wall 'a large charcoal drawing' by John of

> a hairy male nude, arms defiantly folded and a bristling moustache [...] and fronting the stairs that lead upwards where the ladies were learning to be Michelangelos, hung a big painting of Moses and the Brazen Serpent.
>
> Everything in the place was in the 'grand manner': for Professor Tonks [...] had one great canon of draughtsmanship, and that was the giants of the Renaissance. Everyone was attempting to be a giant and please Tonks. None pleased Tonks—none, in their works, bore the least resemblance to Michelangelo.[24]

The one who came closest to Tonks's ideal, however, was John. Although the proportions are somewhat at odds with anatomy (Dorelia's neck is far too wide—not a mistake that Orpen would ever have made), it is nonetheless a bravura piece of work.

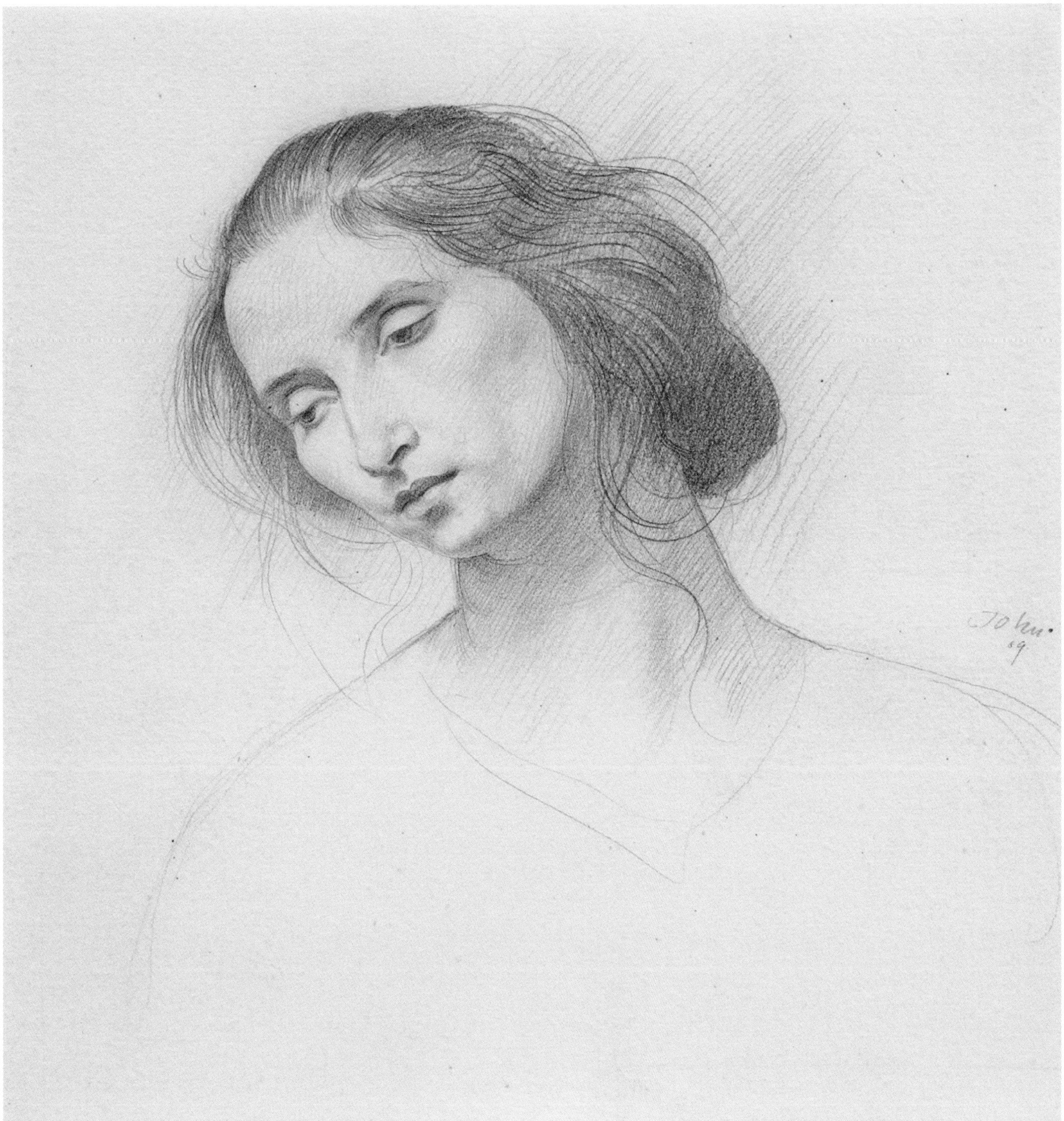
John

9

WYNDHAM LEWIS

Portrait of Helen Saunders, 1913
Signed and dated lower left 'Wyndham Lewis 1913'
Ink, wash and pencil on paper
31.1 × 23.8 cm | 12¼ × 9⅜ in

Provenance

Helen Saunders
Helen Peppin
Private Collection

As a student at the Slade Lewis won a scholarship, and his surviving drawings from his time there reveal he was an accomplished draughtsman from life. Daunted by John's brilliance, however, he was reluctant to exhibit his work until he was liberated from the Slade's classical tradition by Roger Fry's exhibition 'Manet and the Post-Impressionists' in 1910. This portrait of Lewis's friend (and possibly lover), Helen Saunders, shows his move in the direction of Cubism, whilst still retaining some of his debt both to John and to his Slade training.

Lewis's colleagues in the Camden Town Group would be bemused by his increasingly abstracted imagery, which was quite unlike anything being made by any other British artist in London at this time. 'The pictures of Lewis are quite impossible!' Lucien Pissarro complained to their President, Spencer Gore, in 1911 or 1912. 'Either ours is a serious movement or a farce! [...] I don't see why we should put up with such rubbish.'[25]

Saunders (1885–1963) had briefly studied at the Slade before attending the Central School of Arts and Crafts, and she was an early English convert to Cubism. Saunders and Jessica Dismorr joined Lewis (and Kate Lechmere) in the Rebel Art Centre, and they were the only two female members of the Vorticist group, which Lewis founded in 1914. Saunders exhibited in the first and only Vorticist exhibition in London, held at the Doré Gallery in May 1915, as well as at their New York exhibition in 1917. Saunders was also a member of Lewis's short-lived post-war group, X.

In an essay on the Vorticists published in *Vogue* in September 1956, Lewis wrote that it was 'essential that people should believe that there was a kind of army beneath the banner of the Vortex', though in fact, he admitted, 'there were only a couple of women and one or two not very reliable men.'[26] Lewis and Saunders may well have had an affair in 1918: Lewis's biographer Paul O'Keeffe writes of her 'dog-like devotion' to him.[27] In 2022 it was discovered that Saunders's lost painting *Atlantic City*, which had been reproduced in *BLAST*, had been painted over beneath Lewis's 1921 painting *Praxitella*, a portrait of the film critic Iris Barry. Interest in Saunders's life and work has increased considerably in recent years, and an exhibition of her drawings and watercolours was held at the Courtauld Gallery in 2022–23.

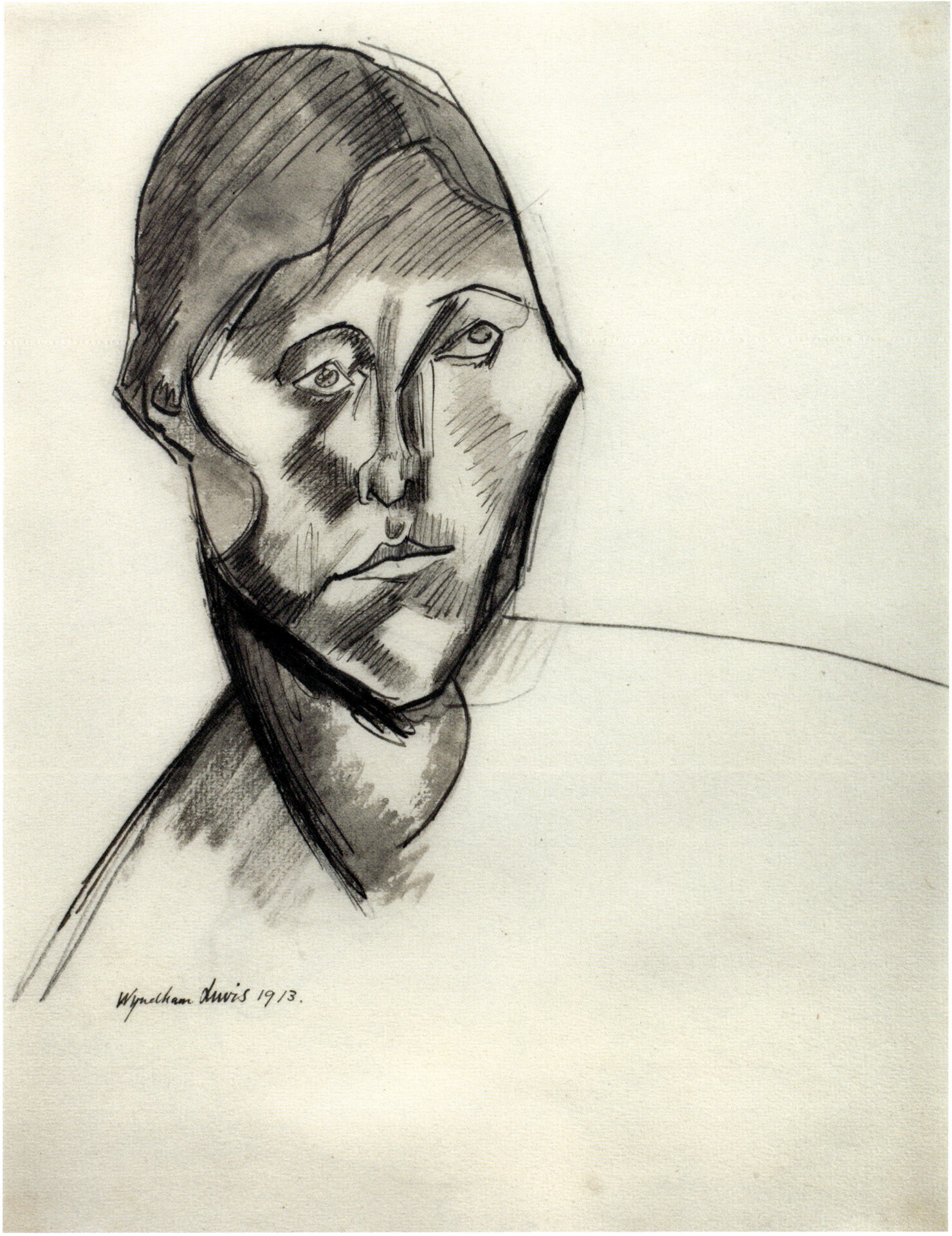
Wyndham Lewis 1913.

10

JACOB EPSTEIN

Romilly John, conceived 1907
Bronze
Height 20.3 cm | Height 8 in

Provenance

Lady Epstein
Edward P. Schinman
Private Collection, by descent
Martin Diamond Fine Arts, New York
Private Collection, 1978
Long-term loan to Ben Uri Gallery & Museum, London

Exhibitions

New York, The Jewish Museum, *The Immigrant Generations: Jewish Artists in Britain 1900–1945*, 24 May – 25 Oct. 1983

Literature

Bernard van Dieren, *Epstein*, John Lane, 1920, pl. XIV (listed as 'Head of a Boy')
Robert Black, *The Art of Jacob Epstein*, World Publishing, 1942, cat. no. 2, pl. 87 (illus.)
Richard Buckle, *Jacob Epstein, Sculptor*, Faber & Faber, 1963, pp. 22–23, pl. 16–17
B.L. Reid, *The Man from New York: John Quinn and His Friends*, Oxford University Press, 1968, p. 191
Edward P. Schinman and Barbara Ann Schinman, eds., *Jacob Epstein. A Catalogue of Edward P. Schinman*, Farleigh Dickinson University Press, 1970, p. 94 (illus.)
Evelyn Silber, *The Sculpture of Epstein*, Bucknell University Press, 1986, cat. no. 8, p. 120 (illus.)
Stephen Gardiner, *Epstein: Artist Against the Establishment*, Flamingo, 1993, pp. 53, 123–125

Jacob Epstein (1880–1959) was born in New York City, the son of Polish emigrants. He moved to Paris in 1902, coming under the influence of Rodin, and then to London in 1905. He soon met John, and he would be impressed by what he later called John's 'wildness, an untamed quality that is the essence of the man.'[28] For his first few years in London Epstein was very short of money, and in 1907 John commissioned this bronze bust of his and Dorelia's son Romilly, who had been born two years before. The critic T.E. Hulme, who would be Epstein's greatest supporter in the years up to the First World War, wrote in *The New Age* in 1913 that this bust of Romilly 'has been universally admitted to be one of the finest bronzes since the Renaissance.'[29]

By the time of this work Epstein was fascinated by the African, Egyptian and Assyrian sculpture he studied in the British Museum, as well as by Hindu erotic sculpture. In this same year he received a major commission to carve a series of large figures to decorate the British Medical Association's new building in the Strand. John considered the eroticism in Epstein's 'monstrous' work for this project 'simply sickening'. The figures caused a scandal when unveiled in 1908, but John defended them. Epstein, however, had a bolder, more modernist outlook than John, and a franker approach to depicting human life in all its forms. He later remarked that it was the job of the 'great artist' to express something 'that is of predominant interest in his own time, but that is [also] true of all time. He goes right down to the very depth of things, while the small master gives things their surface value alone and therefore only expresses his [own] time.'[30] However, as John told Dorelia in 1911, he thought that 'sex is [Epstein's] weak point'.[31]

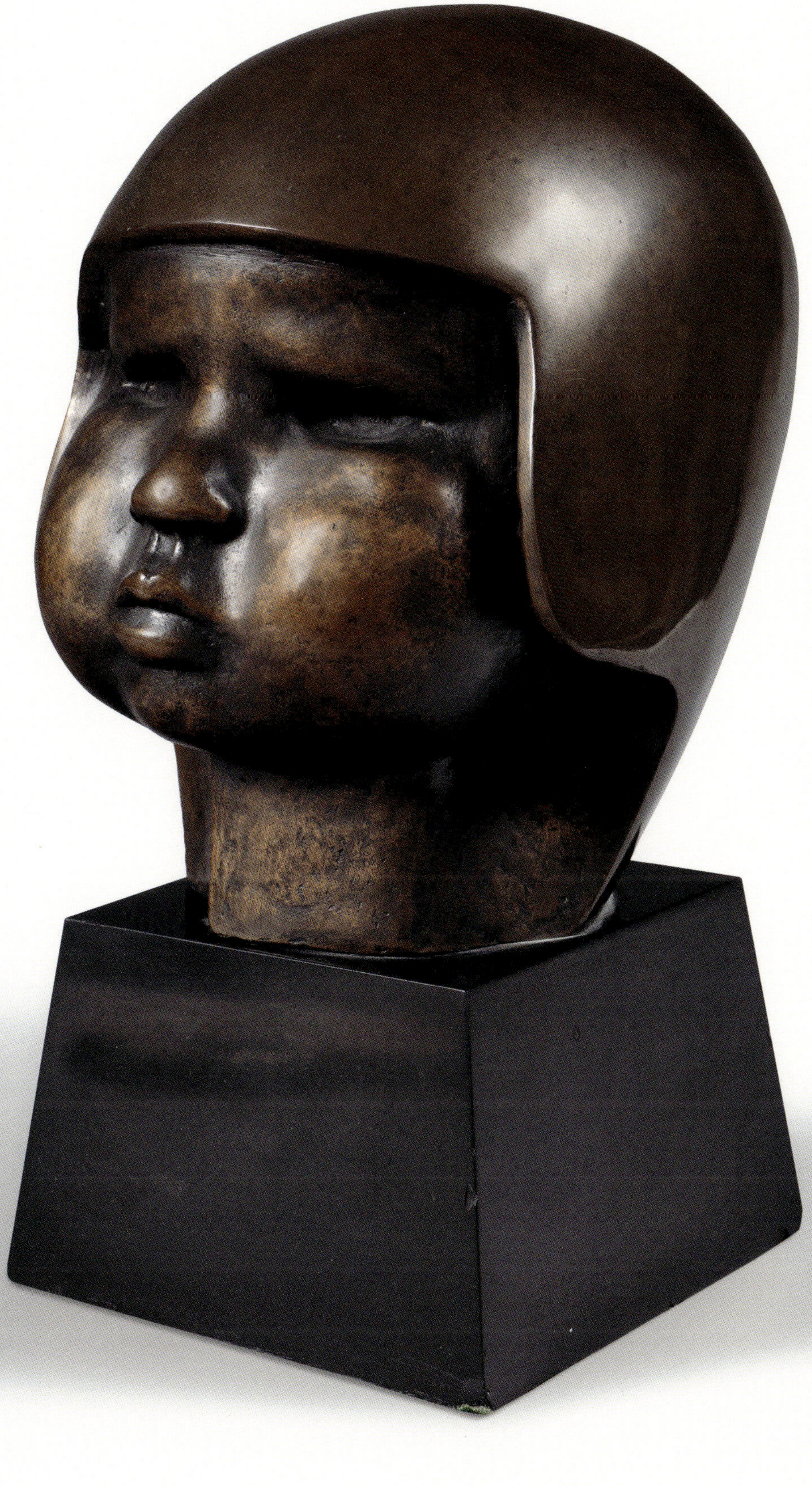

11

AUGUSTUS JOHN

Three Children Bathing, c. 1910
Signed lower left 'John'
Oil on panel
24 × 32.5 cm | 9½ × 12¾ in

Provenance

Arthur Tooth & Sons, London
Private Collection, London
At Swann Galleries, New York, 20 Sept. 2018, lot 425
Private Collection

John's drawings of his young sons are among his finest, most sought-after works, and he can be claimed as one of the best draughtsman of children that has ever lived. Having grown up by the seaside he had a life-long love of the sea, and was a strong, keen swimmer. In *Chiaroscuro* he recalled how, as a boy, the 'beaches, caves, sand dunes and burrows in the neighbourhood of Tenby provided ideal playgrounds [...]. Long days were spent in and out of the sea at Lydstep, Monkstone and other lonely spots along the coast.' He remembered making long, solitary explorations down precipitous cliffs 'to narrow virgin beaches of wet shingle.' He often stripped off his clothes and ran naked in the dunes.[32]

Although he could be a stern, rather distant father (as his own had been), John loved his children, and was keen they should not be brought up conventional Edwardian boys. He frequently took them on holiday to the seaside—Provence, Normandy, Dorset and Wales—where, like him, they ran naked. In his memoir, *The Seventh Child*, Romilly John remembered how, as a little boy of nearly four, when the family was living at Martigues in the summer of 1910, the sea was 'something mysterious and terrifying.' Even though he spent the greater part of each day in the sea, he admitted it was many years before he learnt to swim.[33]

John's financial backer, the wealthy American solicitor John Quinn, acquired a number of his 'Provençal Studies', and they would be among the thirty-six works by John exhibited at the International Exhibition of Modern Art in New York in 1913. Only one other artist, Odilon Redon, had more works in this exhibition, now known to history as the Armory show; Gwen John was also represented by two works from Quinn's collection, including *Girl Reading at the Window* (1911), now in the Museum of Modern Art, New York.

At the time Frank Jewett Mather, Marquand Professor of Art and Archaeology at Princeton, praised John's contributions to the Armory show, writing that he 'can go some way with Matisse because he never forgets Manet and Botticelli.'[34] The most controversial work was Marcel Duchamp's cubo-futurist painting, *Nude Descending a Staircase, No. 2* (1912). It caused a sensation, and revealed how fast the *avant garde* was moving in Europe, and how John, though classed among the moderns, was starting to be left behind.

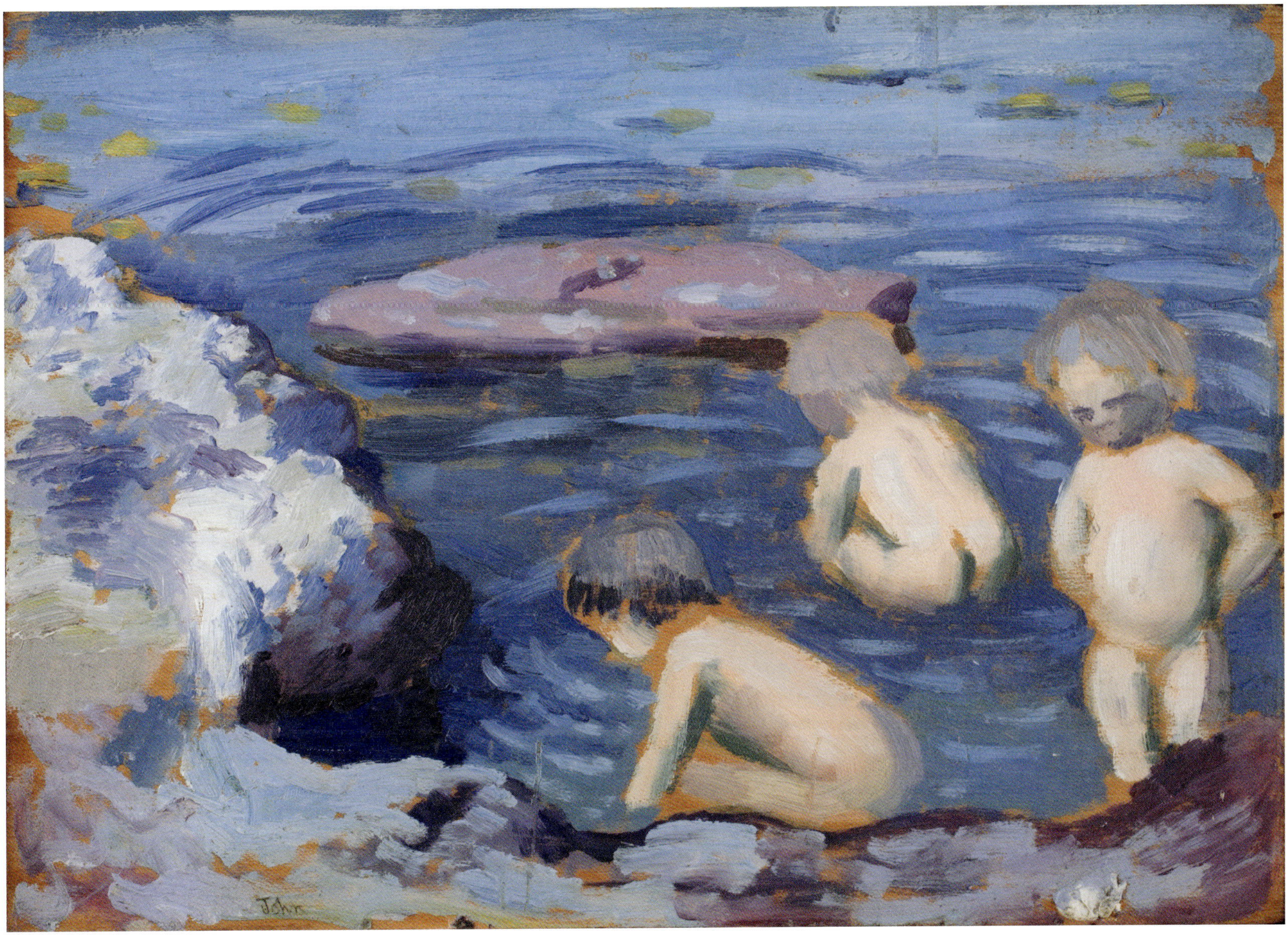
John

12

HENRY LAMB

Edwin John, c. 1912
Graphite pencil on paper
21.6 × 13.3 cm | 8½ × 5¼ in

Provenance

The Artist
Lady Pansy Lamb, by descent
New Grafton Gallery, London
Wolseley Fine Arts, London, 2002
At Cheffins, Cambridge, 13 Feb. 2020, lot 292
Private Collection

Exhibitions

London, J.L.W. Bird, *Winter Exhibition*, 7 – 11 Nov. 1983, cat. no. 27

In the later summer of 1903 John and Orpen rented two large rooms in the Rossetti Studios at 72 Flood Street, Chelsea, and opened an art school. As their prospectus explained, once a week they would teach classes in life drawing and painting, still life, figure composition, landscape and decorative painting. In return for an annual fee of nineteen guineas, prospective students were promised that they would, 'by advice and suggestion,' stimulate 'the most personal artistic aims.'[35]

Two years later, in the summer of 1905, a young medical student, Henry Lamb (1883–1960), abandoned his studies in Manchester and moved to London to train as an artist. Handsome and intelligent, Lamb soon proved himself a talented student, and he and John quickly became friends. For a while Lamb imitated John's appearance—he grew his hair longer, and for a while sported a beard and gold earrings. He would also soon begin drawing like John. This portrait of John's fourth son with Ida, born in Paris in 1905, shows Lamb's closeness to his mentor, and his family. Well into the 1930s he would be a regular visitor to the John household, wherever it was located, and he developed a close attachment to Dorelia (with whom he had, for a while, an affair) and the children. One of Romilly John's earliest memories was of being taken for walks by Lamb when they were staying at the Villa Ste Anne in Martigues, Provence, in the summer of 1910. Lamb is mentioned frequently and with fondness in Romilly's 1932 memoir, *Seventh Child*. He liked all of the children, Romilly wrote, and encouraged them to draw. Lamb was a more stable character than their father who, as Romilly noted, was an 'overwhelming' personality.[36]

According to Lamb's biographer, Keith Clements, Lamb could never quite shake off the early influence of John on his drawing: even in the 1920s he would be complaining of a sketch getting 'infected with something of Augustus's brazenness.'[37] Although this drawing is dated to around 1912, there is perhaps something here reminiscent of Stanley Spencer's graphic technique. Like John, Spencer had trained under Tonks at the Slade, where he was a student from 1908 to 1912. Lamb would meet Spencer for the first time late in 1913, and they became very close for a while.

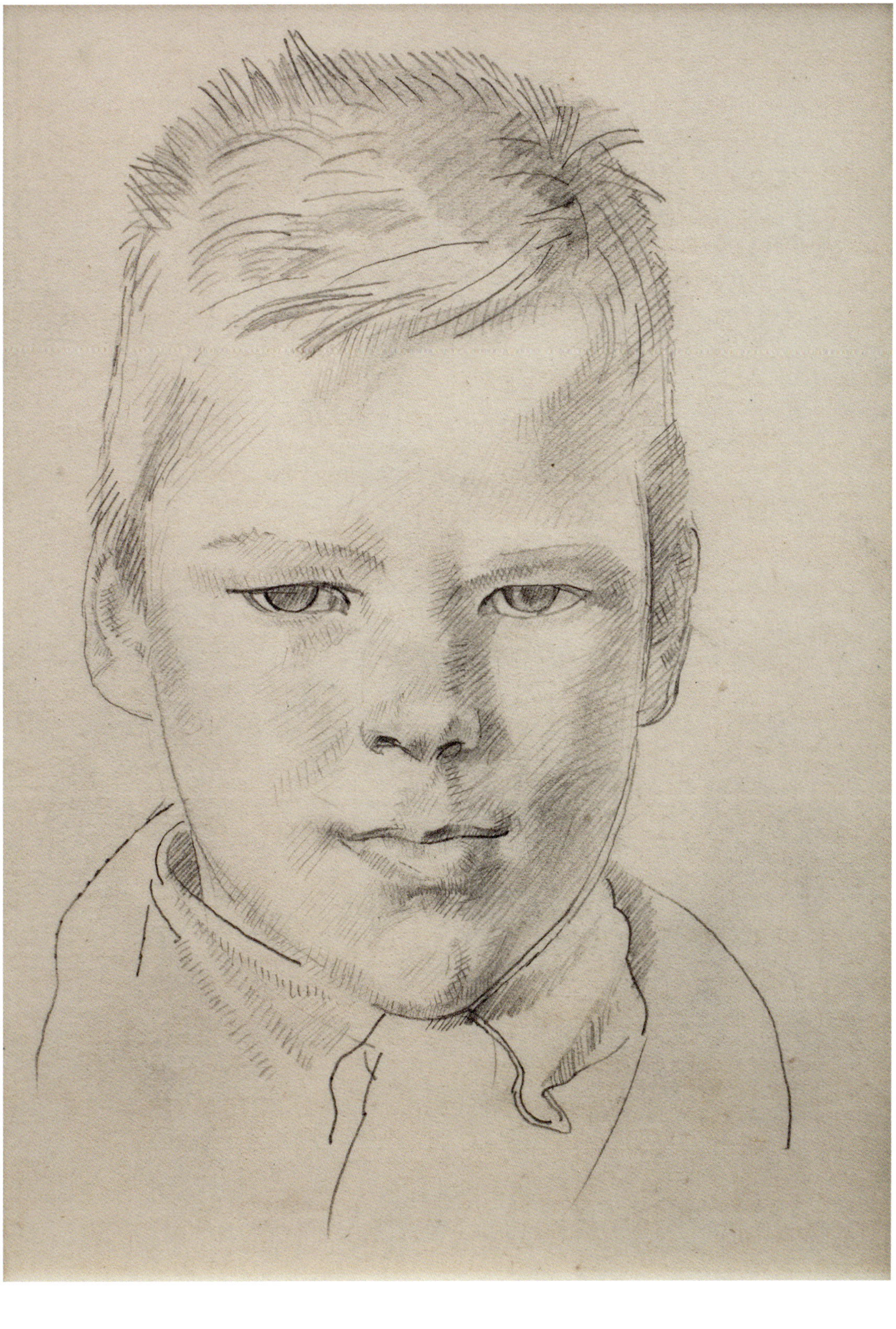

13

HENRY LAMB

Euphemia, 1906

Signed and dated lower left 'Lamb/1906'
Titled lower right 'Euphemia'
Graphite pencil on paper
29.5 × 23 cm | 11⅝ × 9 in

Provenance

Euphemia Lamb
Private Collection

Exhibitions

Manchester, Manchester City Art Gallery, *Henry Lamb 1883–1960*, 9 May – 16 June 1984, cat. no. 7

Literature

Keith Clements, *Henry Lamb: The Artist and his Friends*, Redcliffe, 1985, n.p. (illus.)

When Henry Lamb arrived in London in the summer of 1905 he was accompanied by his beautiful young girlfriend, Nina Forrest (who was generally known as Euphemia). Lamb's father was an eminent mathematician and a Fellow of the Royal Society, but Euphemia came from a working-class family in Manchester. Although she had told Lamb that she was nineteen, he thought she was more probably sixteen. Lytton Strachey described her at the time as Lamb's 'quasi-mistress, a very young woman dressed in the regulation harlot clothes', by which Strachey may have meant home-made dresses and jackets, perhaps copied from the ones Dorelia was making, and which emulated bohemian, gypsy fashions.[38] Over the coming years she would model for various artists in John's circle, including Ambrose McEvoy and Jacob Epstein.

Euphemia, though, was a difficult and confusing personality. 'We are landed with Miss Forrest,' Virginia Woolf complained in April 1906. 'She sits vaguely in the drawing room for hours, and forgets whether she had tea or dinner last, whether children have meat or wine. My head spins with her stories, until I say sternly, "Miss Forrest take my advice and learn Greek," it is like a nightmare.'[39]

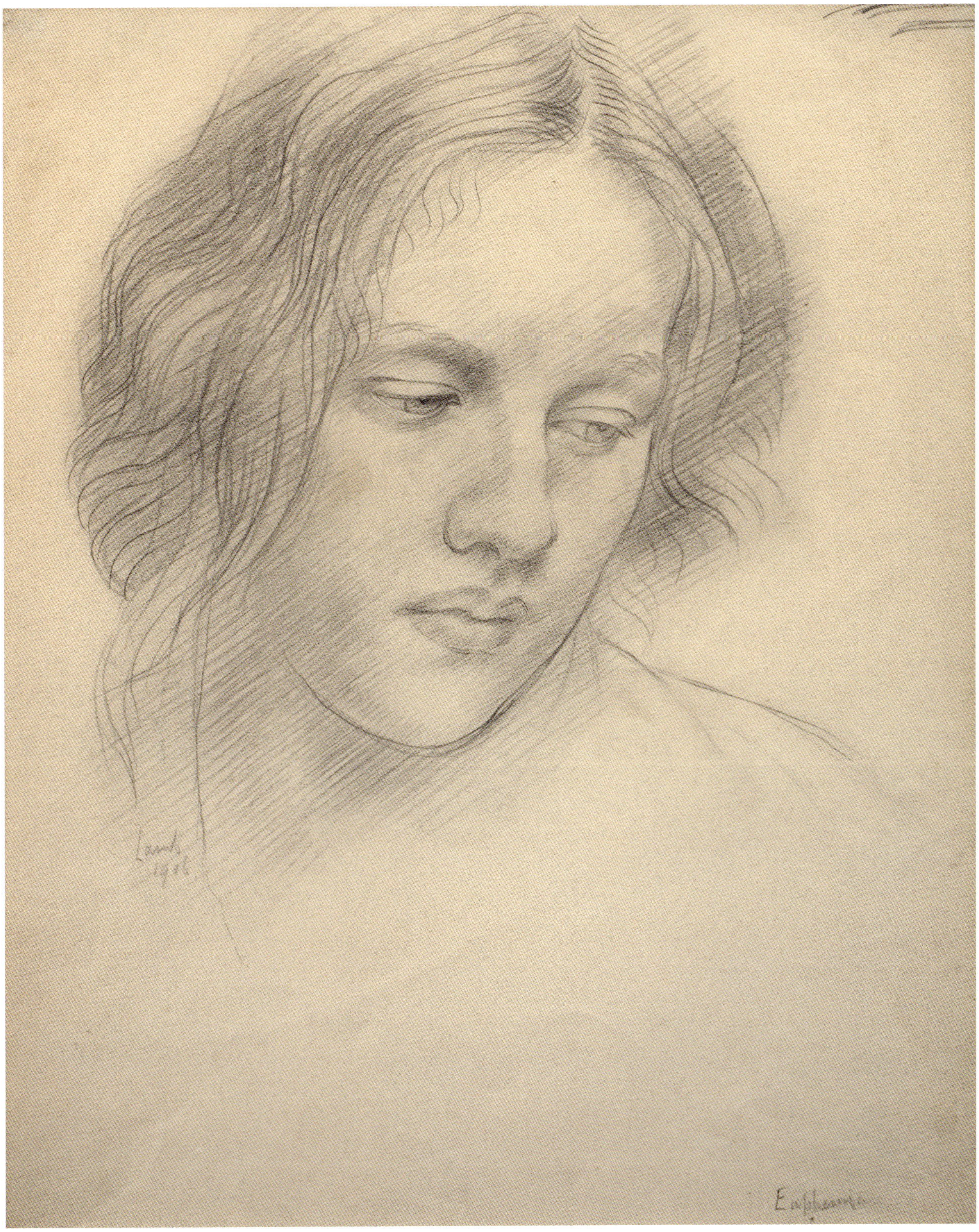
Lamb
1906
Euphemia

14

AUGUSTUS JOHN

Euphemia, c. 1907
Signed lower left 'John'
Graphite pencil on paper
30.5 × 24.1 cm | 12 × 9½ in

Provenance

Euphemia Lamb
Private Collection

Exhibitions

London, National Gallery, *British Painting Since Whistler,* 1940, cat. no. 520

As we have seen, John's style influenced Lamb, and he had encouraged him to look at the work of Rubens and Rembrandt, old masters who had been early influences on John.[40] But another student at John and Orpen's Chelsea Art School, Charles Maresco Pearce, would write in his unpublished memoir that 'Lamb was an exquisite draughtsman in a decidedly Leonardo-esque manner, and the great John himself fell under his influence and produced Leonardo-like drawings of great beauty for some time after this.'[41] Although it is impossible to verify this claim, John's drawings from after 1906 do differ from his earlier works; they are more majestic, more flourishing, with much greater emphasis to the hatching in the features of face and hair, not unlike that to be found in Leonardo da Vinci's drawings.

By the spring of 1906 Euphemia was pregnant, and on 10 May 1906 she and Lamb married at the Chelsea Register Office, with John as a witness.[42] Shortly afterwards they moved to a cottage on the Wiltshire Downs, where Euphemia suffered a miscarriage.[43] A little while later, Lamb reappeared in London. 'He wants to be my apprentice,' John told Dorelia. This pleased John, though he had demurred when Lamb called him 'a Master'.[44] 'I'm not quite a Master,' he replied, '– yet. I keep forgetting myself often. But I am learning loyalty. We must have no rivals and no fickleness.' As he added, he wished that he had 'some demon' to whip him along, to motivate him, to make him work.[45]

In 1907 Henry and Euphemia Lamb moved to Paris, but not long afterwards they separated for ever. John invited Lamb to join him on a summer break in Normandy, and in his letters family news rubbed shoulders with reports of recent artistic encounters:

> You might visit Equihen for some bathing. I saw a young artist called Picasso whose work is wonderful in Paris. We are rather harassed by babies. We ought to have a few vigorous old women to attend to them.

'Yes, Picasso is a wonder,' John added in another letter. 'Have you met him? I have seen some reproductions of wonderful pictures by Gauguin.'[46]

Like John's friendship with Wyndham Lewis, the one with Lamb would also be troubled. Whilst Lewis told his friends that he disliked Dorelia, Lamb was deeply in love with her. Eventually he grew frustrated by John's treatment of Dorelia, and following one (undated) visit to John's household he called him 'that tarantula Augustus [...] in his customary nimbus of boredom, silence and helpless gloom.'[47]

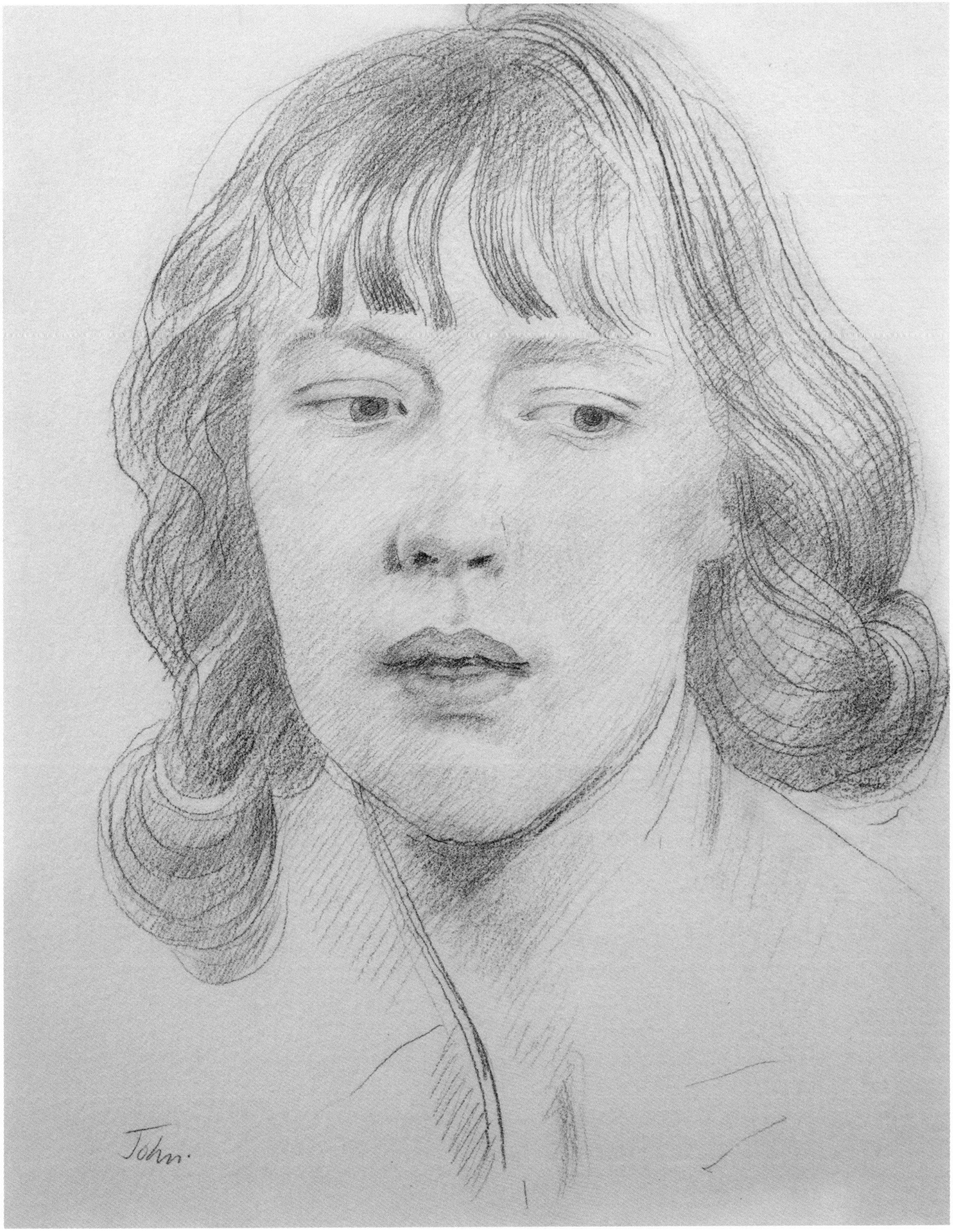
John.

15

JAMES DICKSON INNES

Euphemia Lamb, c. 1909–11
Graphite pencil and watercolour on paper
26 × 22 cm | 10¼ × 8⅝ in

Provenance

Randolph Schwabe
Private Collection
At Phillips, London, 7 March 1995, lot 9
Private Collection

James Dickson Innes (1887–1914) was born in Llanelli, south Wales, and arrived at the Slade from Carmarthen Art School in 1906. Working largely in watercolour, he painted bad figures and good landscapes that at first, in their slightly dreamlike quality, owed a debt to Turner, Steer, John and Conder.

Innes's friend John Fothergill later wrote that Innes's 'lack of craftsmanship not only in his figures but other objects [...] was a sort of ignorance that, like the mistakes of children, is appealing and is evidence of his independence.' In Fothergill's opinion, the most notable qualities of Innes's landscapes were their 'spontaneity, atmosphere, colour and originality.' Diagnosed with tuberculosis, Innes knew he had little prospect of a long life, and he spent the time he had recklessly: 'impelled by the premonition that he hadn't long to live,' Fothergill explained, Innes 'was in a hurry.'[48]

In 1908 Innes and Fothergill travelled to the south of France, eventually reaching Collioure, the seaside town on the Mediterranean coast where Henri Matisse and André Derain had spent a summer a few years before, creating the bold, dramatically coloured paintings that had soon found them labelled by a hostile critic *les Fauves*—'the wild beasts.' After a brief spell back in London, working with his young Australian friend, Derwent Lees, as a part-time teacher at the Slade, in 1909 he moved to Paris to continues his studies. There he met Euphemia Lamb, falling precipitously in love with her. They travelled to Collioure, and later to Wales together in the company of John.

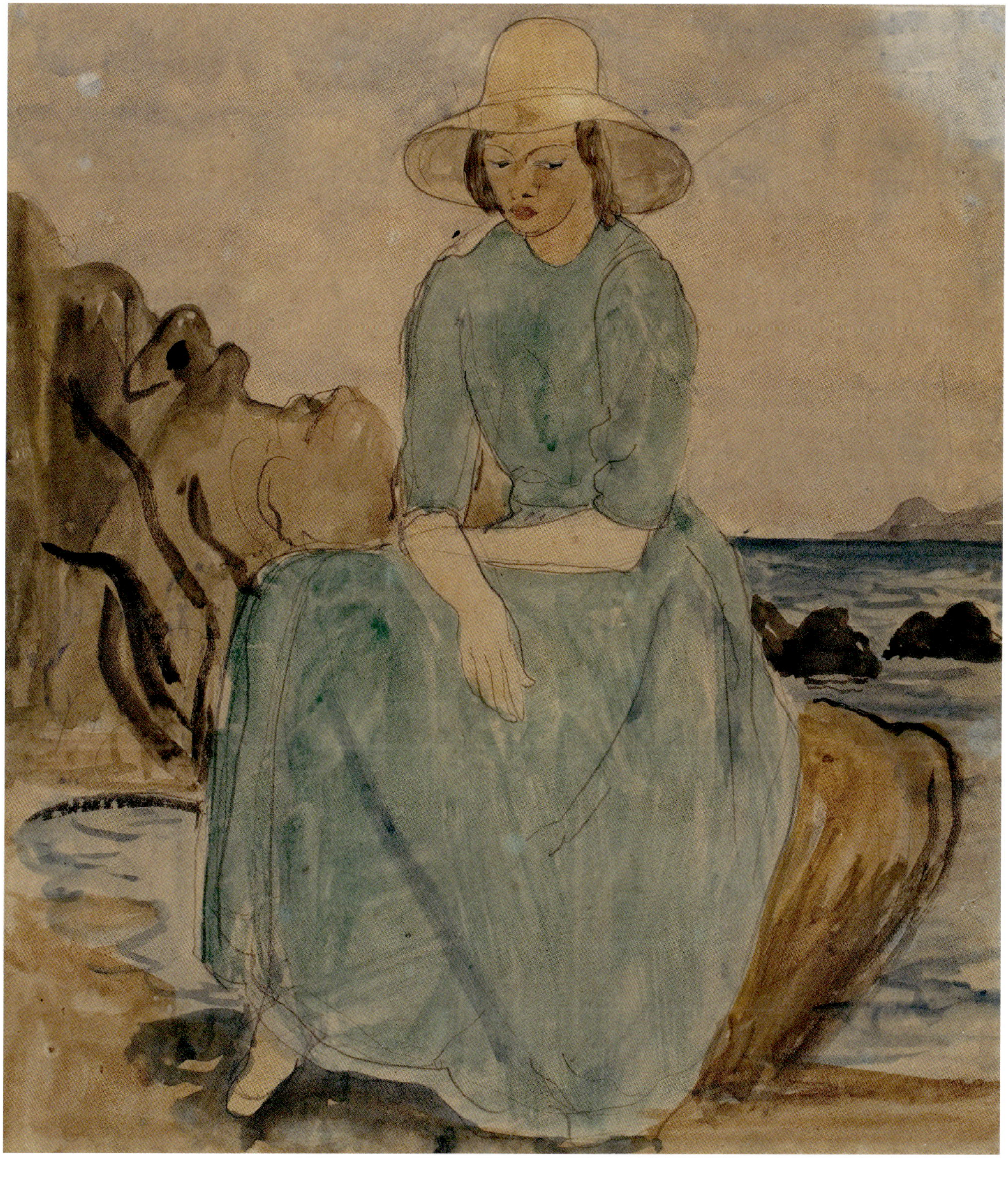

16

JACOB EPSTEIN

Second Portrait of Euphemia Lamb, 1911 (conceived and cast)
Bronze
Height 52.5 cm | Height 20⅝ in

Provenance

Robert Bevan
Anthony d'Offay, London, 1977
At Christie's, London, 6 Nov. 1992, lot 34
J.C. Horwood
Private Collection, UK, and by descent
Piano Nobile, London

Exhibitions

London, Grosvenor Gallery, *The Third Exhibition of the National Portrait Society*, Feb. – March 1914, cat. no. 86 (listed as 'Euphemia')
London, Leicester Galleries, *An Exhibition of Sculpture and Drawings from 1900 to 1932 by Sir Jacob Epstein (1880–1959)*, 17 June – 17 July 1971, cat. no. 17 (another cast) (listed as 'Euphemia (First bust)')
New York, Hirschl & Adler Galleries, *British Modernist Art 1905–1930*, Nov. 1987 – Jan. 1988, cat. no. 56

Literature

Bernard van Dieren, *Epstein*, John Lane, 1920, pl. XVII
Arnold Haskell, *The Sculptor Speaks: Jacob Epstein to Arnold Haskell*, Heinemann, 1931, p. 168
Robert Black, *The Art of Jacob Epstein*, World Publishing, 1942, cat. no. 21, pl. 82
Richard Buckle, *Jacob Epstein Sculptor*, Faber & Faber, 1963, p. 52, pl. 74 (plaster cast illus.) (listed as 'First Bust of Euphemia')
Evelyn Silber, *The Sculpture of Epstein*, Bucknell University Press, 1986, cat. no. 33.3, pp. 128–129 (illus.)
British Modernist Art 1905–1930, exh. cat., Hirschl & Adler, 1987, cat. no. 56, p. 65 (col. illus.)

Euphemia Lamb first sat for Epstein in 1908, and a bronze of that bust is in the Tate collection. In this second version she takes a different pose, her head tilted up rather than down, her hair tied back rather than hanging loose. By 1911 Epstein had completed his large works for the British Medical Association building in the Strand, and he now wanted to return to smaller works, to train himself in what he called 'a more intensive method of working'. Euphemia was one of the models he employed for this process, and as he explained in his autobiography,

> With that in view, I began a series of studies from the model, which were as exact as I could make them. I worked with great care, and followed the forms of the model by quarter-inches [...] not letting up on any detail of construction of plane, but always keeping the final composition in view.[49]

The year after completing this work Epstein was commissioned to sculpt another major work: the large memorial for the grave of Oscar Wilde in Père Lachaise Cemetery in Paris. He would also be working on one of his greatest achievements, *The Rock Drill*. It would not impress John. Seeing it in 1915 he called it 'altogether the most hideous thing I've seen.'[50] Others were equally hostile. 'To be attacked in the press is almost my daily portion', Epstein complained to John Quinn in July 1917. 'I loom too large, for our feeble small folk of the brush and the chisel. I consider my life in England as a sculptor a failure.'[51] By the time of his death in 1959 he was considered on both sides of the Atlantic to be, as *The New York Times*'s obituary stated, 'a sculptor of world renown'.

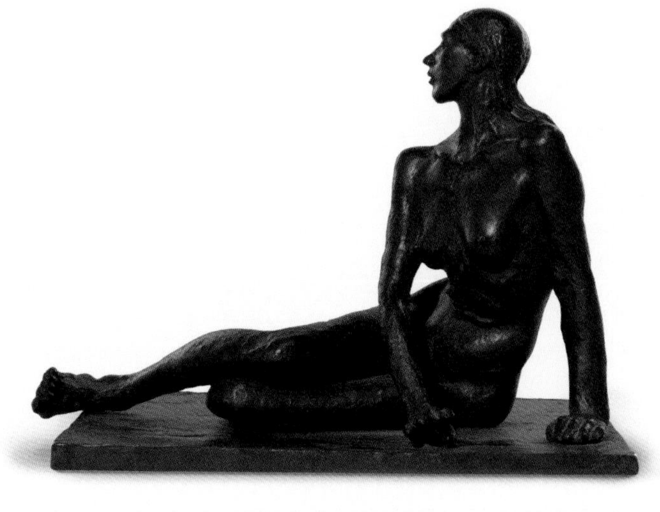

Fig. 10. Jacob Epstein, *Nan (The Dreamer)*, 1910, Private Collection

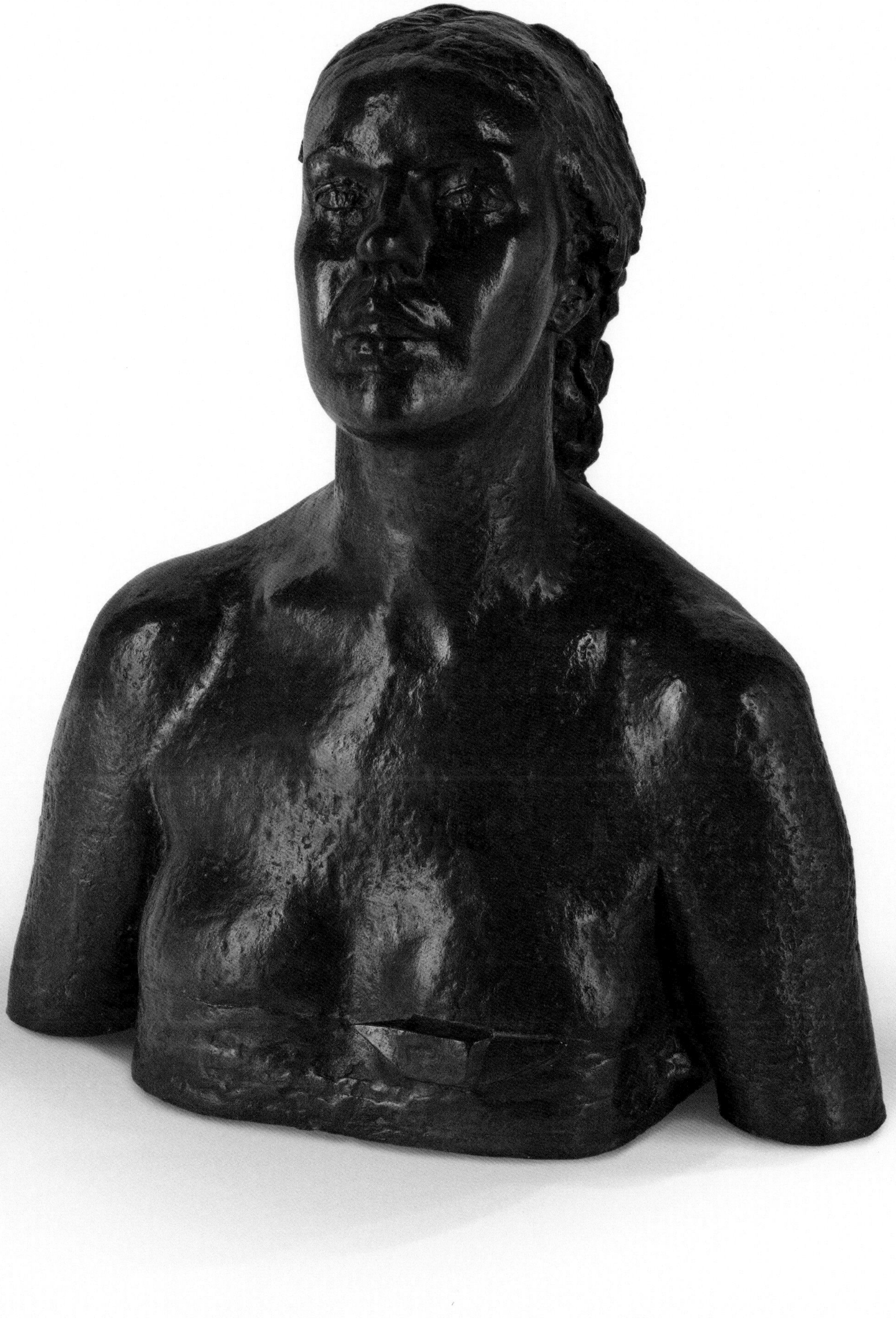

17

AUGUSTUS JOHN

Two Irish Girls, 1908–10
Signed lower left 'John'
Oil on canvas
39.4 × 31.8 cm | 15½ × 12½ in

Provenance

Sir Cyril Kendall Butler
J. Leger and Son, London
Kerrison Preston
Private Collection, by descent

Like William Orpen and Henry Lamb, John was drawn to Ireland and what he saw as the ancient, 'primitive' aspect of the country's heritage, and a distant, almost pagan past that echoed what he had seen in Normandy and among the Romany peoples that so fascinated him wherever he travelled in Europe. Like the Romany, the ancient folk customs of rural Ireland suggested an older, more spiritual (and certainly far less corrupted) world—distant from big European cities, industry, modernity and all its trappings, conventions and social restrictions.

John first visited Ireland in 1907, not long after the death of Ida in Paris. He travelled to Galway to make a portrait of the poet W.B. Yeats, and returned a number of times to the west coast before and during the Great War. On one occasion in Galway City he met James Dickson Innes by chance, and they talked of taking a studio there together.

A new friend, Francis Macnamara, took John to little back street pubs where they listened to Irish sagas and songs: 'At dusk', John recalled, 'dark forms could be espied, lurking among the fallen balks of the old timber-yard beyond, and women still lingered, murmuring, by the Spanish Gate—a face, or part of a face, blooming for an instant from shadowy veils and quickly averted.'[52] John was entranced, and made numerous studies like this one of the Galway people, often working very quickly, abandoning technical finesse in order to capture character. His visits led to his major mural series, *Galway* (1916 and 1920), now in the Tate collection.

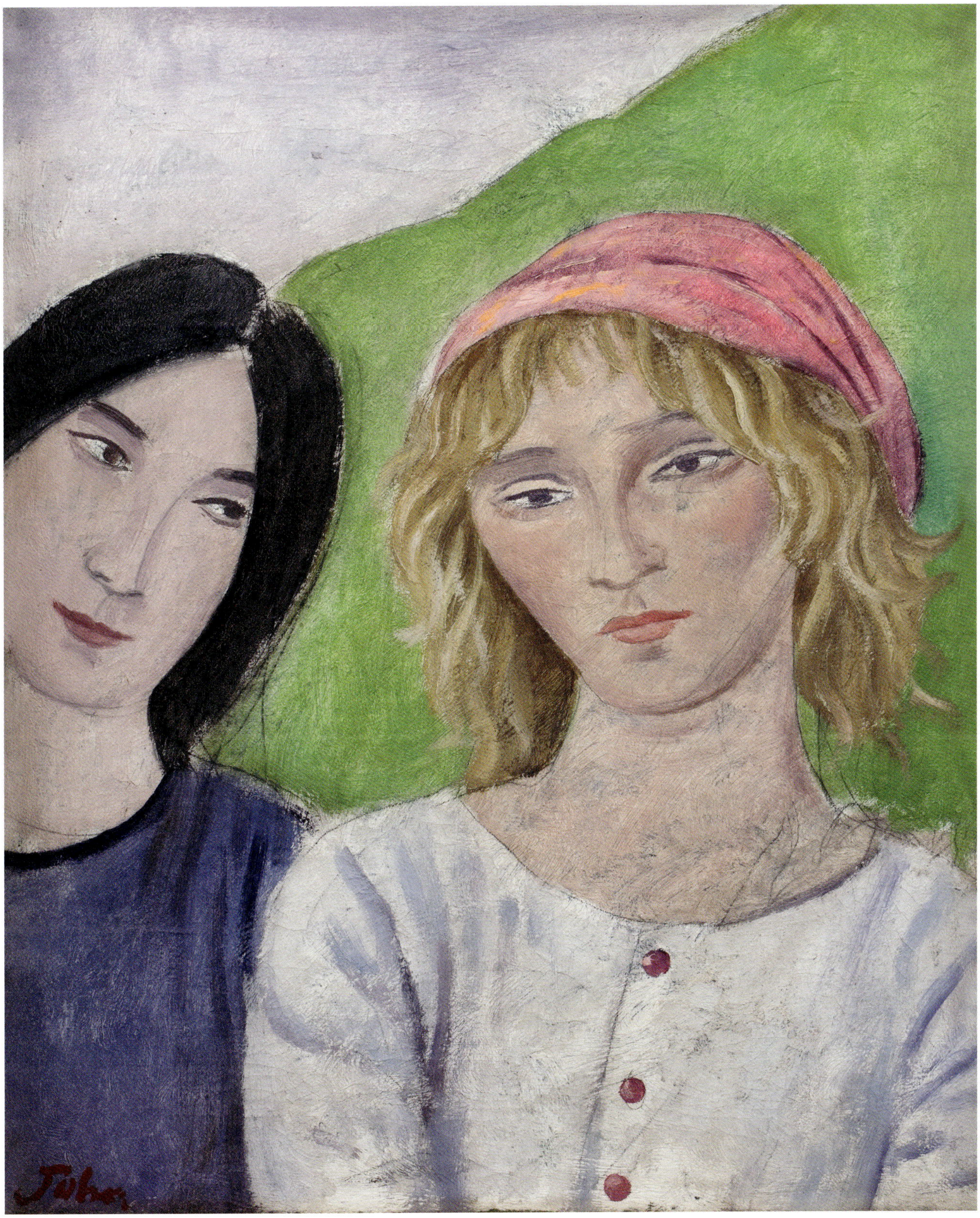

18

HENRY LAMB

Edie McNeill, 1911
Signed and dated lower right 'Lamb/ 1911'
Oil on canvas
127.5 × 76.2 cm | 50¼ × 30 in
Southampton City Art Gallery

Provenance

Sir Michael Sadler
Southampton City Art Gallery, purchased with the assistance of the Chipperfield Bequest Fund, 1938

Exhibitions

Salisbury, Salisbury Museum and Poole, Poole Museum, *Henry Lamb: Out of the Shadows*, 26 May – 30 Sept. 2018 and 18 May – 29 Sept. 2019, cat. no. 9

Literature

G.L.K., *Contemporary British Artists: Henry Lamb*, Ernest Benn, 1923, pl. 2 (illus.)
Keith Clements, *Henry Lamb: The Artist and his Friends*, Redcliffe, 1985, n.p. (illus.)
Harry Moore-Gwyn, *Henry Lamb: Out of the Shadows*, exh. cat., Paul Holberton Publishing, 2018, cat. no. 9, pp. 40–41 (col. illus.)

Lamb's visits to Brittany between 1909 and 1911 were an important stage in his career. The region had been popular with artists since at least the 1860s, but it was Paul Gauguin (1848–1903) who made the little south-coast village of Pont Aven famous. He had first visited in 1886, and it is likely that it was seeing Gauguin's work in Paris that prompted Lamb's visits. When he went to Brittany in 1911 he took Dorelia's sister Edie with him as a model. Nicolette Devas, who as a child knew and was partly brought up by Edie, described her as

> docile and gentle in her ways [...] a thin, sad woman keeping to herself. With her black hair parted in the middle, and the John tradition of clothes, her black eyes and dark skin, she reminded me of an elegant Indian woman [...] With her reticence she revealed nothing, and her black eyes concentrated, it seemed, on the mystery of her soul.[53]

Lamb wrote of this painting that it began 'sublimely', but he was then 'too intimidated not to spoil it [...] but most of the sublimity was accidental.'[54]

The influence of John is apparent, for there is more than a little of John's atmospheric cliff-side paintings of young women about it. But the influences on John himself are also at play here (as they are in a number of Lamb's work from this period), in particular Puvis de Chavannes and Picasso of his 'Blue' and 'Rose' periods. The painting was by and large well received when exhibited with the NEAC in November 1911. For *The Times* it was a 'very interesting portrait,' whilst *The Glasgow Herald* called it 'an exquisite and subtle harmony of greys.'[55]

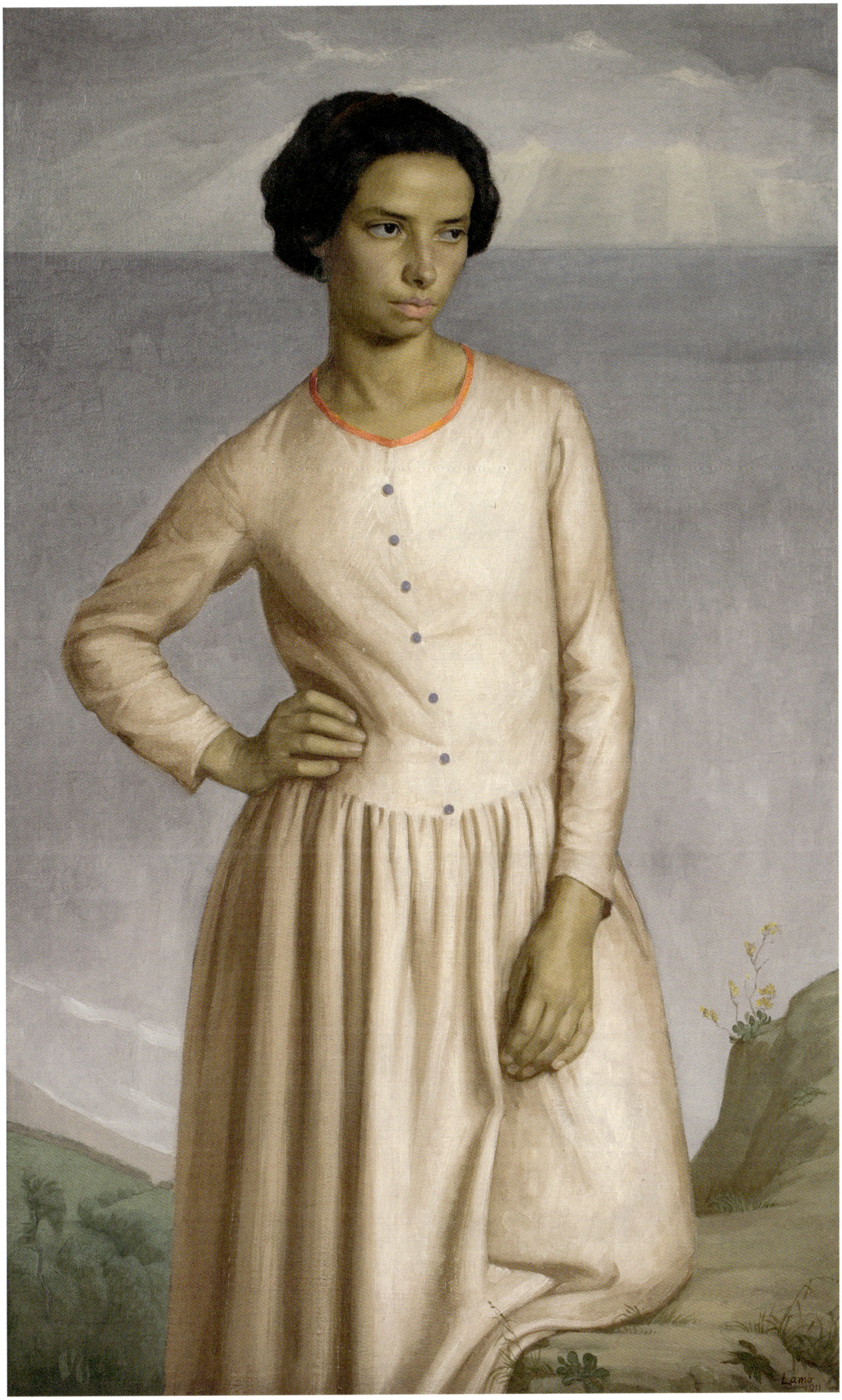

19

HENRY LAMB

Breton Boy, c. 1911
Oil on panel
23.8 × 18.5 cm | 9⅜ × 7¼ in

Provenance

Private Collection
At Gorringe's, Lewes, 3 Sept. 2009
Private Collection

According to at least one contemporary critic, Lamb's early work lacked finesse, as was to be seen in comments by P.G. Konody in a review of an NEAC exhibition in November 1906, only a year after Lamb had begun his artistic studies in earnest:

> There was a time when sterling merit was the only qualification for admission to the 'New English,' and when it would have been impossible to find on these walls so childish, incompetent and ugly a thing—badly conceived, badly drawn and villainously painted—as Mr. H. Lamb's 'Girl with a Necklace.'[56]

But in Konody's opinion, even after his period studying in France there was still little improvement in Lamb's work. Writing a review of an NEAC exhibition in May 1909, he railed against those artists who, he felt, were imitating 'the extravagance' of John's 'more "advanced" style [...] Mr. Henry Lamb seems to be deadly serious in his emulation of all that is disconcerting in Mr. John, and the results are truly deplorable.'[57] As Harry Moore-Gwyn has written, 'Lamb would forever owe a debt to John for his transformation from the workmanlike draughtsman and portraitist of 1905 to the bold and self-assured painter he had become [by 1913], but to fight against the criticism of imitation he would be forced to forge a new direction.'[58] This, Moore-Gwyn argues, Lamb achieved by going to the south coast of Brittany and working there in isolation.

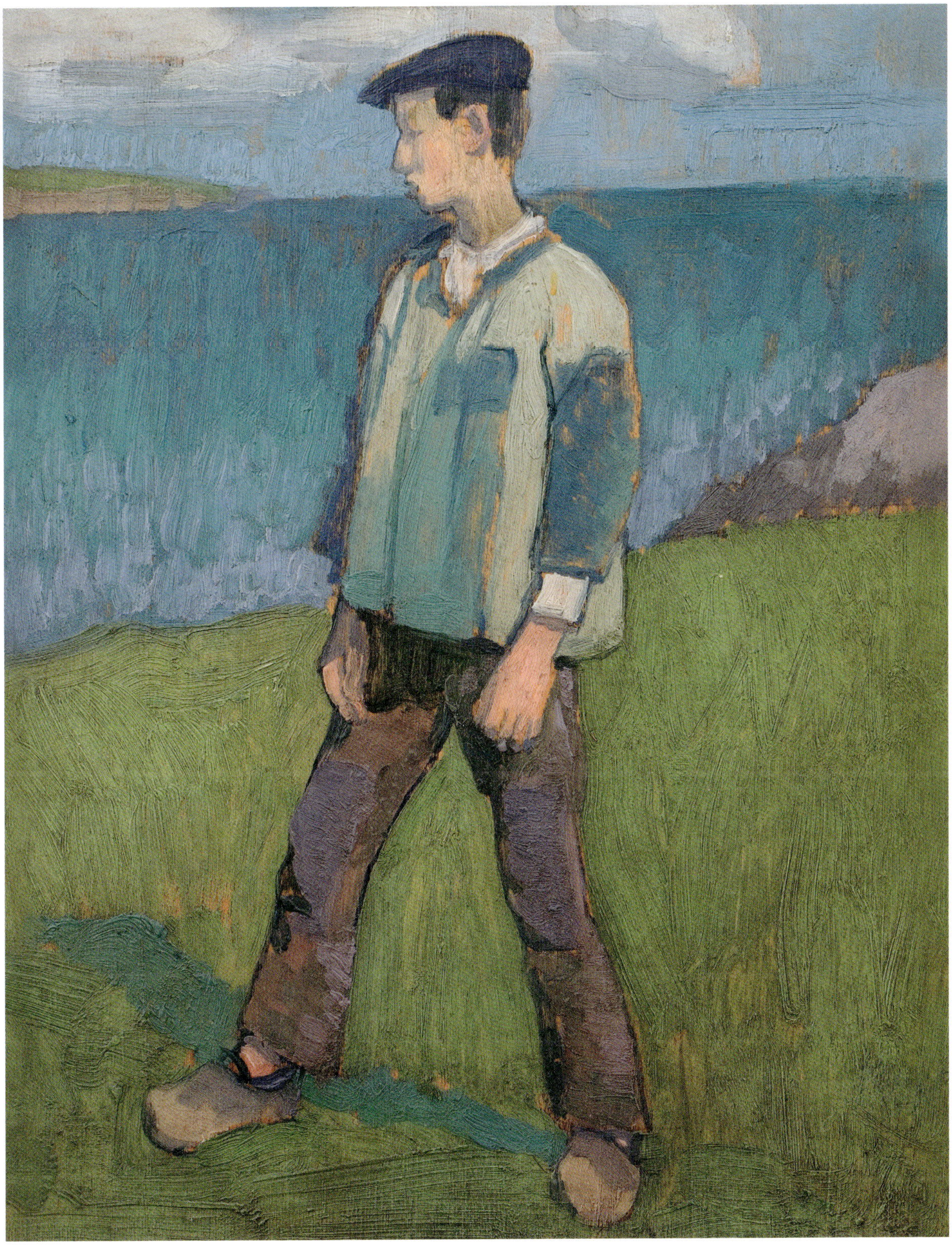

20

HENRY LAMB

Peasant Women with Sickles, c. 1911
Stamped lower right 'Lamb'
Graphite pencil and watercolour on paper
26.7 × 20.6 cm | 10½ × 8⅛ in

Provenance

At Skinner, Boston, 9 Sept. 2011, lot 511
Private Collection

In the summer of 1908, when John, Dorelia and their children were on holiday in Normandy, Lamb was staying nearby. He was struggling financially, and John wrote to Ottoline Morrell, his wealthy lover, pointing out a number of such artists in need of monetary assistance. Lamb had 'just 40 francs left to carry him on through the summer and back to Paris', he explained. 'He is no ordinary personage and has the divine mark on his brow [...] he studies the colours of the world as though nothing else matters.'[59] Part of the appeal of Brittany for many artists in this period was both its cheapness and its remoteness from modernity. Lewis visited the same time that Lamb was there, claiming later that they spent a long summer together. As Lewis explained, '[t]he coastal villages of Finisterre [...] introduced one to a more primitive society.' But unlike Lamb, Lewis found it a difficult environment in which to work: 'The Atlantic air, the raw rich visual food of the barbaric environment, the squealing of the [bagpipes], the crashing of the ocean, induced a creative torpor.' He spent his time writing rather than painting.[60]

Lamb, too, was struck by the simple energy of the landscape. 'The grass in the orchards and meadows is long now and the cows are kept picketted on narrow strips of over-grazed ground at the edges', he would write. 'It is after tea when the boys are back from school and from the sea that one has most chance of sittings.'[61] Although sitting for artists was one way for the locals to make money, Lamb struggled to find willing subjects to sit for long. 'If I am to do any large Breton pictures,' he wrote, 'I shall have to learn how to coax the right people away from their work and sit for love or money.'[62]

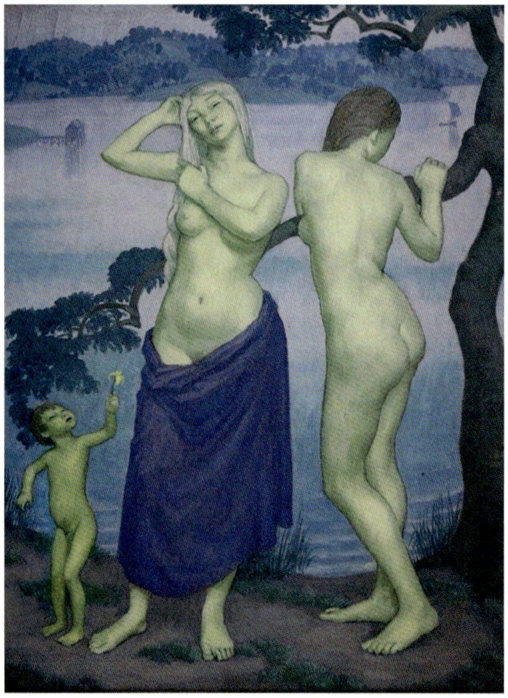

Fig. 11. Henry Lamb, *The Lake*, 1911, Private Collection

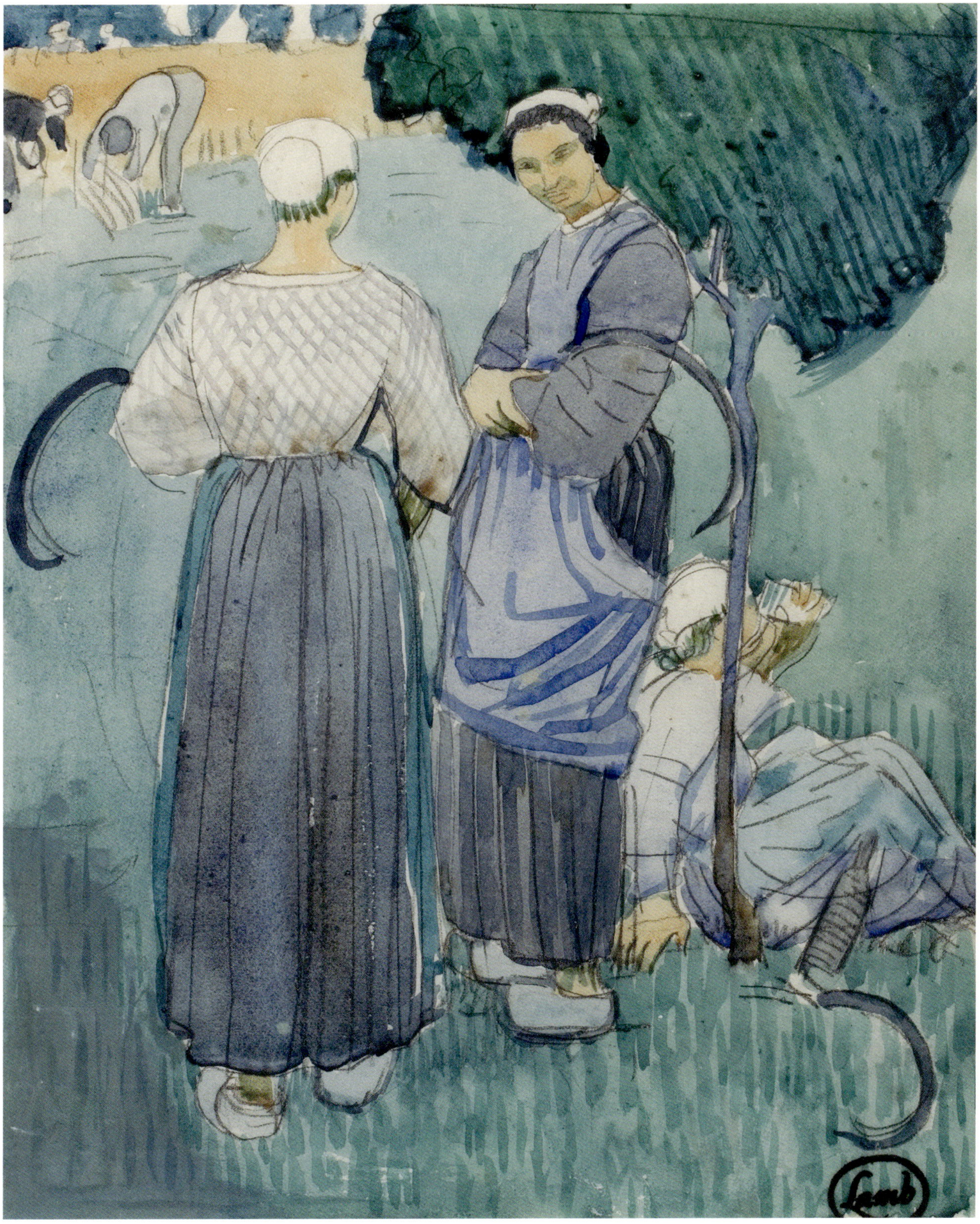
Lamb

21

HENRY LAMB

Portrait of Gola Islander
Stamped lower right 'Lamb'
Inscribed lower right 'Gola Island'
Black chalk and watercolour on paper
29 × 23 cm | 11$^{3}/_{8}$ × 9 in

Provenance

Deborah Devonshire, Duchess of Devonshire
At Sotheby's, London, 2 March 2016, lot 52 (B.I.)
Private Collection

After his visits to Brittany Lamb made two trips to north-west Ireland in 1912 and 1913. It was during this time that he visited the tiny island of Gola, off the coast of Donegal. Like Brittany, Gola was an inspiring environment, speaking of an older, simpler world. Again, Lamb stayed in the home of a local farming family. 'I find myself in a paradise', he wrote from there. 'There are mountains, a lake, rocks, cliffs, caves and white strands: the people are more lovely and even more angelically dispositioned than on the mainland and certainly more sensible.' He was delighted that they 'all promise to sit for me. So I should pass a month agreeable enough even if the weather is bad: at present it is brilliant, only too breezy. The wind never drops [...]. This makes outdoor sketching out of the question [...].'[63]

Lamb sent some of the oil portraits he made in Ireland to the third exhibition of the Camden Town Group, which opened in London in December 1912. Two works made during this visit, *Head of an Irish Girl* and *Irish Girls*, are now in the Tate collection.

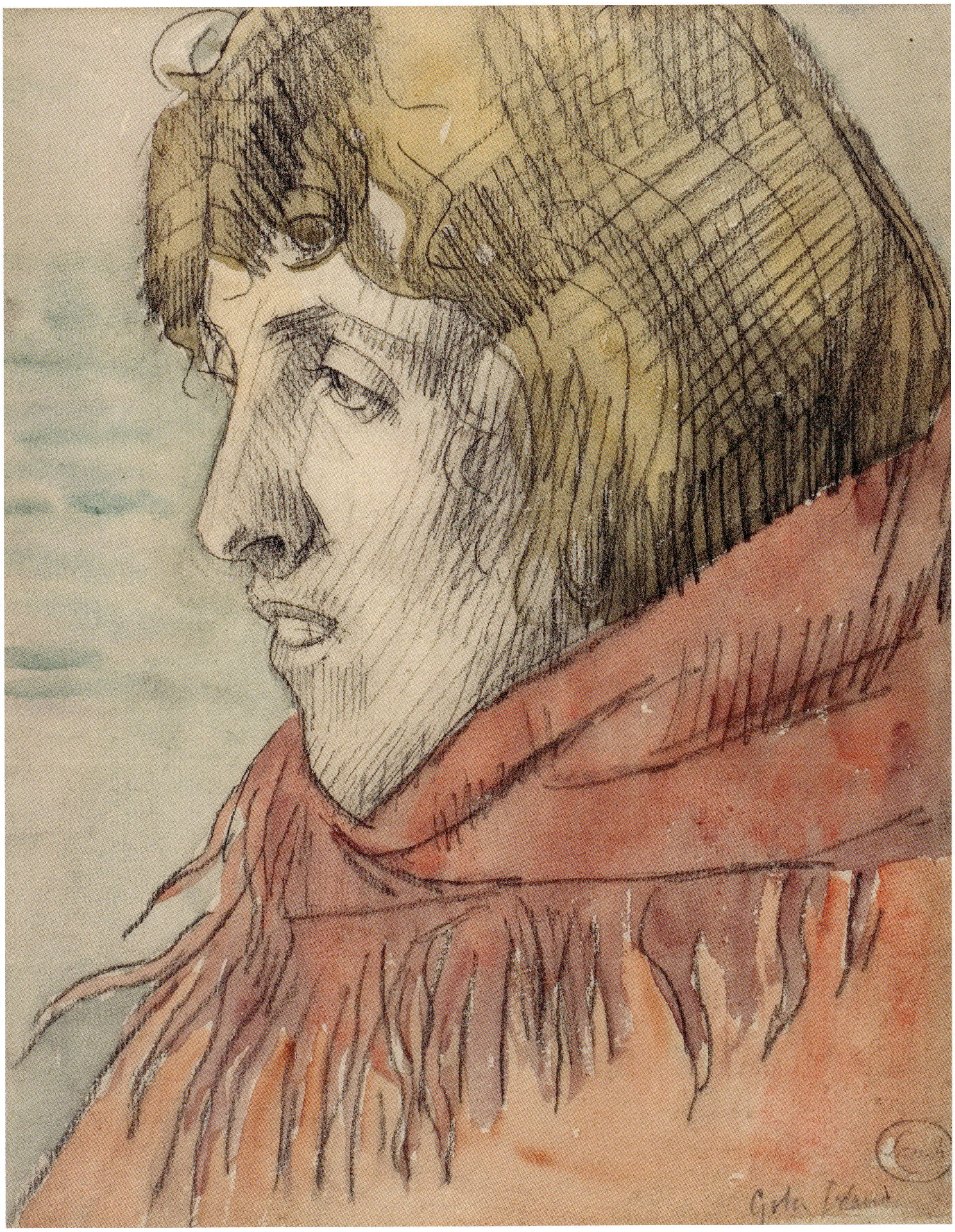

22

DERWENT LEES

Lyndra, 1909

Signed and dated lower left 'Lees Nov. 09'
Graphite pencil on paper
33 × 24.8 cm | 13 × 9¾ in

Provenance

Private Collection
At Lawrences, Crewkerne, 23 April 2010, lot 1625
Private Collection

Literature

This painting will be included in the forthcoming catalogue raisonné of works by Derwent Lees, which is currently being prepared by Lynn Davies.

Derwent Lees (1884–1931) was born and grew up in Australia where as a young man, following a riding accident, his foot was amputated. After a brief period in Paris he studied at the Slade between 1905 and 1907, and made a close friendship with fellow student James Dickson Innes. Lees won prizes for his fine draughtsmanship, and was invited by Tonks to return to the Slade as a drawing assistant. He remained as a teacher there from 1907 to 1918, and he appears standing at the back of the famous 1912 Slade picnic photograph (fig. 14) , along with Gertler, Nevinson, Carrington, Bomberg, Spencer and others. Edith Gilbert Price, known to her friends as Lyndra, was a model who had also posed for John (cat. 23); she and Lees married in 1913.

'His teaching was highly thought of by his colleagues,' Randolph Schwabe would write, 'and by those who came after him. He had remarkable facility, and, over and above his very skillful drawings from life, adopted himself, chameleon-like, to the styles of John, Innes and McEvoy.' Of these three, for a while Lees came nearest to Innes, explained Schwabe, before suddenly turning his style in the direction of McEvoy's watercolours.[64] A *Times* review of a posthumous exhibition at the Redfern Gallery in 1934 acknowledged all three of these artistic influences, whilst also noting Lees's own particular qualities: 'Rich, and rather strange, colour and a curious intensity of statement are characteristic of all his work.'[65]

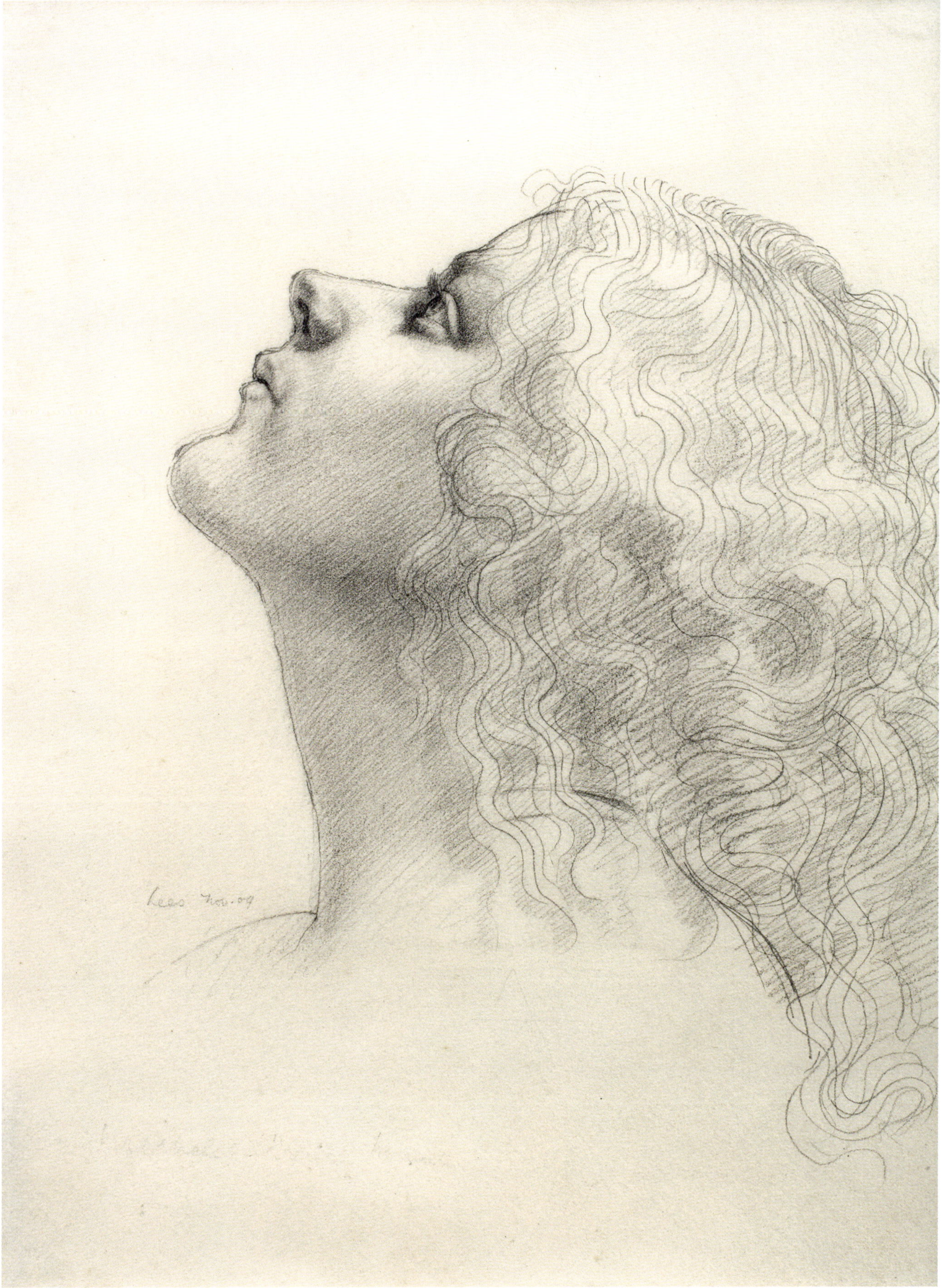
Lees Nov.09

23

AUGUSTUS JOHN

Edith Lees, c. 1910
Signed lower right 'John'
Graphite pencil on paper
39.5 × 20 cm | 15½ × 7¾ in

Provenance

At Christie's, London, 12 June 1981, lot 42
At Christie's, London, 4 March 1983, lot 93
Gerard O'Keeffe, Kanturk, Co. Cork
Private Collection

Edna Clarke-Hall, who studied at the Slade at the same time as John, was for a while a student at Orpen and John's Chelsea Art School. She later described watching as John gave instruction to a young woman who was struggling in his life class:

> She had been doing a ghastly drawing of this model. Then John came along. He looked at this awful drawing which was all sloppy but made no criticism. He just said: 'Would you kindly move and let me sit by your side?' [...] I watched with fascination—you did not often see John draw. He would take a piece of charcoal or a pencil with a very shaky hand but when he started to draw it was perfectly steady. He was doing a clean line drawing of this nude model, simple but very beautiful and absolutely true to the model. It was a great privilege to have John drawing for you because he knew how to draw [...].[66]

John, however, did not find life as a teacher very easy (he needed the money, which was his chief motivation for teaching, a role he did not pursue much longer than he had to). But it was not without its uses. 'My students don't seem to make any progress,' he told Ambrose McEvoy. 'I on the other hand am become so dexterous with a piece of charcoal I astonish myself.'[67]

Whilst some critics found John's work uneven, others were immediately attracted to it. The writer Lytton Strachey saw almost at once that the contradictions at the heart of John's work—the mixture of exquisite technique with sometimes unattractive subjects—were equally its very essence. 'I wish you could see the drawings of Augustus John,' he told Leonard Woolf in 1905, 'his pictures are mere violent beauty and degradation. They'd be very suitable on your walls—visions of awful women in theatric and deathly landscapes, moving idyllically through a quite mad and filthy world. The beauty of line and shape is incomparable.'[68] The bare-foot woman depicted in this drawing is Edith Lees, commonly known as Lyndra, who married John's friend Derwent Lees in 1913.

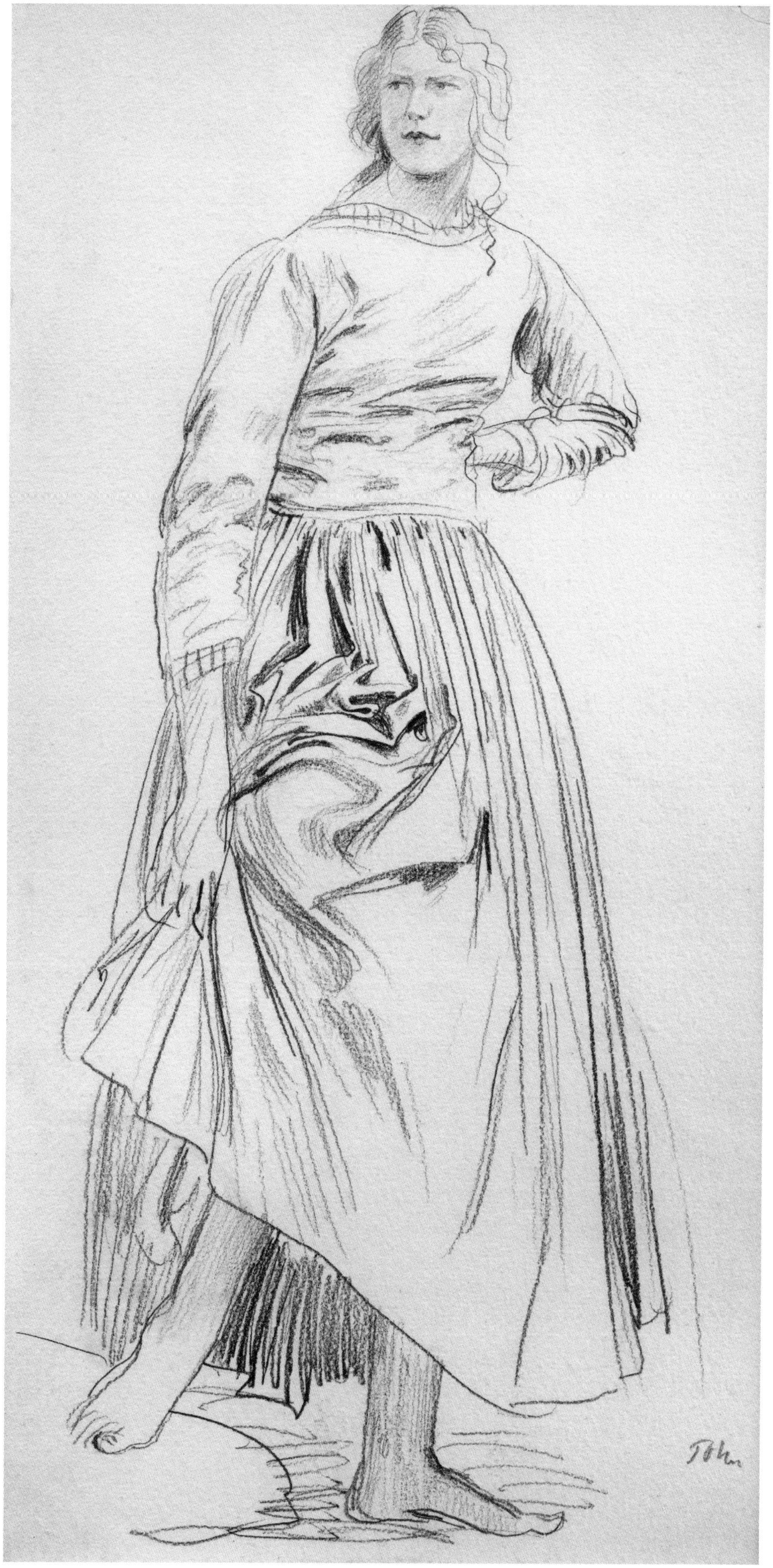
John

24

AUGUSTUS JOHN

Portrait of Edith Lees, c. 1910
Signed lower right 'John'
Pencil on paper
34.3 × 24.4 cm | 13½ × 9⅝ in

Provenance

Private Collection, before 1950
Private Collection, by descent

In 1907, the Irish poet W.B. Yeats wrote that, according to the students of the Slade, John was 'the greatest living draughtsman [...] the only modern who draws like an old master.'[69] The precise crosshatching, sinuous outlines and delicate effects of shading in drawings such as *Portrait of Edith Lees* explain why aspiring young artists held John in such high regard. When Yeats met him later that same year he would be deeply impressed: 'He is himself a delight, the most innocent, wicked man I have ever met,' he informed his friend, the wealthy New York lawyer and collector, John Quinn.[70] In his turn, Quinn would be deeply impressed when he eventually met John in person in London in 1909. Quinn recorded that John was 'one of the most interesting men I have ever met'—and 'probably the greatest painter in England after [John Singer] Sargent.'[71]

In 1907 a former Slade student, John Fothergill, edited an illustrated book, *The Slade: A Collection of Drawings and some Pictures Done by Past and Present Students of the London Slade School of Art, 1893–1907*. It included essays on both Orpen and John, the one on the latter written by Scottish artist and critic, D.S. MacColl (who had himself been at the Slade a few years before John). As MacColl wrote,

> The temper of Mr. John is rebellious against the ordinary and scornful of the pretty, and the anarch [sic] young [man] has not yet controlled or concentrated his passion to the creation of great pictures; but he has given us some measure of his powers and indication of their quality. He has made imaginative sketches ... he has followed the tramps and gypsies ... he has painted portraits first-rate in character ... he has scattered broadcast drawings with a wild flame of life in them [...] He is not, I think, very popular; he has not, I hope, arrived, but I do hope he is going on, and that prodigal sketching will not be the last chapter of his story. So lusty an appetite promises growth.

MacColl then added that the illustrations of John's drawings reproduced in the book were 'a casual handful, but one or two of them will justify to the unacquainted what some of us think of their author.'[72] In this respect they succeeded, in so far that it was on seeing them in this publication that C.R.W. Nevinson decided that he had to go to the Slade, in order that he too might learn to draw like John.

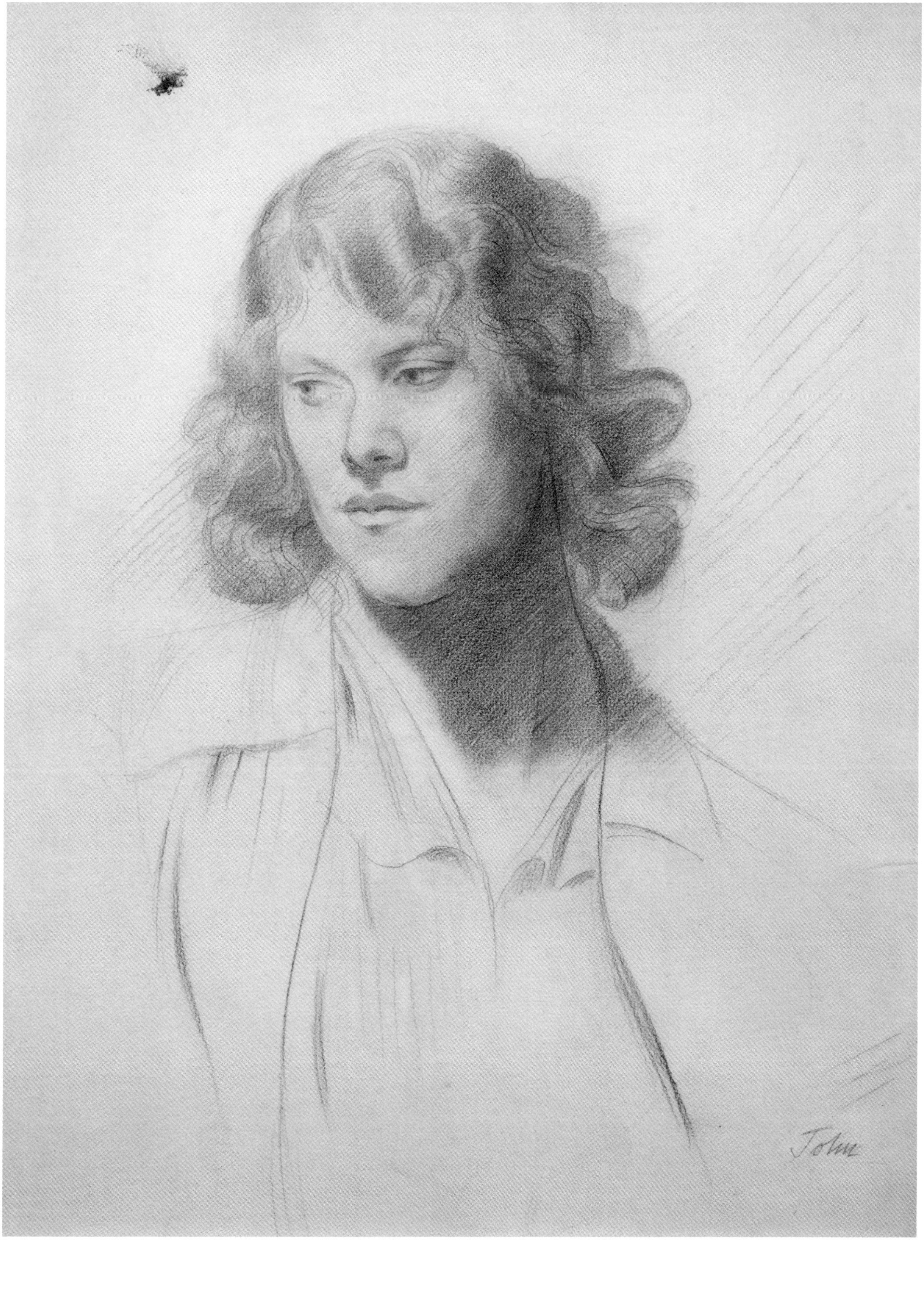
John

25

DERWENT LEES

Lyndra in the Garden, c. 1913
Oil on board
50.8 × 35.6 cm | 20 × 14 in

Provenance

Leger Galleries, London
Private Collection, Aug. 1963
At Roseberys, London, 9 Dec. 2008, lot 721
Private Collection

Literature

This painting will be included in the forthcoming catalogue raisonné of works by Derwent Lees, which is currently being prepared by Lynn Davies.

It took some years for John to translate his aptitude as a draughtsman into a similar, consistent ability working with oil paint. His portrait of Ida, *Merikli*, with its clear debt to Rembrandt, generated some excitement when it was exhibited at the NEAC's 1902 winter exhibition. (It was this painting that prompted *The Athenaeum's* critic to remark that John was 'evidently a genius, if by that we understand the power of seeing things in a new and personal manner; but his work shows a perverse disregard of beauty which is to be regretted.')[73]

But it was not until his large portrait of Dorelia, *Smiling Woman*, was exhibited at the International Society's 'Exhibition of Fair Women' at London's New Gallery in February 1909 that John really established himself as a British painter of recognised importance. 'Here at last Mr. John has "arrived",' Roger Fry declared in *The Burlington Magazine*, 'in painting as definitely as he has long ago done in drawing.' The portrait seemed comfortably to unite the old with the new. 'This woman is essentially modern,' wrote Fry, 'but she belongs nonetheless to the fifteenth century.'[74] The following month, Laurence Binyon praised John's large portraits of women for their 'character, life and rhythmic power.'[75] This full-length figure painting, one of several that Derwent Lees painted of his wife, shows the younger artist responding to John's example.

As Kenneth McConkey has argued, John's example—his 'message about "the spirit of place"—in practice a rocky landscape uniformly lit and inhabited by "gypsy-esque" females—found receptive eyes and ears among his immediate following in works by James Dickson Innes, Derwent Lees, Henry Lamb and Ian Strang.' Even Paul Nash and Gerald Brockhurst were among those influenced by John's romantic imagery, 'the woman in place', in their early work.[76] In 1915 Wyndham Lewis would complain of the 'the pseudo-gypsy hordes' John had 'launched against' London. By this date, he claimed, John was 'an institution like Madame Tussauds, never, I hope, to be pulled down. He quite deserves this classic eminence and habitual security.'[77]

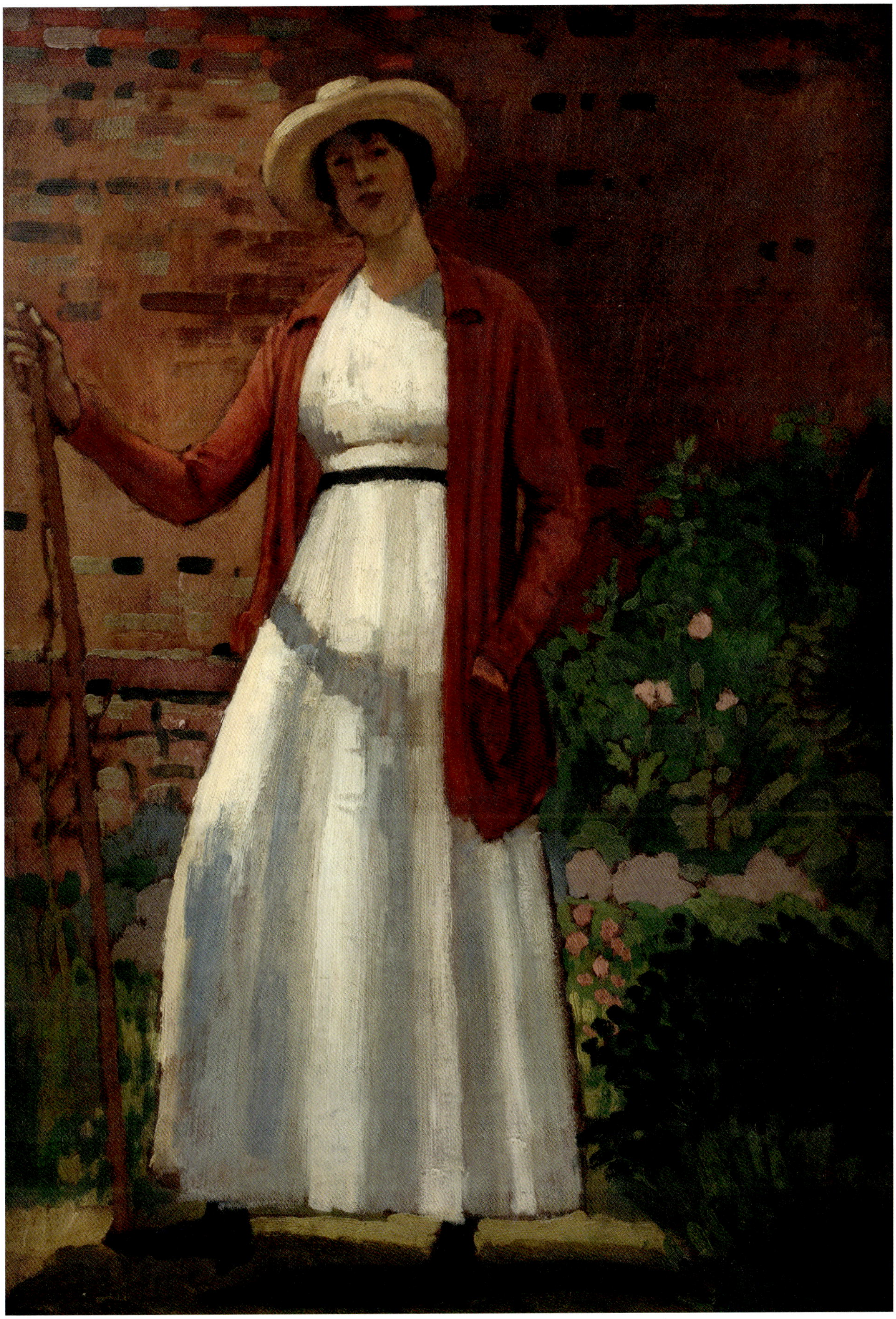

26

AUGUSTUS JOHN

Girl in a Blue Striped Coat, c. 1910
Signed lower left 'JOHN'
Oil on panel
33 × 23.5 cm | 13 × 9¼ in

Provenance

Thomas Agnew & Sons, London
F.W. Burman
David Jones' Gallery, Sydney
Private Collection, Sydney
At Shapiro Auctioneers, Chippendale, 24 May 2022, lot 25
Private Collection

In May 1909 the critic C.J. Holmes wrote in *The Burlington Magazine* that John was now to be aligned with the moderns, not with the old masters he had previously revered:

> He sides with Manet rather than with Van Dyck, and his power and originality excuse this preference. Fortunately there are many mansions in the house of Art; and if a remarkable talent chooses one of them we should be content to let him have his place there, even if we think he might be somewhat better accommodated elsewhere.[78]

In this period from 1907 to 1914 the female figure—often, but not always, Dorelia, and as often as not painted out of doors—became a key motif in John's repertoire. John was generally at his best when he did not linger too long on a drawing or painting. William Rothenstein wrote that the freshness of John's 1902 oil painting of Ida, *Merikli*, was spoilt by bad glazing. 'That was the worst of John', he suggested: 'he was impetuous, undisciplined, and had scant respect for his materials.'[79] The model for this freely painted panel has not been identified, though it was most likely Dorelia.

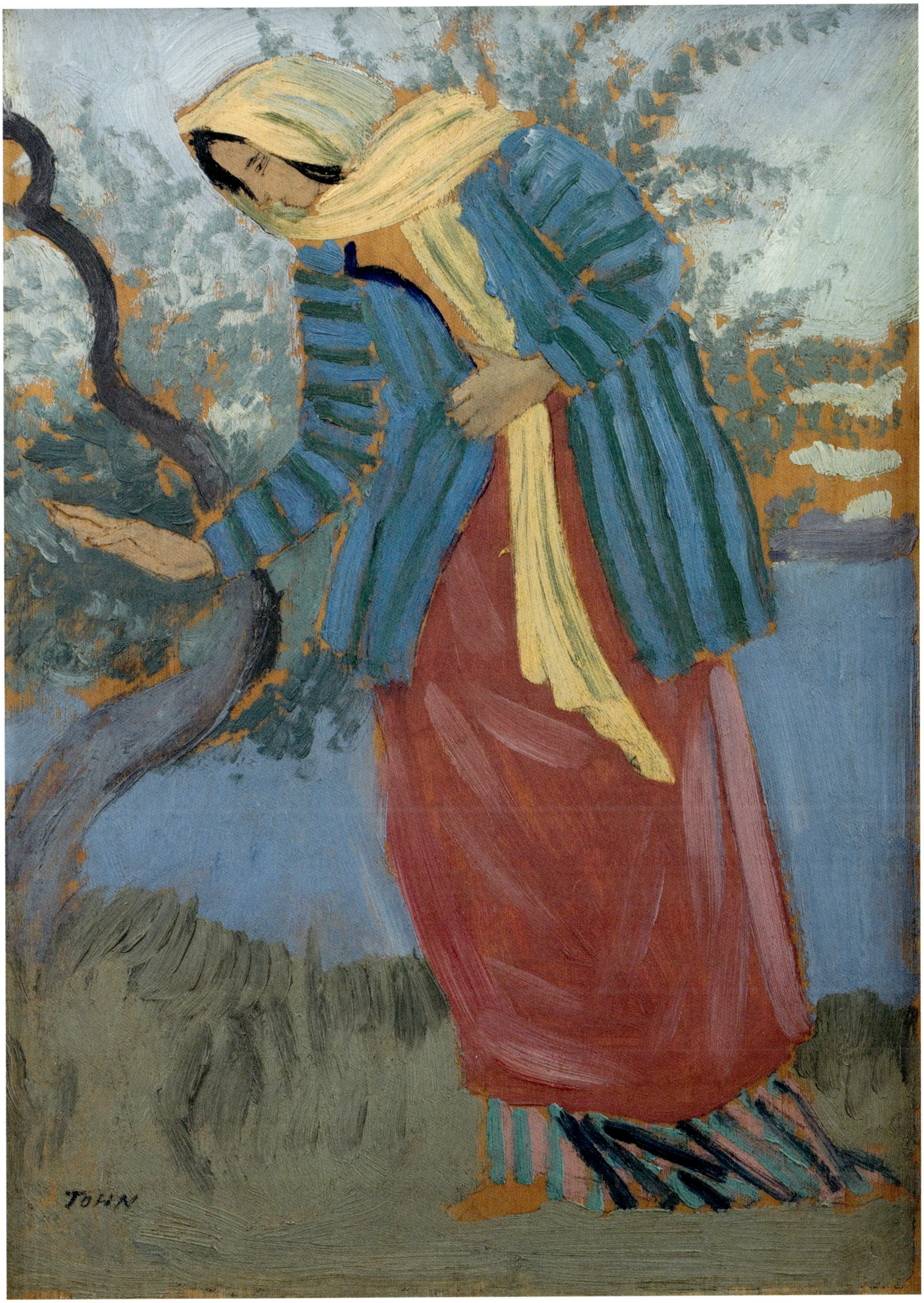
JOHN

27

AUGUSTUS JOHN

Lady on Clifftop, 1910
Signed lower right 'John'
Oil on panel
23.25 × 33 cm | 9¼ × 13 in

Provenance

Viscount Cowdray
Woolley & Wallis, Salisbury, 10 Dec. 2014, lot 303
Private Collection

John's success with *Laughing Woman* was soon followed by another large work, *The Way Down to the Sea* (fig. 1), a major work from this hugely productive and important period of John's career. Both paintings came from the burst of activity that followed Dorelia's insistence that they find a more permanent home in London, which led John to taking a lease on a handsome Georgian villa at 153 Church Street, Chelsea. *The Way Down to the Sea* was itself inspired by John's period in France, and in particular his on-going interest in the work of Pierre Puvis de Chavannes. The adult figures in the painting centre on Ida (who had died in Paris two years before). Her pose is taken from a series of life drawings possibly made whilst they were camping together on Dartmoor following the birth of Pyramus in 1905. Ida, rather enigmatically, holds a ball over the head of one of her sons, whilst Dorelia stands behind her. The two other female figures are probably Euphemia Lamb and Dorelia's sister, Jessie.

When the influential art critic P.G. Konody saw the painting in 1909 he was ambivalent, writing in *The Observer* that John's achievements were both 'ambitious and wayward.' There was, Konody felt, too much 'willful eccentricity' in the picture, as well as too many 'echoes of the art of the past'. For these reasons, he wrote, he could not accept *The Way Down to the Sea* 'as the final utterance of Mr. John's art. It holds the germ of real greatness, but can only be accepted as a transitory phase in this interesting artist's evolution.' Konody would have preferred it if John, like William Nicholson, would devote his obvious talents to what he called 'serious straightforward portraiture.'[80] Instead, John kept painting the people who interested him: Dorelia, his children, the occasional female friend, and the landscape around him. *Lady on Clifftop*, probably painted beside the Étang de Berre, depicts an enigmatic female figure silhouetted against the blue waters of the lake and an atmospheric coast scene beyond.

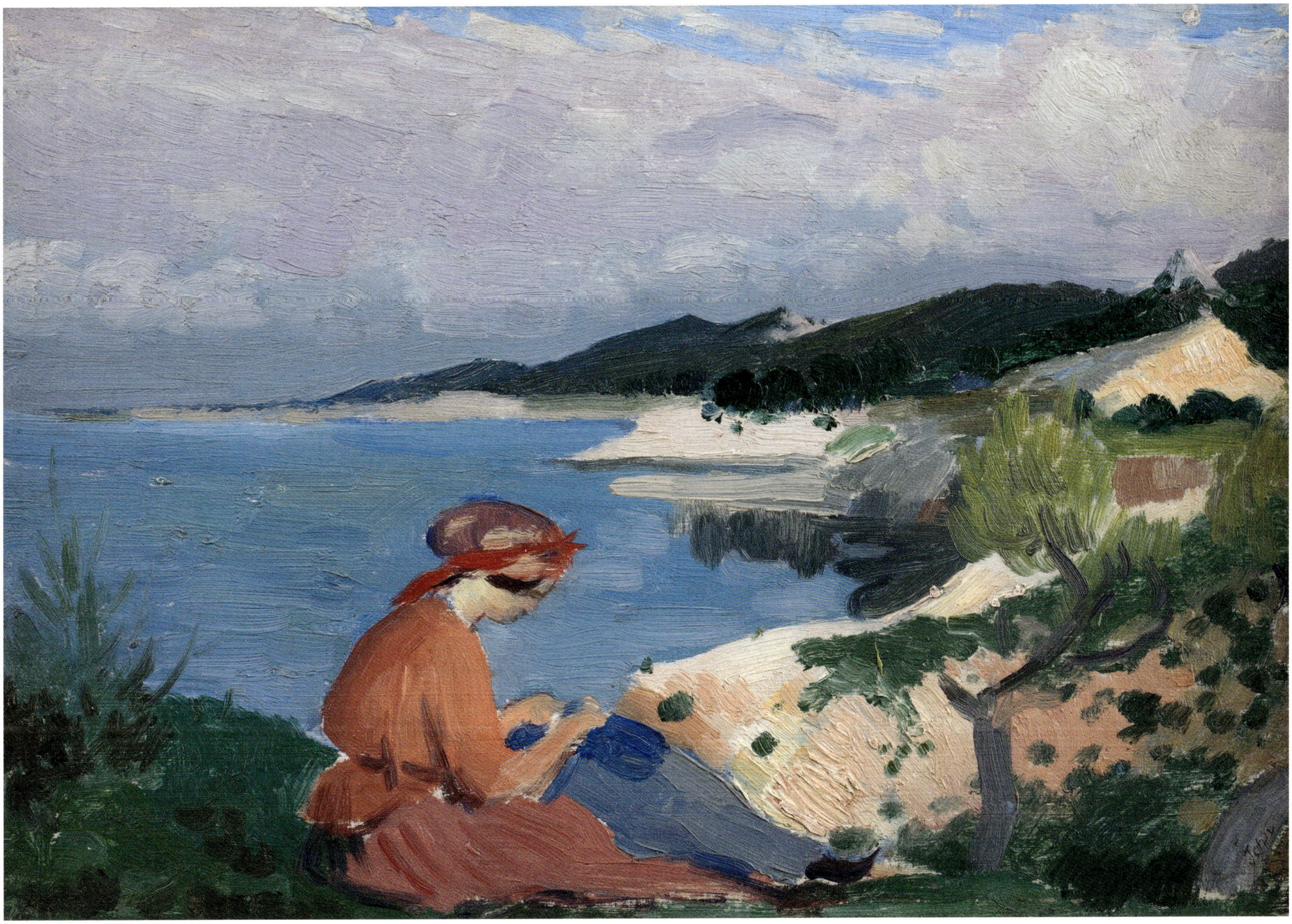

28

JAMES DICKSON INNES

Girl Reading in a Landscape, 1913

Signed and dated lower right 'J D Innes 13'
Oil on panel
40.6 × 61 cm | 16 × 24 in

Provenance

Private Collection, acquired directly from the artist
At Sotheby's, London, 2 June 2004, lot 28
Private Collection

Literature

John Hoole and Margaret Simons, *James Dickson Innes 1887–1914*, Lund Humphries, 2013, cat. no. JDI 345, pp. 152, 153, 181, fig. 167 (col. illus.)

Following his trips to the south of France Innes returned to Wales, making a journey that eventually took him to Arenig Fawr, a small mountain near the lakeside town of Bala. Like Collioure, Arenig would be a revelation and an inspiration. Returning once more to London in the autumn of 1910, he arrived there at around the same time that John returned to England from Martigues. That winter, Innes visited both Fry's ground-breaking exhibition 'Manet and the Post-Impressionists' and John's exhibition of 'Provençal studies' at the Chenil Gallery.[81] He and John met, and quickly formed a close bond.

Innes had an exhibition of his recent work at the Chenil Gallery, and John recommended his work to Quinn. 'He's a really gifted chap,' he explained, 'and shows a rare imagination in his landscapes. It is true he has not done much yet, being quite young, but if he can keep it up there can be no doubt about his future.'[82] John lent him 'a good deal of money,' and Quinn bought a number of Innes's watercolours.[83] But John also led Innes into more drinking, and more trouble: in 1911 Fothergill recorded that Innes had been 'wounded in the head in a back street in Chelsea along with John in a fight. What stupidities some people allow themselves to indulge in because they call themselves artists.'[84]

But Fothergill remained impressed by Innes's work. In his opinion, after the two trips to Collioure Innes's painting had 'suddenly flowered', and 'he gave to Wales the same vivid greens, purples and changing colours that he had seen in France.' Instead of remaining 'just one more exponent of pale English sunshine and veiled charm', Innes tore the veil away altogether 'and got nature with the brilliance of stained glass.'[85]

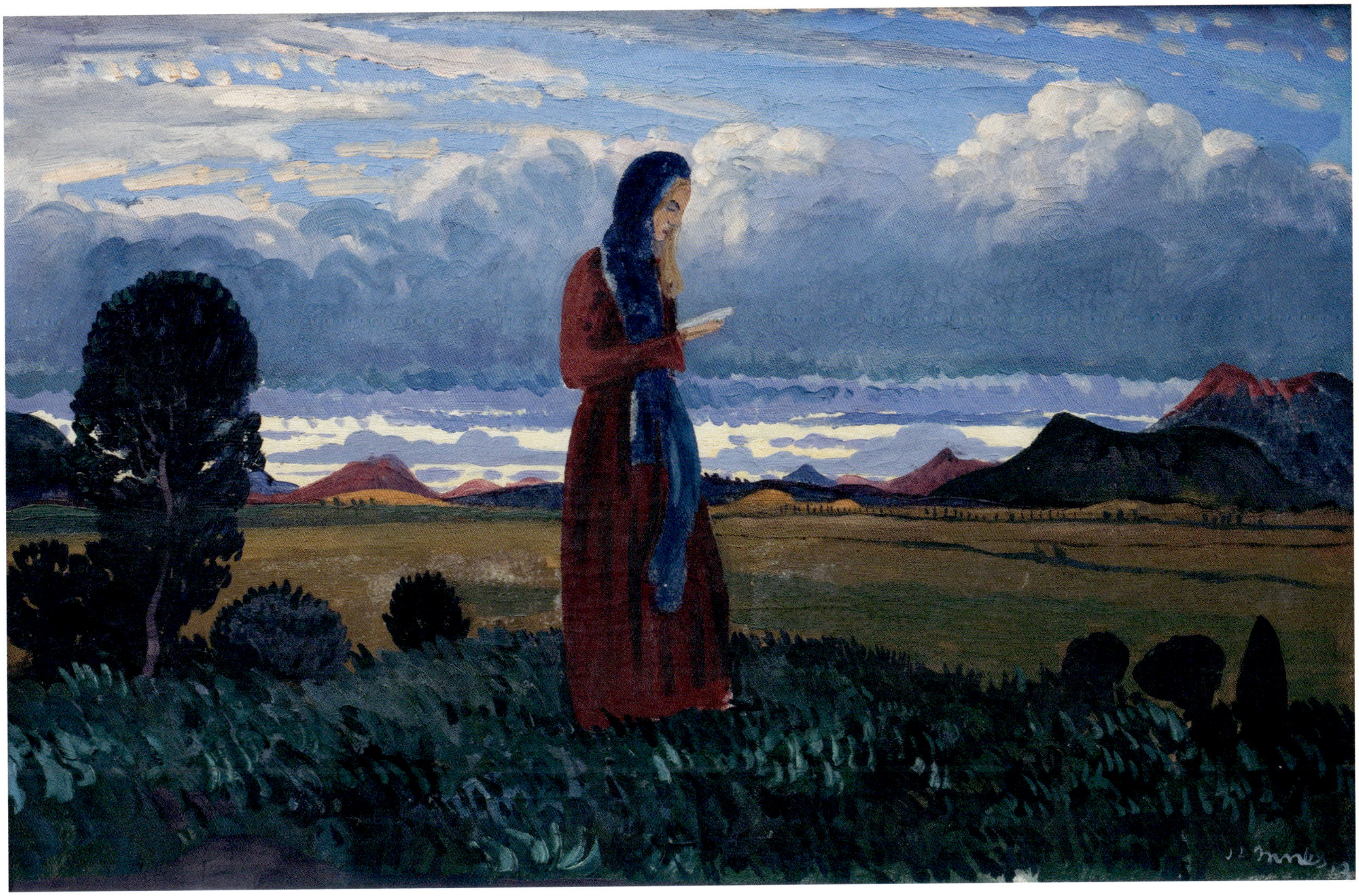

29

AUGUSTUS JOHN

Port de Bouc, 1910
Signed lower right 'John'
Oil on wood
23.5 × 31.7 cm | 9¼ × 12½ in
Southampton City Art Gallery

Provenance

Southampton City Art Gallery, purchased with the assistance of the Frederick William Smith Bequest Fund, 1955

Exhibitions

Possibly London, Chenil Gallery, *Provençal Studies and Other Works by Augustus E. John*, Nov. – Dec. 1910, cat. no. 43 (listed as 'Near Port de Bouc')
Poole, Poole Museum and Salisbury, Salisbury Museum, *Augustus John: Drawn from Life*, 26 May – 30 Sept. 2018 and 18 May – 29 Sept. 2019, cat. no. 29

Literature

John Hoole and Margaret Simons, *James Dickson Innes 1887–1914*, Lund Humphries, 2013, p. 90, fig. 89 (col. illus.)
David Boyd Haycock, *Augustus John: Drawn from Nature*, exh. cat., Paul Holberton Publishing, 2018, cat. no. 29, pp. 69–70 (illus.)

John's difficulties and strengths as a painter became clear at around the same time Picasso and Braque were revolutionising art for ever with their invention of Cubism, and Filippo Marinetti was announcing the arrival of the Futurists in the pages of *Le Figaro*. It was in 1909 that John painted one of his finest pre-1914 works, *The Way Down to the Sea* (fig. 1), as well as one of his worst, his large portrait, *The Rt. Hon. Harold Chaloner Dowdall, Lord Mayor of Liverpool and his Sword-bearer*. This rather pompous painting added to the sense in certain quarters that here was an artist not in full command of his abilities.

John's clearest motive in taking the commission, beside his debt of friendship to the sitter, was the money—which he needed to sustain his ever-expanding family. John was in a 'very bad way,' Wyndham Lewis told a friend, 'not so much in what he is actually doing, which seems to be portraits of Mayors and Mayoresses, but in his state of mind. That cursed family of children is his excuse,' Lewis explained—but he blamed 'that sickening bitch' Dorelia most of all, calling her 'his accomplice in the muzzle of his genius.'[86] A commission at this same time from the wealthy dealer Sir Hugh Lane to paint a series of large canvases for his new home in Chelsea was much more successful. From this would eventually come one of John's best-known (though unfinished) works, *Lyric Fantasy* (c. 1913–14), now in the Tate collection.

Further significant assistance came from John Quinn. At the end of 1909 he offered John an annual sum of £300 in return for first choice of the resulting paintings. In early 1910 John used this opportunity to travel to Italy, and then to settle for the summer in Provence. There he would paint a series of rapid oil paintings on panel, of Dorelia, of his children, and of the landscape, including this one. They made the most of the bright light and sunshine, and these 'Provençal Sketches' were an immense success when exhibited at the Carfax Gallery on his return to London at the end of the year.

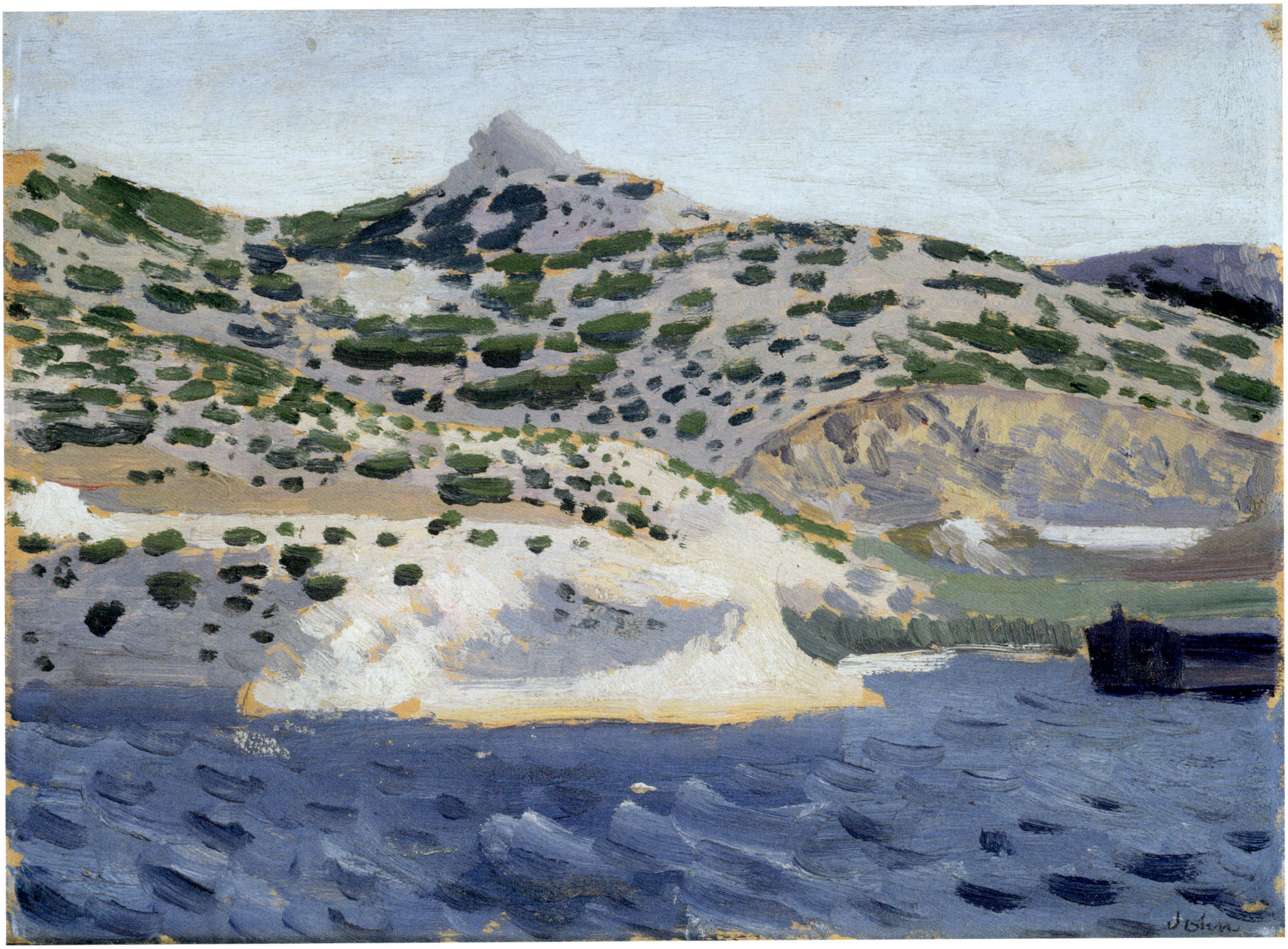
John

30

DERWENT LEES

Near Cassis, 1911
Oil on panel
25.4 × 35.6 cm | 10 × 14 in

Provenance

Mr and Mrs J.B. Priestley, 1947
Jane Wyndham Lewis, 1951, following her divorce from the above
The Fine Art Society, London, 1971
At Christie's, London, 8 June 1990, lot 245
Private Collection

Literature

This painting will be included in the forthcoming catalogue raisonné of works by Derwent Lees, which is currently being prepared by Lynn Davies.

John, Innes and Lees worked together for a while in the south of France and around Bala in Wales, as well as in Dorset between 1911 and 1913, and Lees and Innes would both be visitors to John's home at Alderney Manor. John encouraged Quinn to buy Lees's work, and three of his paintings were shown in the Armory Show in New York in 1913. John and Lees would exhibit together at the Chenil Gallery in December 1913. Paintings by Lees are in numerous collections, including the Tate, Manchester City Art Gallery and the Art Gallery of South Australia.

According to John, 'Lees owed much to the example of Innes: he found in his friend's approach to nature a means of release from his academic shackles, and with immense will and intelligence strove to adapt himself to a new outlook.'[87] Although some of Lees's paintings are almost indistinguishable from those by Innes, he could, at times, actually be a better landscape painter than either of the companions whose work he emulated in France, Dorset and Wales.

John had made friends with the wealthy patron of the arts and first president of the newly founded Contemporary Art Society, Thomas Scott-Ellis, 8th Lord Howard de Walden. In 1912 he and Lees visited him and his wife at their home at Chirk Castle in Shropshire, on the English-Welsh border. According to Lady Howard de Walden,

> I used to hear a knock on my bedroom door at any hour of the night, and wake up, imagining hearing breathing. And there [Lees] stood, quite quietly and said, 'I come to your door for protection, now I will go to bed.' Every day I took him for a walk, but he would only come if I wore white gloves. So white gloves I wore over hills and dales. He did paint rather well, but was as mad as a hatter.[88]

Lees eventually suffered a complete mental breakdown in 1918. According to Frank Rutter, it was caused by Lees 'brooding' over his inability to serve in the Great War due to his damaged leg, but the affliction was clearly incipient long before this.[89] Lees spent the final thirteen years of his life in a psychiatric institution in Surrey, where he died in 1931. His early work continued to be exhibited at the Redfern Gallery, and the Tate holds a number of his works in its collection. This includes his jewel-like landscape, *Métaire des Abeilles* (1912), painted near Collioure.

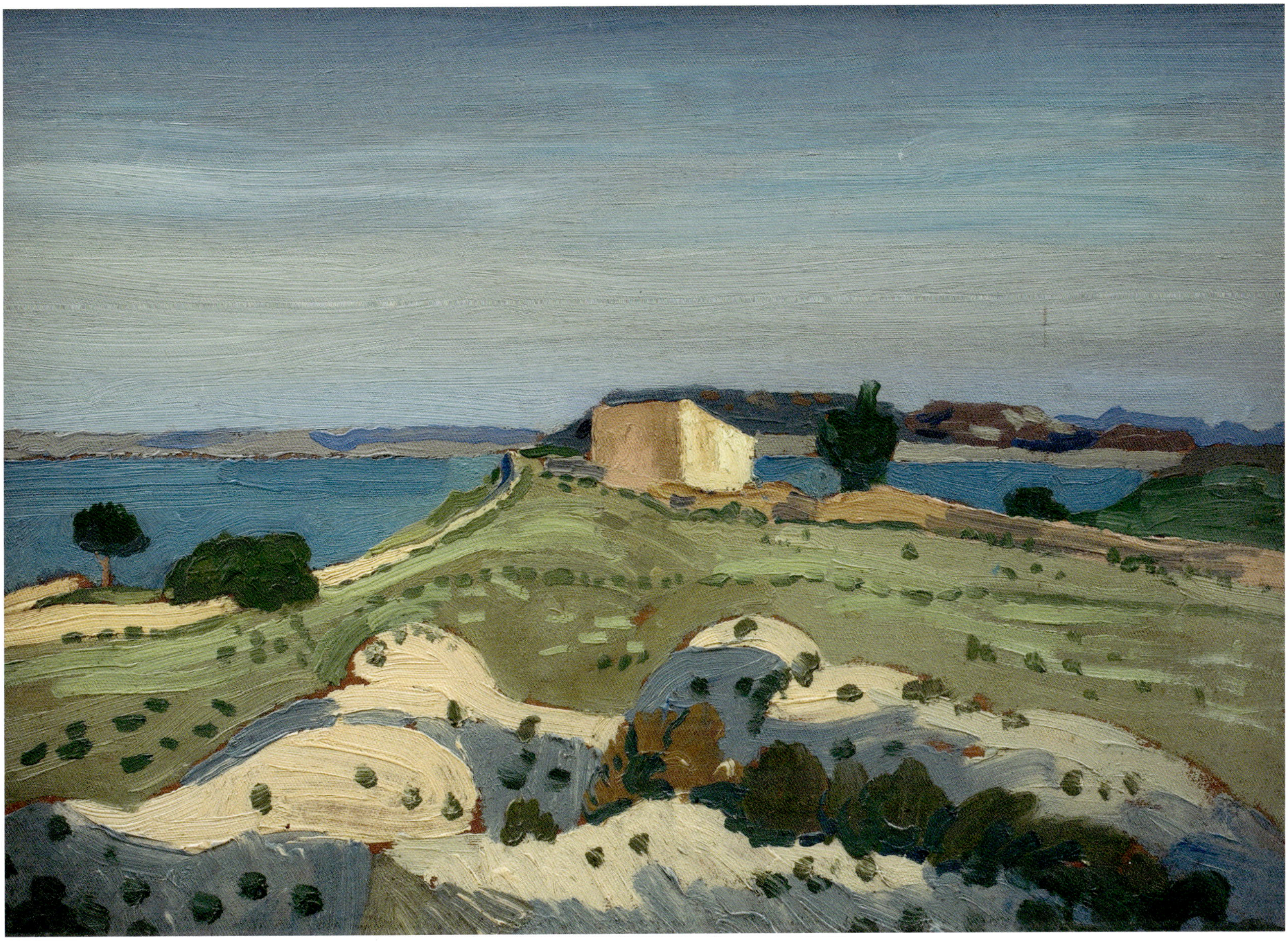

31

AUGUSTUS JOHN

The Arenig Fach, c. 1911
Oil on panel
30.5 × 40.6 cm | 12 × 16 in

Provenance

Thomas Agnew & Sons, London
Elizabeth Taylor, 1979
At Christie's, London, 8 Feb. 2012, lot 509
Private Collection

In the spring of 1911 Innes invited John to come and see 'his' mountain, Arenig. 'This is the most wonderful place I've seen', John wrote to Dorelia shortly after their arrival. 'The air is superb and the mountains wonderful.'[90] As their paintings reveal, at times they painted virtually shoulder-to-shoulder. Following the technique John had developed in Provence of working rapidly in oil, Innes began using oil paints almost in the same way he used watercolours.

Innes painted even faster than John, who was impressed as his new friend worked with 'swiftness and decision', setting down in a single sitting 'view after jewelled view of the delectable mountains he loved.'[91] It is possible some of Innes's approach rubbed off on John—though John would be careful not to identify too close a link. 'My mountains were never Innes-conceived,' he told John Rothenstein in 1952. This was just '[a]nother silly legend. They were conceived by neither of us but seen by both, though more effectively by him, for I lacked his superstition and drew better. His limitations actually helped him.'[92]

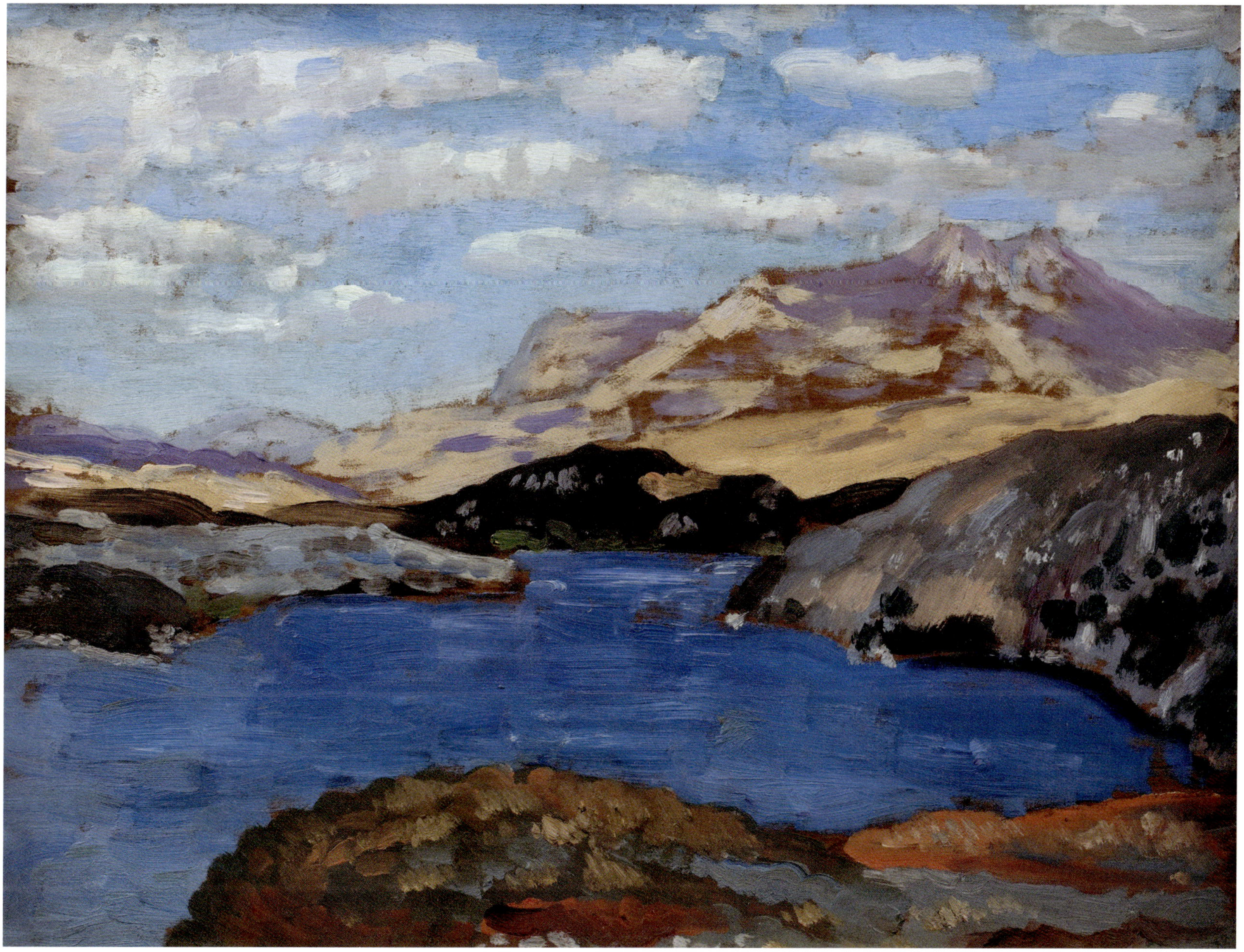

32

JAMES DICKSON INNES

Sunset, Arenig, c. 1911–12
Oil on panel
22.9 × 33 cm | 9 × 13 in

Provenance

Horace de Vere Cole
C.M. Palairet
At Christie's, London, 3 March 1989, lot 319
Private Collection

Exhibitions

London, National Gallery of British Art, *Loan Exhibition of Works of J.D. Innes*, Nov. 1921, cat. no. 88
London, Leicester Galleries, *Paintings by J.D. Innes*, April 1928, cat. no. 113

Literature

John Hoole and Margaret Simons, *James Dickson Innes 1887–1914*, Lund Humphries, 2013, cat. no. JDI 226, p. 175 (listed as 'Arenig, Sunset')

Dorelia and Euphemia briefly joined Innes and John during their painting trip to Wales in 1911, and both men made numerous paintings of their lovers in the landscape of hills, rivers and waterfalls. But when they were alone they pursued other women—Innes less successfully, as John admitted: 'if we both loved the same wandering girl, it was I who embraced her and obtained her response.'[93] When they met a party of gypsies Innes vanished for a week in pursuit of one of the women. 'But the chase was too much for him', John recorded. 'Somewhere in the outskirts of Ruabon he collapsed—from fatigue or worse.'[94] Still not fully recovered, Innes returned to Collioure with Derwent Lees later in the year—though, like John, he would become irritated with Lees's way of mimicking their style. Nevertheless, the work John, Innes and Lees produced that year was vivid and electrifying, representing some of the most exciting Post-Impressionist painting being done by any British artists, anywhere.

In 1911 Innes and John were invited to join the Camden Town Group, though like Wyndham Lewis, who also showed with the group, their work did not fit comfortably with Walter Sickert, Spencer Gore and Lucien Pissarro's scenes of suburban London life. Innes and John continued to be close through 1912, and in January 1913 John, Innes and Lees were in the south of France together. Later in the year they would be in Wales again, but John was starting to tire of Innes. 'I can't stand him for long', he had already told Dorelia: it was another friendship that had run its course.[95]

In the final few years of his short life Innes spent time in Spain and North Africa in a vain attempt to overcome his illness. By the time of the outbreak of the Great War in August 1914 Innes was in a nursing home in Kent, and John visited him there with Euphemia. Innes died shortly afterwards; he was only twenty-seven.

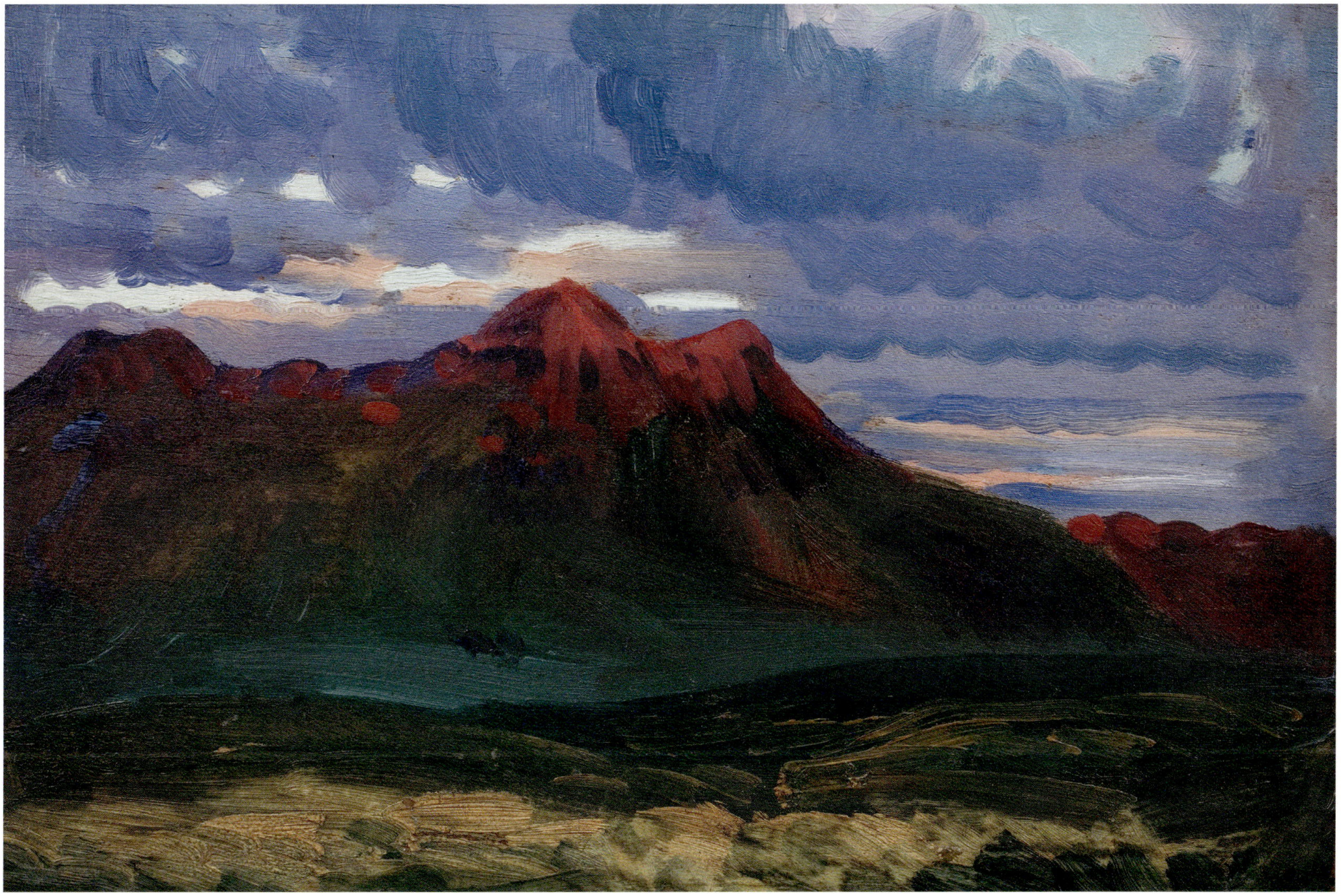

33

AUGUSTUS JOHN

Landscape in Wales, c. 1911–13
Signed lower right 'John'
Oil on panel
32.5 × 40.6 cm | 12¾ × 16 in

Provenance

With Arthur Tooth & Sons, London
Private Collection
Private Collection, by descent
Piano Nobile, London

Although John was born and brought up in Wales, it was only through the encouragement of fellow Welshman James Dickson Innes that in 1911 he returned there to paint. As John recounted of his first visit to Wales with Innes,

> Our meeting at Arenig was cordial, and yet I seemed to detect a certain reserve on his part: he was experiencing, I fancy, the scruples of a lover on introducing a friend to his best girl—in this case, the mountain before us which he regarded, with good reason, as his spiritual property. Had he not been the first discover and surmount it?[96]

These paintings proved successful. In his autobiography *Chiaroscuro*, John wrote that the house he commissioned to be built for him in Mallord Street, Chelsea, was paid for with the proceeds of an exhibition at the Goupil Gallery that 'consisted of pictures done in North Wales.'[97] This painting, known only as 'Landscape in Wales', most likely depicts the environs of Arenig.

Yet landscape painting would become less and less a part of John's oeuvre after this date. For a while, back in London, he continued to focus on the grand compositions Sir Hugh Lane had commissioned, and which resulted in *Lyric Fantasy*—unfinished on account of Lane's untimely death in the sinking of the RMS *Lusitania* in 1915. The First World War marked a change in John's personality and outlook. Encountering him at a theatre in London in July 1917, the young New Zealand writer Katherine Mansfield would describe him as looking 'really impressive'. But as she added, 'I seemed to see his mind, his haggard mind, like a strange forbidding country [...]. Everything exhausted and finished—great black rings where the fires had been, and not a single fire even left to smoulder.' She went on, 'I expect this is all rubbish, and he's really a happy man and fond of his bottle and a goo-goo eye. But I don't think so.'[98]

Having failed to complete the enormous canvas that had been commissioned from him by the Canadian government to commemorate their army's achievements in France, more and more of John's time would be taken up with portraiture. This transformation into a society portraitist would mark the second stage of John's career: the age of great fame and greater fortune. No longer was he the Bohemian outsider; he had become a part of the establishment.

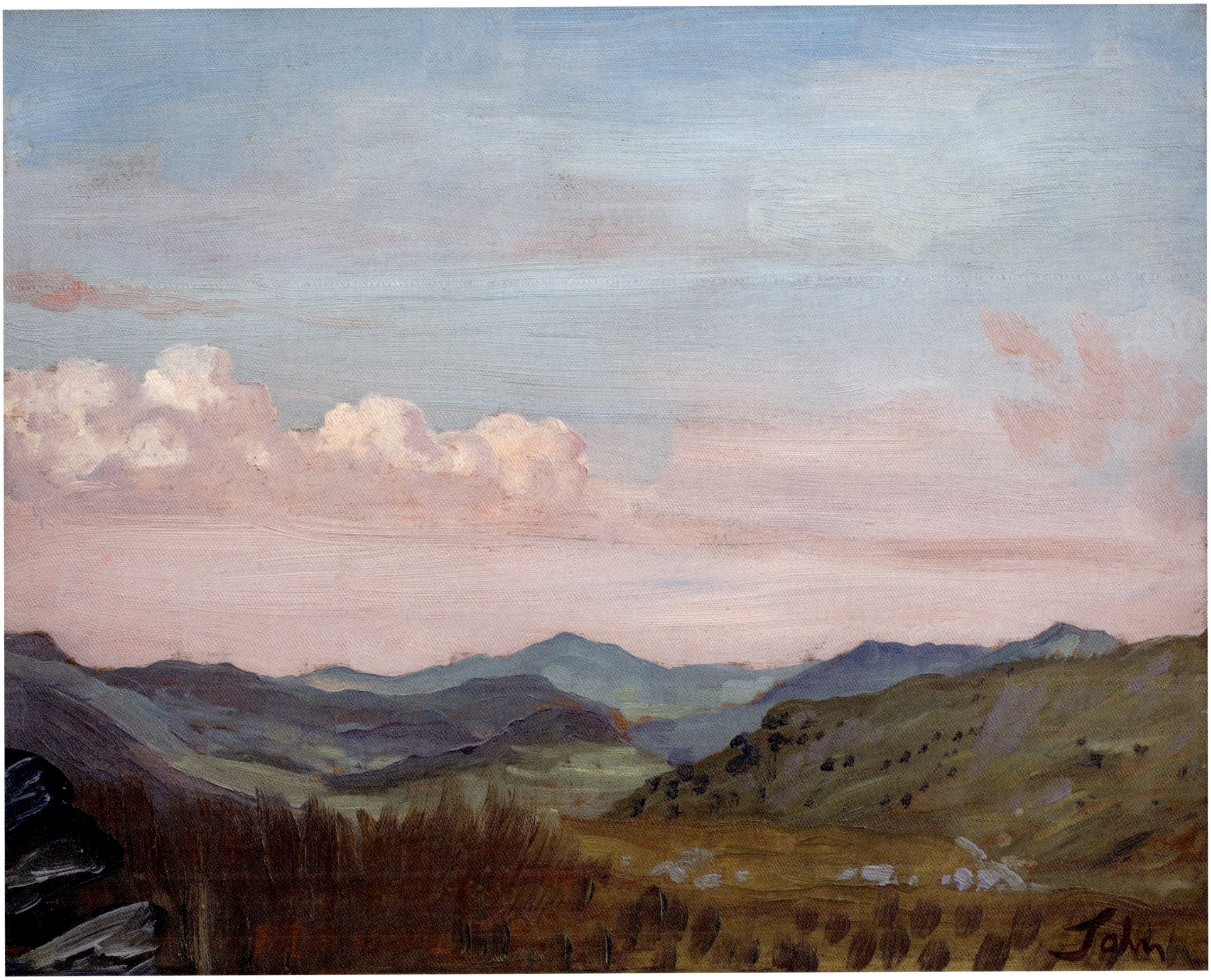
John

34

HENRY LAMB

Errigal, Donegal, 1913
Oil on panel
23.5 × 31.1 cm | 9¼ × 12¼ in

Provenance

Private Collection, acquired from the artist, 1913
At Christie's, London, 22 June 1962, lot 101
Sandra Lummis Fine Art, London
At Dreweatts, Newbury, 22 Oct. 2022, lot 40
Private Collection

Lamb first visited Donegal in 1912, and returned the following year. At just under 2,500 feet Errigal is a relatively small mountain but iconic nevertheless. During his time in Ireland Lamb made numerous *pochades*—small outdoor studies of the landscape. The weather hampered his efforts, however. It was 'hopelessly bad', he wrote, and the poor light 'makes it almost impossible to invent good colours.'[99]

But by the spring of 1914 Lamb was emerging as a serious presence in the British art scene. In a review of the Whitechapel Art Gallery's retrospective of twentieth century art held in May 1914, the critic Sir Claude Phillips picked him out for particular praise: 'The art of Mr. Henry Lamb, unique in its combination of the decadent with the austere, is marked by an inventiveness, a nobility of design, with which nothing here can be paralleled.'[100] Then came the war, and Lamb would eventually enlist with the Royal Army Medical Corps. He would be gassed in France during the late stages of the conflict, and received the Military Cross for bravery shown in action in Palestine. Shortly afterwards he was commissioned by the government to paint a number of large official records. These—along with his earlier portrait of the writer Lytton Strachey, now in the Tate collection—are among his greatest works.

Little of real greatness was to follow, however. He appears to have picked up Walter Sickert's muted palette, and began painting in varying shades of brown. As was the case with Epstein and John, the war had denuded him of something. The colour had gone. Although he would be elected as a Royal Academician in 1949 he had lost the glow of youth. He would not really thrive in the new, post-war world.

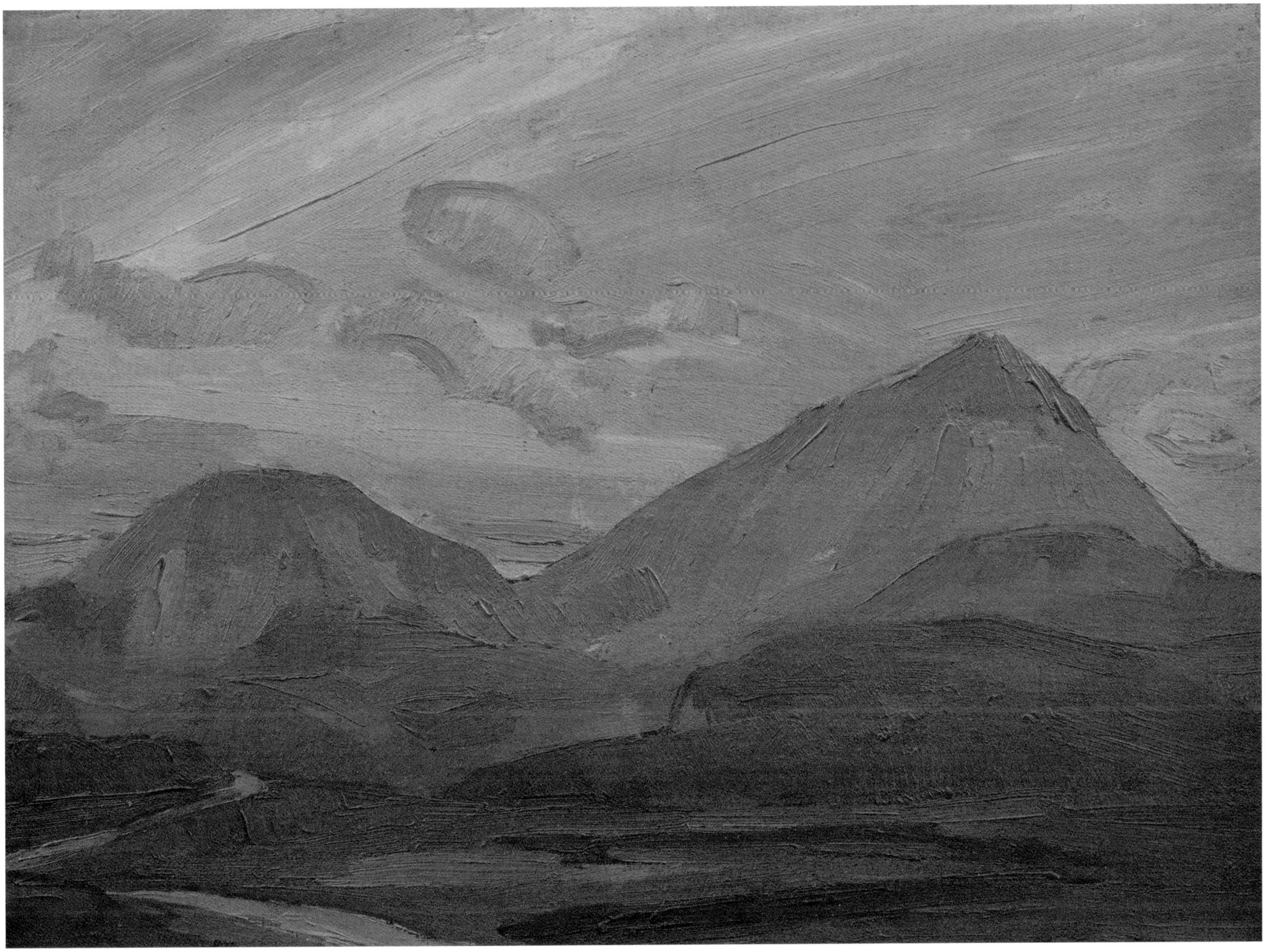

35

WILLIAM ORPEN

The Yacht Race (Sighting the Boat), c. 1913
Signed lower right 'ORPEN'
Graphite pencil and watercolour on paper
53.5 × 76.5 cm | 21 × 30⅛ in

Provenance

Herschel V. Jones, by March 1916
At Sotheby's, London, 22 May 1997, lot 254 (listed as 'Watching the Yacht Race (On the Cliffs Howth)')
Peter Nahum at The Leicester Galleries, London
Pyms Gallery, London
Private Collection, 2004

Exhibitions

London, Goupil Gallery, *Goupil Gallery Salon*, Oct. – Dec. 1913, cat. no. 307 (listed as 'Sighting the Boat')
New York, M. Knoedler & Co., *Recent Works by William Orpen*, 23 March – 4 April 1914, cat. no. 14
Buffalo, Albright-Knox Art Gallery, *Recent Works by William Orpen*, 15 April – 4 May 1914, cat. no. 13
London, Chenil Galleries, *Drawings by William Orpen A.R.A.*, Jan. 1915
London, Pyms Gallery, *The Art of a Nation: Three Centuries of Irish Painting*, June 2002, cat. no. 31

Literature

'Studio Talk', *The Studio*, vol. LX (Oct. 1913), p. 222
'A Great Draughtsman', *Liverpool Daily Post*, 5 Jan. 1914, p. 6
E.S. Grew, 'The Severe Art of Drawing', *The Graphic*, 17 Jan. 1914, p. 104 (illus.)
The Ladies Field, vol. LXIV (31 Jan. 1914), p. 473 (illus.)
The Art News, vol. I, no. 1 (9 Feb. 1914), p. 3 (illus.)
'Fine Arts – Portfolio of Drawings by W. Orpen', *The Athenaeum*, 14 Feb. 1914, p. 235
New York American, 30 March 1914, p. 8
Colour Magazine, vol. 4, no. 3 (April 1916), p. 92 (illus.)
Alan and Mary Hobart, *The Art of a Nation: Three Centuries of Irish Painting*, exh. cat., Pyms Gallery, 2002, cat. no. 31, pp. 109–112 (illus.)

Every summer between 1902 and 1914 Orpen returned to Ireland to teach at the Metropolitan School of Art in Dublin. His 'brilliant teaching', the Irish art historian John Turpin has written, followed the example of the Slade, and 'inspired a whole generation of Irish artists.'[101] Orpen rented a house on the coast at Howth, where he had grown up and where this watercolour was painted.

'The view looking towards the mainland in the evening, from the top of the Hill of Howth, is wonderful and ever-changing', Orpen wrote in his memoir, *Stories of Old Ireland*. 'Of an evening, as the sun dips, the water of the bay becomes brilliant gold [...]. And the Sheerwater gulls start their laughter, like a bunch of young girls at the side of a road laughing at the passers-by. Ireland! Romance, laughter, and tears!'[102]

When Max Beerbohm came to caricature Orpen in 1914, a drawing later acquired by the Tate collection, it was as a personification of 'bravura'. Orpen's capabilities as a draughtsman were almost as renowned as those of Augustus John, being similarly well-practiced and informed by a rich sense of art's history. In *The Yacht Race*, *Life Class on the Beach* (fig. 12), and other tinted drawings made at Howth, Orpen showed men, women and children engrossed in leisure pursuits. The seated child in *The Yacht Race* was repeated—her blue dress turned to yellow—in an oil painting called *The Edge of the Cliff, Howth*. These relaxed figures, often barefoot, were drawn in precise, sparing outlines. Strong colours were reserved exclusively for accents, emphasising a green hat or a pink jacket, with skin tones made to seem pale and limpid as the sea and sky, their brilliance conveyed by the whiteness of the paper.

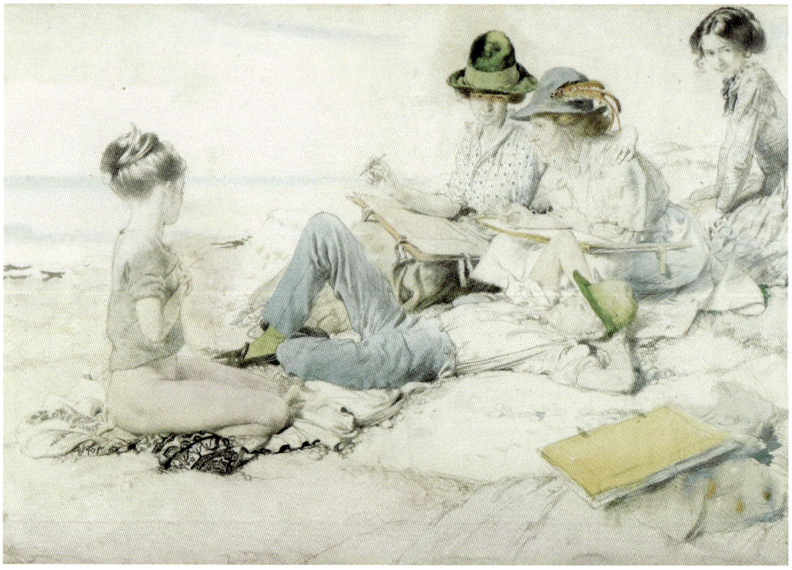

Fig.12. William Orpen, *Life Class on the Beach*, 1910, Private Collection

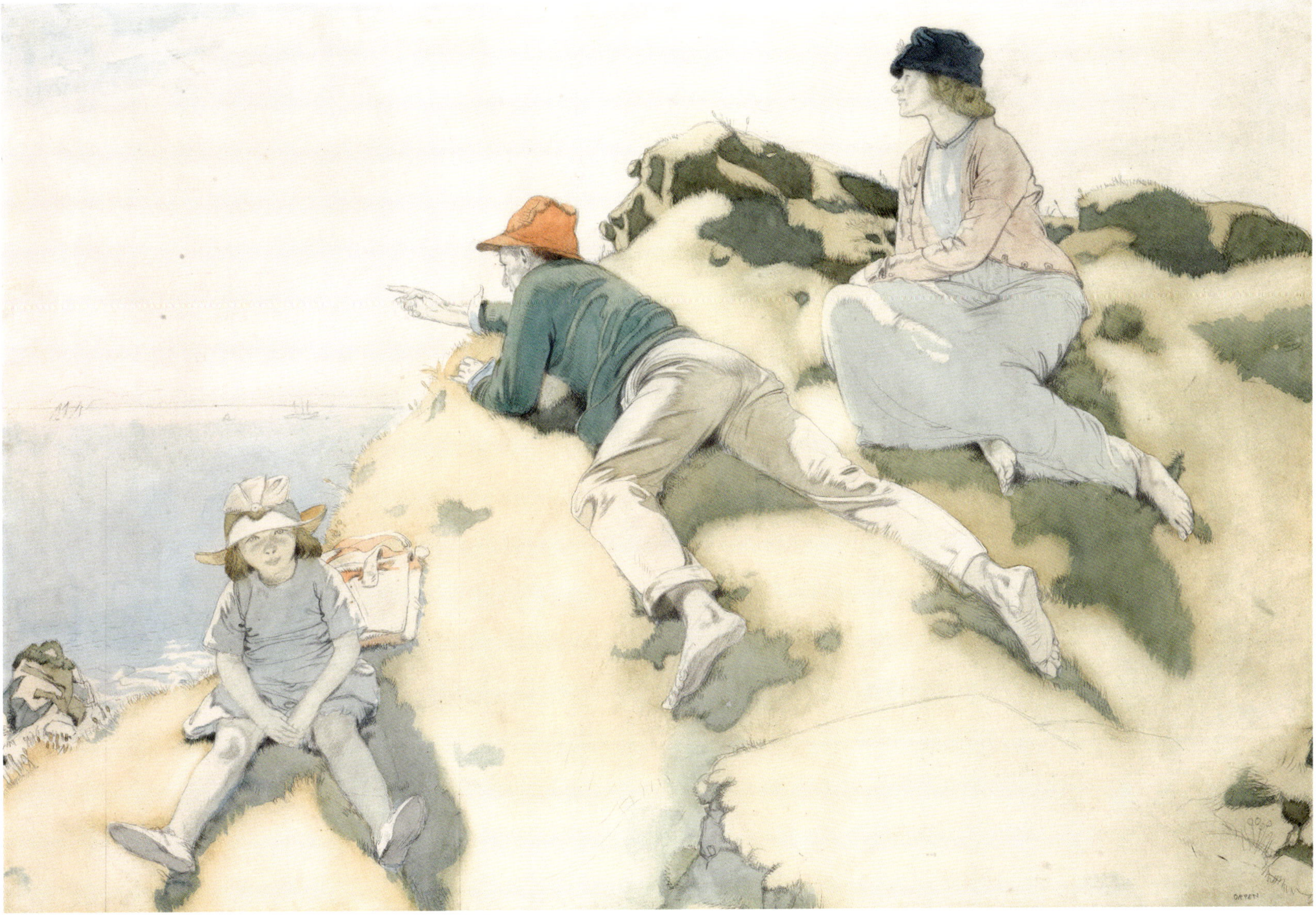

36

WILLIAM ORPEN

Study for The Holy Well: A Nude Couple and a Kneeling Man, c. 1916

Signed lower right 'ORPEN'

Signed, dated and inscribed lower right 'To George Roller/ with many thanks /William Orpen/ December 1930'

Pencil and black chalk on buff paper, partially squared in pencil

64.7 × 42.5 cm | 25½ × 16¾ in

Provenance

George Roller, given by the artist, Dec. 1930

Joseph ('Joe') Childs, Portsmouth, given by the above

Private Collection, by descent

Nude Pattern: The Holy Well (fig. 13) is a large painting in tempera that Orpen completed in 1916, and which is now in the collection of the National Gallery of Ireland. According to John Turpin, Orpen's painting 'dramatizes the ancient pagan roots of primitive Irish Christianity in a West of Ireland setting. The proliferation of nudes and the "flattened" technique convey a sense of unreality. It is a major statement of Irish decorative painting—an aspect, if slightly perverse, of the Celtic Revival in the arts.'[103]

As is the case with John's, references to the works of other, historical artists are more than occasionally to be found in Orpen's work. John's fascination with groups of figures, for example, owed a debt to Botticelli's *Primavera*, as well as to the work of Puvis de Chavannes. In Orpen's drawing, the postures of the male and female figures echo Adam and Eve being expelled from the Garden of Eden in Masaccio's early fifteenth-century fresco in the Brancacci Chapel, Florence. Steeped in the history of art, Orpen would go on to edit the multi-volume series, *The Outline of Art*, published in 1924.

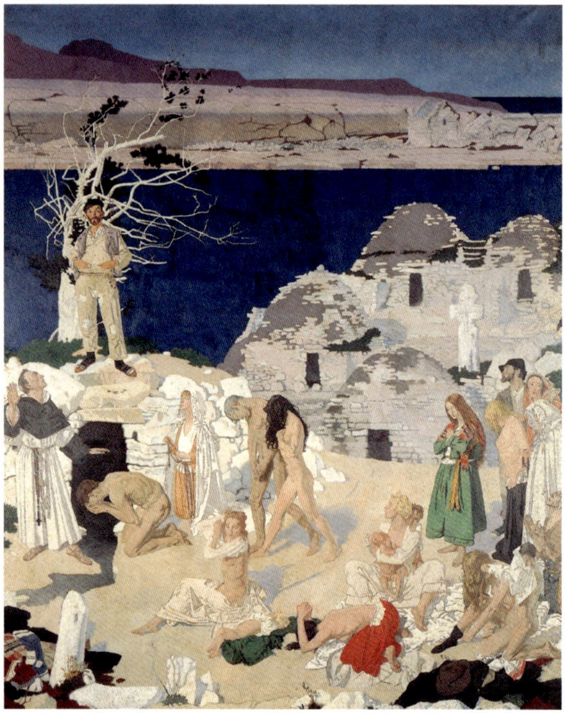

Fig. 13. William Orpen, *Nude Pattern: The Holy Well*, 1916, National Gallery of Ireland, Dublin

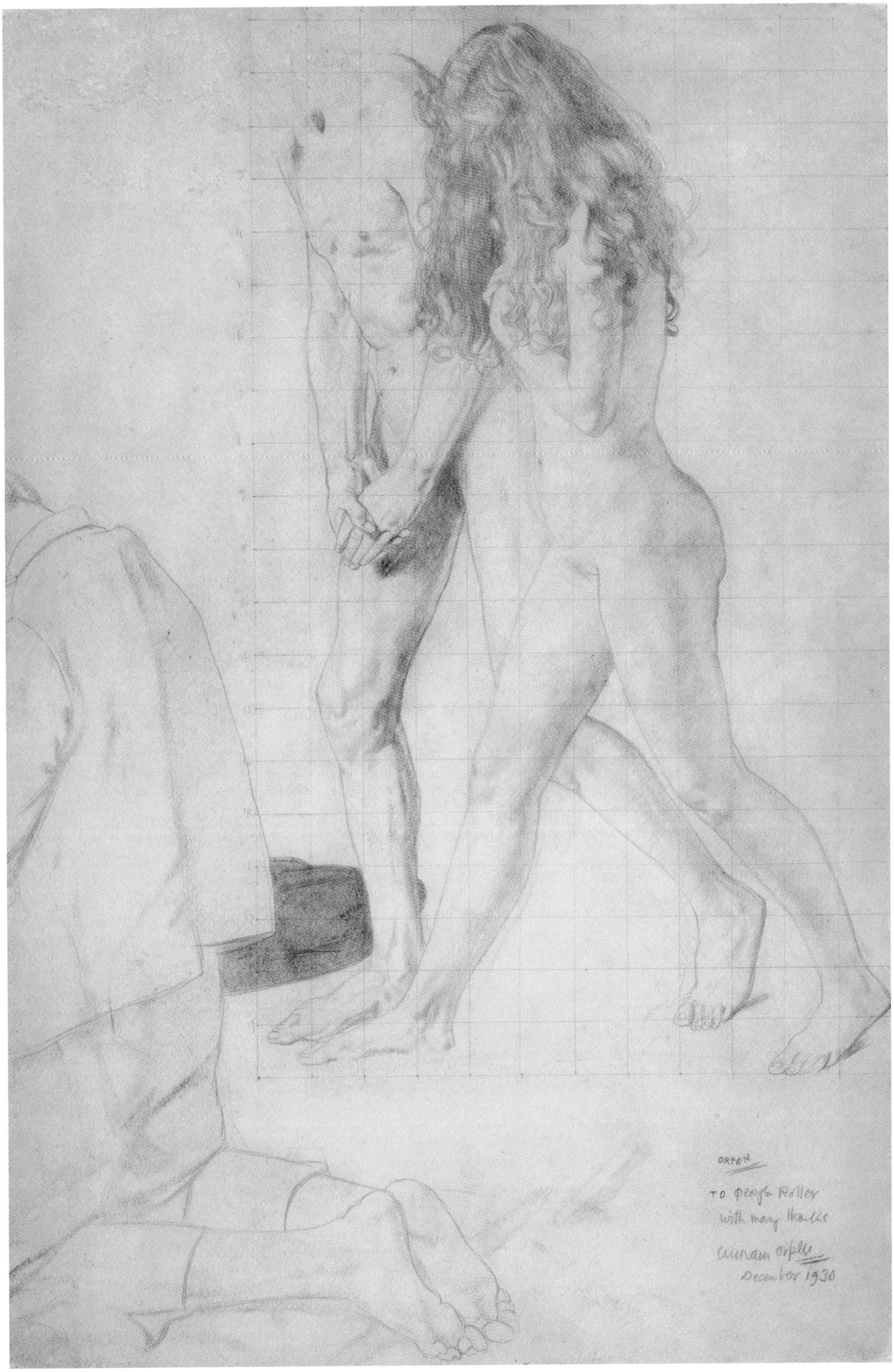
ORPEN
To George Roller
with many thanks
William Orpen
December 1930

37

WILLIAM ORPEN

Portrait of Lady Rocksavage, 1914
Oil on canvas
92 × 80 cm | 36¼ × 31½ in

Provenance

Sybil Rocksavage, Countess of Rocksavage, 1915, acquired in aid of the Red Cross
Private Collection

Exhibitions

New York, M. Knoedler & Co., *Exhibition of Recent Works by William Orpen*, 23 March – 4 April 1914 (listed as 'Lady Rocksavage')

Literature

Recent Works by William Orpen, exh. cat., M. Knoedler & Co., 1914, n.p. (illus.) (captioned as 'Portrait')
Guy Pène du Bois, 'English Art and Onion Soup: The Recent Exhibition of the Work of William Orpen', *Arts & Decoration*, vol. 4, no. 7 (May 1914), p. 261 (illus.)

Through hard work and diligent study, Orpen achieved a confidence and facility of technique in oil paint far sooner than John. And like their Slade friend Ambrose McEvoy, he devoted himself almost exclusively to portraiture at a much earlier stage than John (whose career as a society portraitist did not really begin in earnest until 1919). By around 1910 Orpen was already one of the most successful (and wealthiest) portrait painters in Britain or Ireland. His subjects thus tended to be wealthy socialites: Sybil Sassoon was the daughter of Sir Edward Albert Sassoon and Baroness Aline Caroline de Rothschild, and she married the Earl of Rocksavage, later 5th Marquess of Cholmondeley, in 1913.

This portrait was sold as part of a Red Cross money-raising scheme during the war: blank canvases in the name of famous artists were auctioned at fine venues like Claridge's hotel. In this case, however, the painting had been made at an earlier date and was included in Orpen's exhibition at Knoedler, New York, in spring 1914. It was not until a Red Cross charity auction in 1915 that its sitter, Lady Rocksavage, decided to buy it. Orpen's studio book records that the sale price was £334.[104]

Orpen won great praise for his paintings of the Great War, all of which he gifted to the nation; he would be rewarded with a knighthood in 1918. But it came at great cost. He was burnt out and was drinking heavily. He died in 1931, aged only 52.

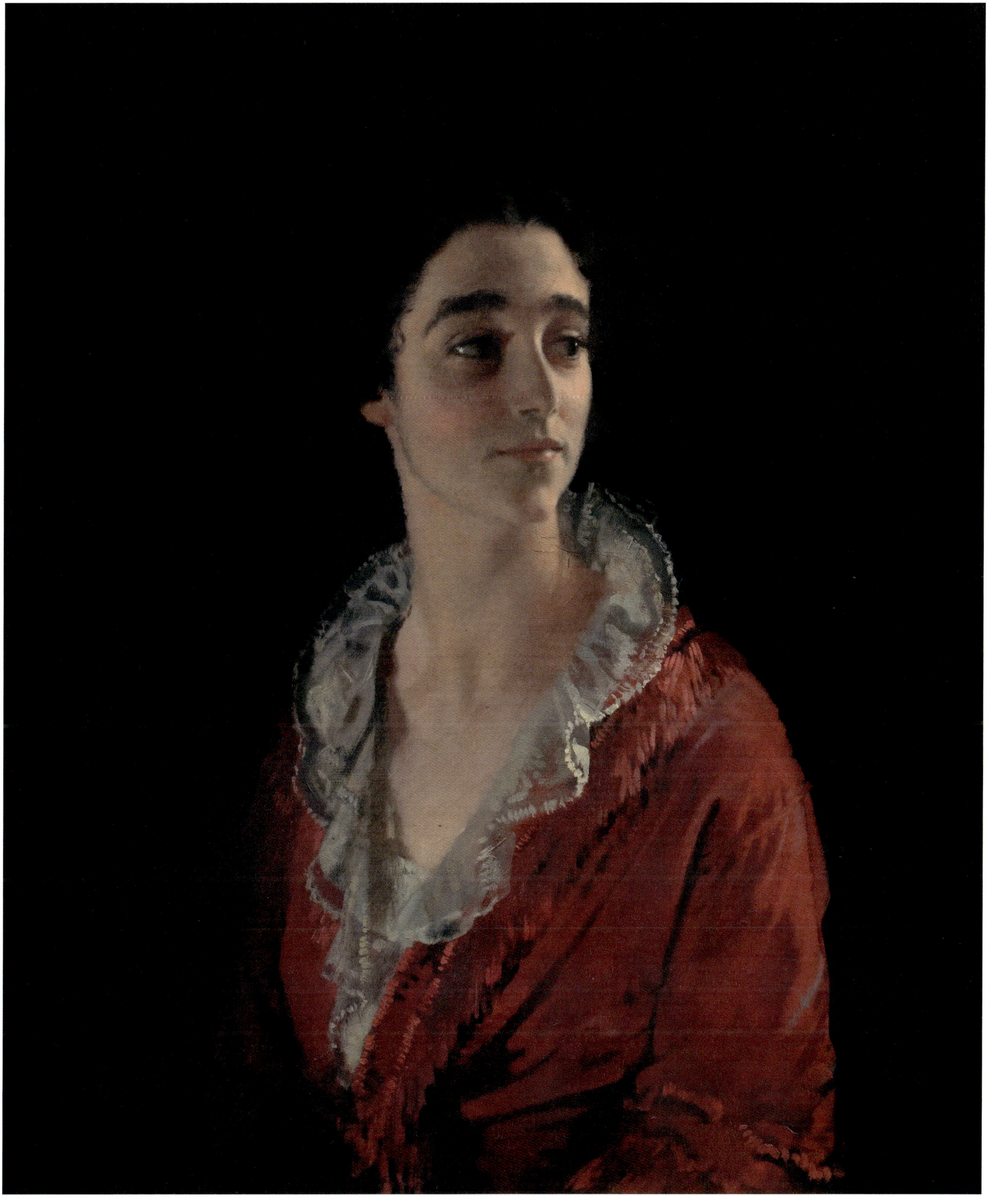

38

GWEN JOHN

Marie Hamonet with Arms Crossed, c. 1918–19
Charcoal and wash on paper
32 × 24.8 cm | 12 5/8 × 9 3/4 in

Provenance

Isabel Bowser
Lucy Bowser
Private Collection, by descent
At Bonhams, London, 30 May 2012, lot 57
Private Collection

Exhibitions

London, Barbican Art Gallery; Manchester, Manchester City Art Gallery; and New Haven, Yale Center for British Art, *Gwen John: An Interior Life*, 12 Sept. – 3 Nov. 1985; 28 Nov. 1985 – 26 Jan. 1986; and 26 Feb. – 20 April 1986, cat. no. 102

Gwendolen Mary John (1876–1939) was the second of Edwin and Augusta John's four children, and Augustus's elder sister by nineteen months. In 1884 their mother died after a long illness; the cause of death was recorded as rheumatic gout and exhaustion.[105] She was only thirty-five. The children were not encouraged to mourn. 'When I was a child', Gwen would write in 1928, 'I used to cry all the time, and they told me, "don't cry now, when you're grown up you'll have something to cry about." So I was afraid of growing up and I never expected any happiness in life.'[106] At the family home in Tenby the regime was strict and silent; out of doors the children ran wild on the beach and in the dunes. Augustus and his brother Thornton were educated in a series of minor private schools, whilst Gwen and their youngest sibling, Winifred, were taught at home. It was a stifling atmosphere that all four children would escape: Gwen to France, Thornton and Winifred to America, and Augustus to London, Dorset, France and Ireland.

Gwen followed her brother to the Slade in 1895, a few months after her nineteenth birthday, and for some of their period as students they shared lodgings together. Compared to her female peers Ida Nettleship, Gwen Salmond and Edna Waugh, who all won scholarships, Gwen's time at the School was relatively undistinguished. She was quiet and very shy. 'Gwen seemed to me a rather odd person,' Edna Waugh would later write, reflecting on their first proper meeting.[107] In 1902 Gwen herself would explain to a friend that she could use letters 'to say what I mean exactly,' since this was 'the only chance I have, for in talking shyness and timidity distort the very meaning of my words in other people's ears. That I think is one reason I am such a waif [...] I don't pretend to know anybody well. People are like shadows to me and I am like a shadow.'[108]

In 1904 Gwen John returned to Paris, eking out a living life modelling, teaching and occasionally sending paintings to the New English Art Club's exhibitions. Her work included portraits, as well as the delicate, carefully observed interiors for which she would eventually be famed. For a while she modelled for Rodin, and they had an intense affair. 'I had desired to be a distinguished artist,' she told him. 'I wanted my part in the sun [...] But now I am in love, I don't envy being known.'[109] In another she claimed, 'I was a little solitaire, no-one helped me or awoke me before I met you.'[110] This work depicts a Breton peasant girl named Marie Hamonet, who sat for John on several occasions in 1918 and 1919 while the artist was staying at Pléneuf.

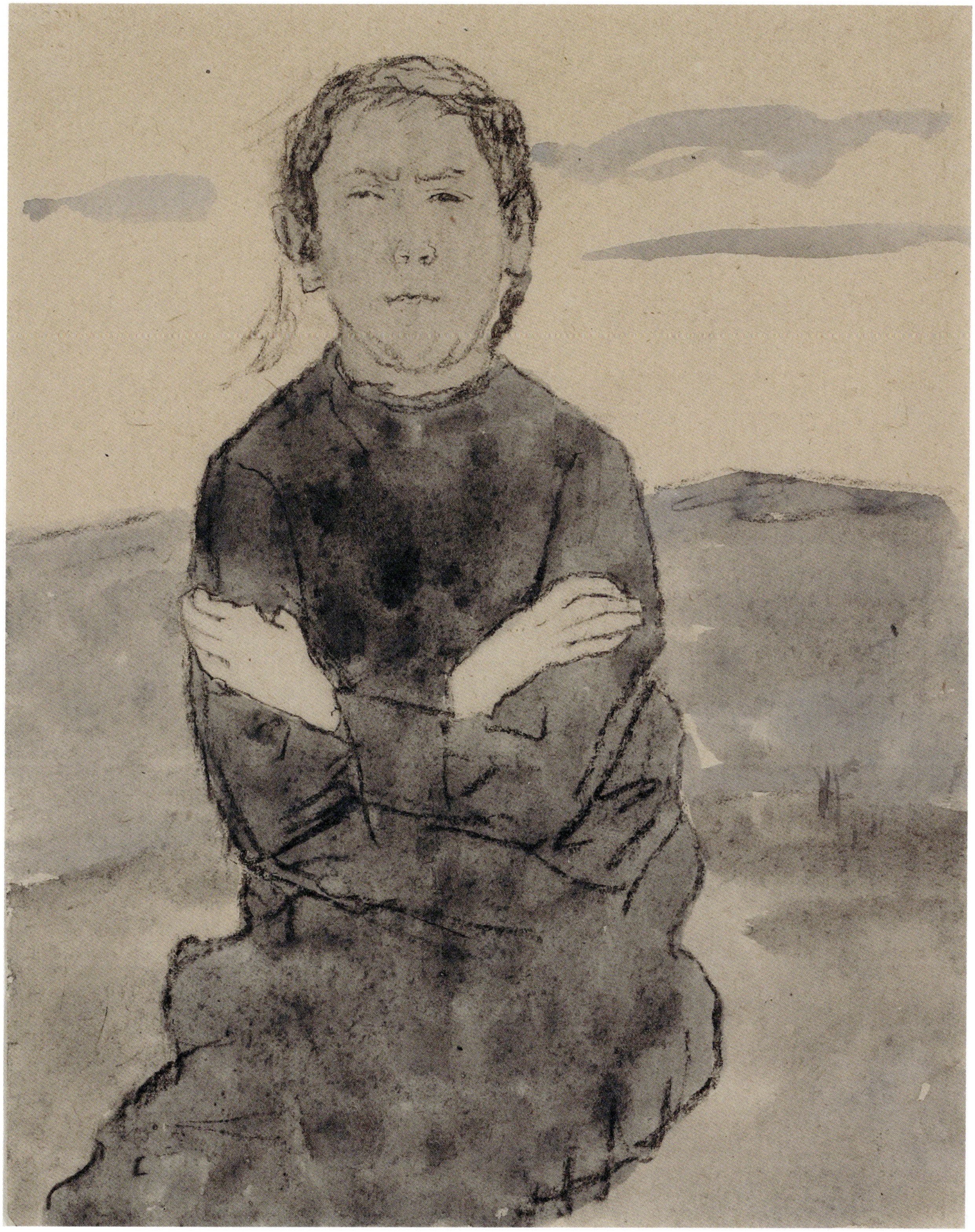

39

GWEN JOHN

Portrait of a Young Nun, c. 1918–19
Oil on canvas
60.3 × 40 cm | 23¾ × 15¾ in

Provenance

The Artist's Estate
With Anthony d'Offay, London
Selby McCreery, 1982
Piano Nobile, London
Private Collection

Exhibitions

London, Matthiesen Gallery, *Gwen John Memorial Exhibition*, 19 Sept. – 19 Oct. 1946, cat. no. 34
Edinburgh, Scottish Society of Women Artists, *Twenty-Second Exhibition*, dates unknown
London, Arts Council Gallery, *British Painting 1925–1950: Second Anthology*, 20 June – 20 Sept. 1951, cat. no. 65 (listed as 'Three Quarter Length of a Young Nun')
London, Matthiesen Gallery, *Gwen John 1876–1939*, 14 Feb. – 8 March 1958, cat. no. 4
London, Matthiesen Gallery, *Gwen John*, 8 June – 8 July 1961, cat. no. 21
London, Faerber & Maison, *Gwen John 1876–1939*, 13 Nov. – 12 Dec. 1964, cat. no. 5
London, Anthony d'Offay, *Gwen John 1876–1939*, 1 July – 22 Aug. 1982, cat. no. 9 (listed as 'Three Quarter Length of a Young Nun')
London, Barbican Art Gallery; Manchester, Manchester City Art Gallery; and New Haven, Yale Center for British Art, *Gwen John: An Interior Life*, 12 Sept. – 3 Nov. 1985; 28 Nov. 1985 – 26 Jan. 1986; and 26 Feb. – 20 April 1986, cat. no. 21
London, National Portrait Gallery, *The Painter's Eye*, 16 April – 13 June 1999
Chichester, Pallant House Gallery, *Gwen John: Art and Life in London and Paris*, 13 May – 8 Oct. 2023, unnumbered

Literature

Cecily Langdale and David Fraser Jenkins, *Gwen John: An Interior Life*, exh. cat., Phaidon, 1985, cat. no. 21 (illus.)
Cecily Langdale, *Gwen John: With a Catalogue Raisonné of the Paintings and a Selection of the Drawings*, Yale University Press, 1987, cat. no. 57, p. 152, pl. 208 (illus.)

Although Rodin continued to encourage and support her, Gwen John was devastated when their affair ended, and found solace in her work, her books, her room and her cats. She had a select circle of friends, but others often found her as complicated as she found them. When Ida and Dorelia moved to Paris in 1906, Ida wrote that Gwen was still 'the same reserved creature, mysterious and flame like and *impitoyable* [ruthless]'.[111]

The world was, in many ways, a mysterious burden to Gwen John. 'I see the sky and the stars from my window,' she told Rodin in a letter of 1906 or 1907:

> I know that we are on an island and the sky is like the sea, all around—I wonder why I am here, what to do and what is this world and where we go after we die [...] It is very strange that you know the answer no more than I do. All the people I see in the street seem so preoccupied with themselves and in their own world, my Master. I am a stranger not only in this country but in the world; I don't feel at home and I am always wondering why I am here [...] when I am not with you, or writing to you or drawing my cat to show it to you, always the same questions come to trouble me.

Whilst Augustus hated the moral and intellectual restrictions imposed by religion, Gwen increasingly found solace in church worship, and in around 1913 she converted to Roman Catholicism. Not long afterwards she would be commissioned by the nuns of the local chapter of the Sœurs de Charité Dominicaines de la Présentation de la Sainte Vierge de Tours to paint a portrait of their (long deceased) founder, Mère Marie Poussepin. At least six of these survive, and they are among her best known works. She also made individual paintings, drawings and watercolours of the nuns including *Portrait of a Young Nun*, which may depict a nun called Soeur Babette. In a notebook entry of 1922 she would call herself 'God's little artist: a seer of strange beauties, a teller of harmonies, a diligent worker.'[112] But by 1933 she had almost completely ceased working, and lived an increasingly reclusive life in Meudon, whence she had moved in 1911 to be close to Rodin's then home.

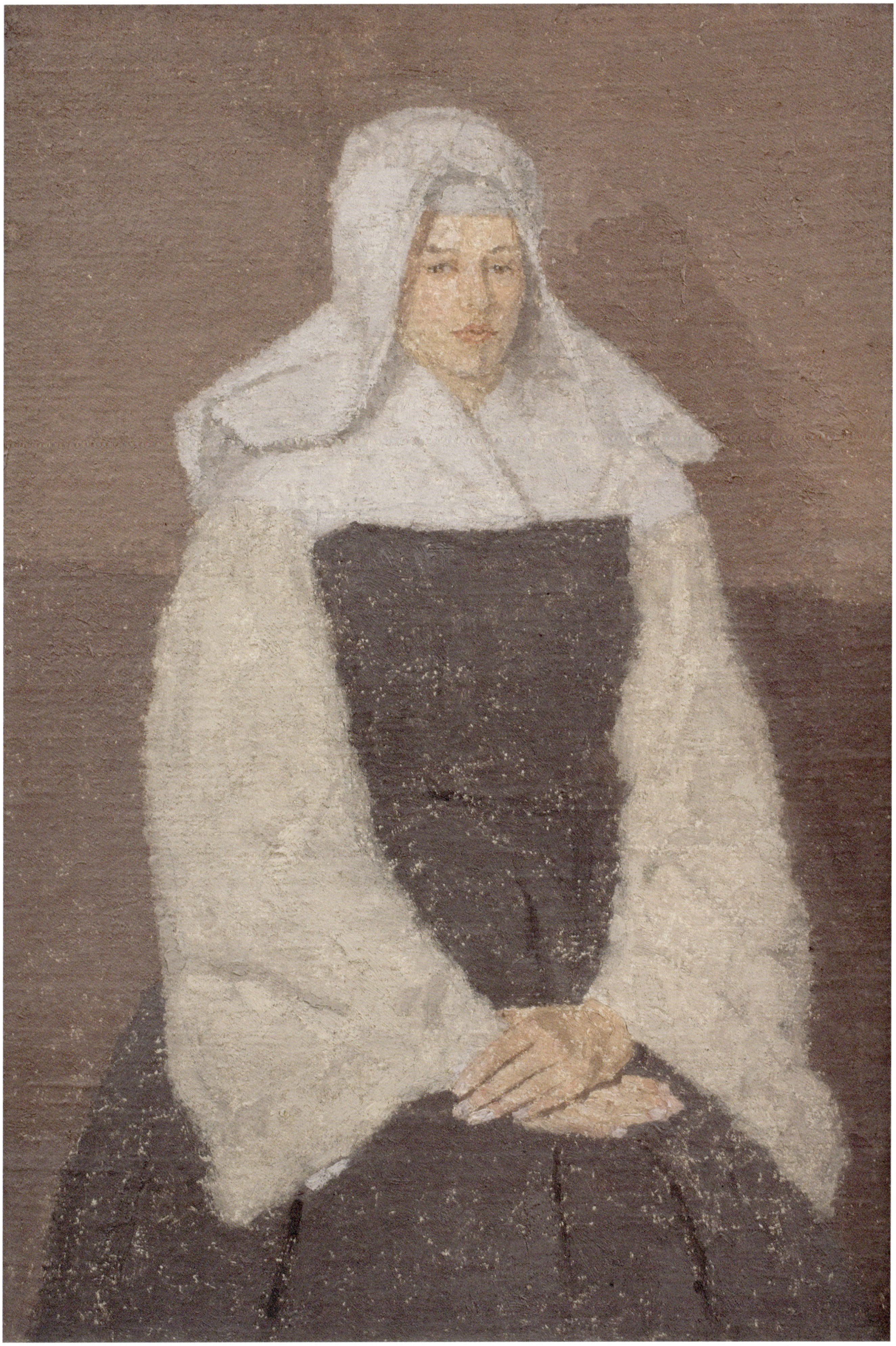

40

GWEN JOHN

Sleeping Nun, c. 1916–18

Stamped lower right 'Gwen John' (estate stamp)
Charcoal, watercolour and gouache
31.8 × 23.8 cm | 12½ × 9⅜ in

Provenance

The Artist's Estate
Anthony d'Offay Gallery, London
Caroline Conran, 1982
Piano Nobile, London
Private Collection

Exhibitions

London, Anthony d'Offay Gallery, *Gwen John 1876–1939*, 1 July – 22 Aug. 1982, cat. no. 41

According to Henry Tonks's biographer, the Slade's drawing master possessed 'a considerable belief in women's power of achievement', and thought women 'easier to teach' than men because they were more likely to do what they were told, and they made 'quicker progress.'[113] Tonks's chief disappointment was that marriage often obliged them to abandon their hard-learnt craft. This was the fate of both Edna Waugh and Ida Nettleship. Gwen, notably, would never marry.

She was a slow, methodical worker, and it took a little while for her carefully nurtured talent to flourish. After leaving the Slade she spent a brief period (some three months) in Paris, where she attended an atelier and learnt from James McNeill Whistler. Returning to London she painted two important self-portraits, one of which, *Self-Portrait in a Red Blouse* (now in the Tate collection), was bought by the Slade's Professor, Fred Brown.[114] For a while she was close to Ambrose McEvoy, who had also studied for a time under Whistler. McEvoy painted a beautiful portrait of Gwen John in around 1900, and it would be claimed by John Rothenstein that he influenced her work. Augustus rejected this claim. 'She had no help from McEvoy,' he told Rothenstein in 1952, 'whom she out-distanced immeasurably from the start.'[115] Especially in her pictures of nuns, including this work portraying a sister of the Dominican nunnery in Meudon, John demonstrated an artistic outlook that was independent from that of her forbears and contemporaries.

Her work hovers somewhere between modernism and tradition, with a life—like its creator—all of its own, subtle and beyond definition. Whilst Gwen lived much of her life in the shadow of her famous brother, Augustus was fully aware of his sister's powerful character, and her immense talent. He would be—despite the often difficult nature of their relationship—one of Gwen's greatest champions. Three years after her premature death in 1939 Augustus wrote that, notwithstanding Gwen's 'extreme timidity in a social sense', she 'was always capable of demonstrating a dauntless courage and a formidable strength of will. Her pride, honesty and devotion to what she took to be her duty, combined, under the compulsion of a sufficient motive, to transform her into an irresistible force. This gentle soul was then adamant in resolution and would [stop] at nothing.'[116] As he also recognised, Gwen possessed 'a mind of exceptional quality [...] She didn't steal through life,' he told one biographer in 1952, 'but preserved a haughty independence which some people mistook for humility.'[117]

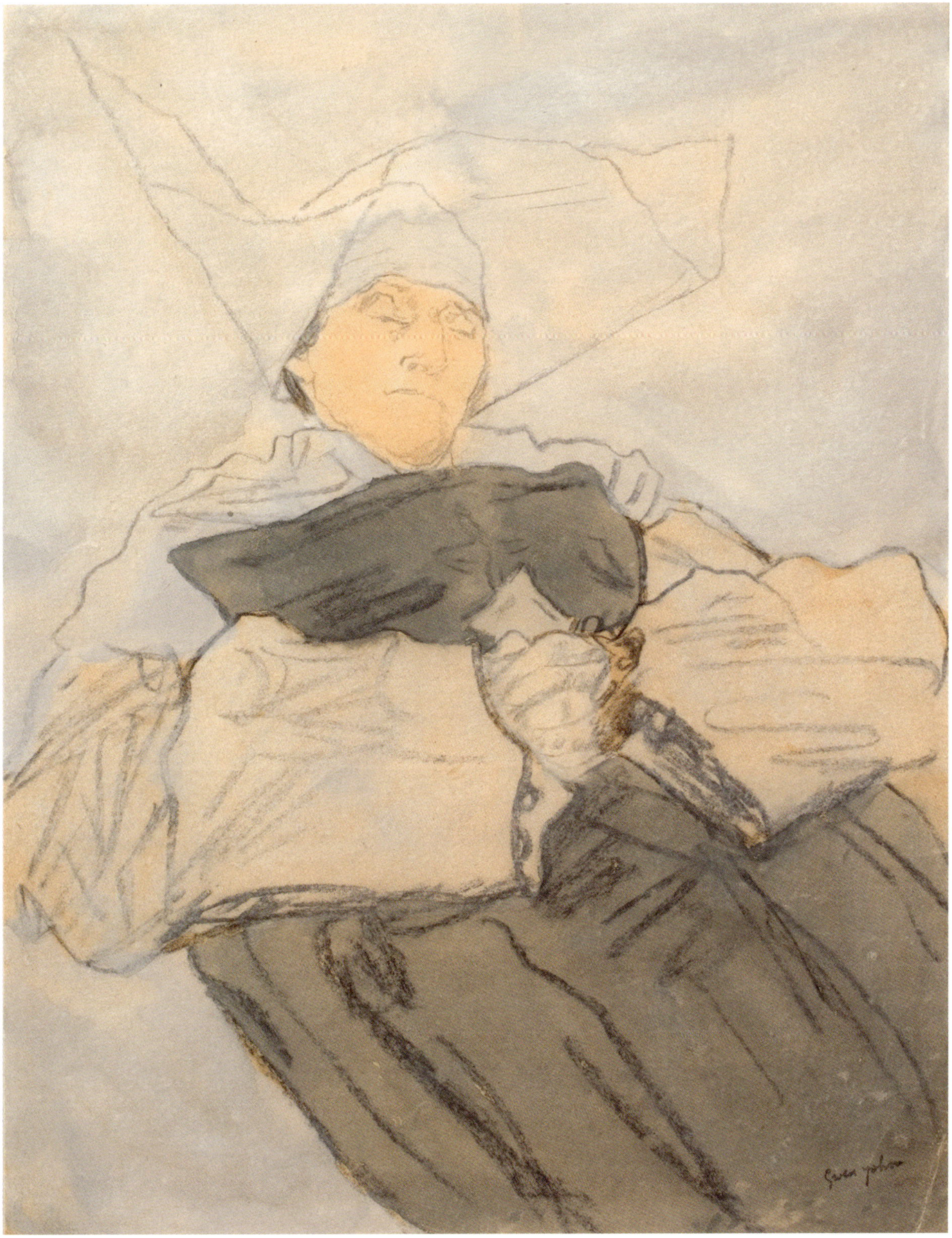

41

WYNDHAM LEWIS

Nine designs for Omega lampshades, 1913
Process engravings on paper
13.3 × 28.3 cm | 5¼ × 11⅛ in

Provenance

Duncan Grant
Private Collection

Lewis was invited by Roger Fry to join the Omega Workshops in February 1912. An artist and critic, Fry was one of the leading critics of the period, and a key figure in the Bloomsbury Group, and he had curated the ground-breaking exhibition 'Manet and the Post-Impressionists' in 1910. The idea behind the Omega Workshops was a combination of assisting young artists by giving them regular paid employment (30 shillings a week), whilst simultaneously bringing decorative modernism to the British public. Lewis, who was frequently struggling for money, was a relatively reluctant participant. His contributions included a screen showing circus performers, as well as this set of nine fan-shaped figurative designs for lampshades.[118]

In October 1913, following an acrimonious falling out, Lewis split from Fry and the Omega group. He took fellow artists Edward Wadsworth and Frederick Etchells with him to form a rival organisation, the Rebel Art Centre, alongside Kate Lechmere and C.R.W. Nevinson. Lewis would later write disparagingly of 'the rather jaded and amateur tastefulness of the Omega workshops', of all its 'colour-matching, match-box making, dressmaking, chair-painting game, carried on in a spirit of distinguished amateurish gallantry and refinement [...].'[119]

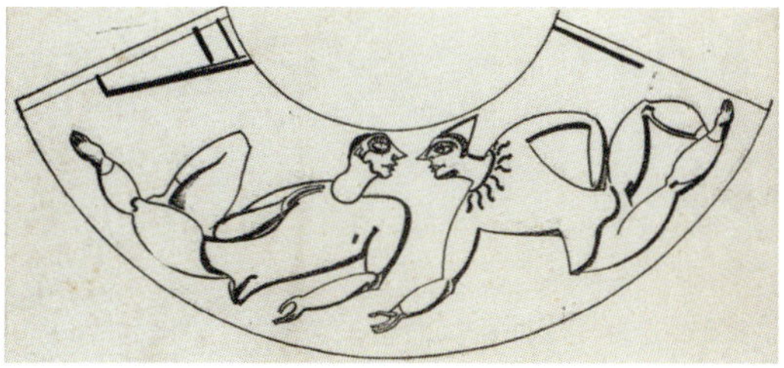
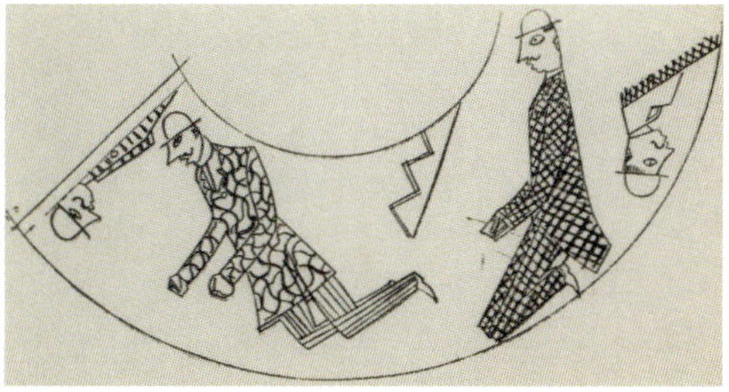
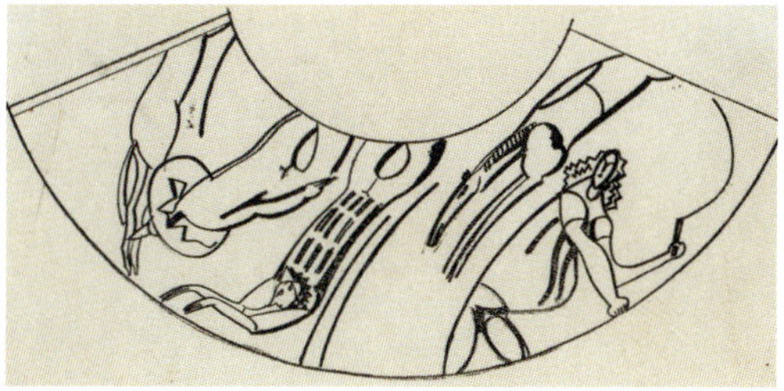
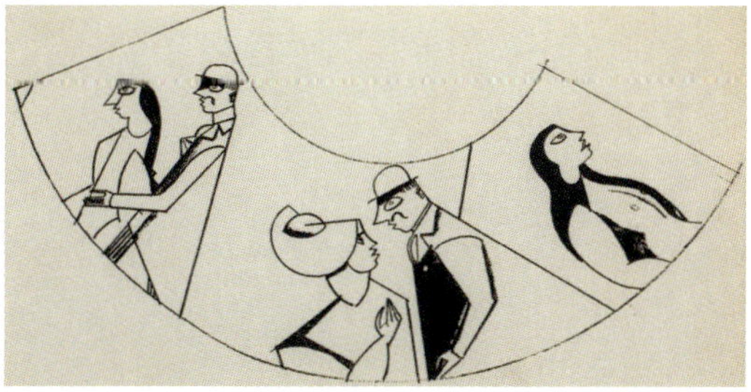
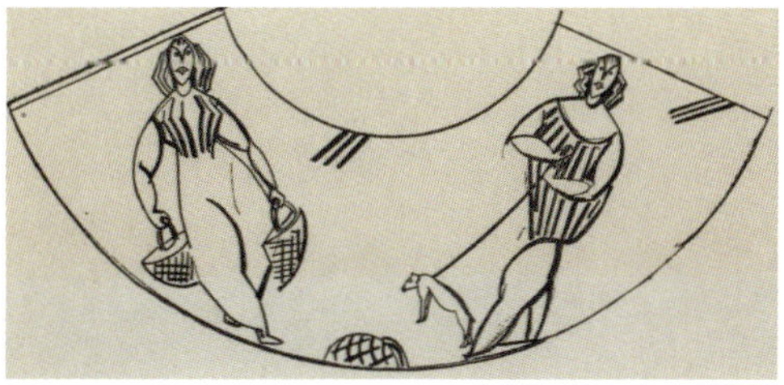
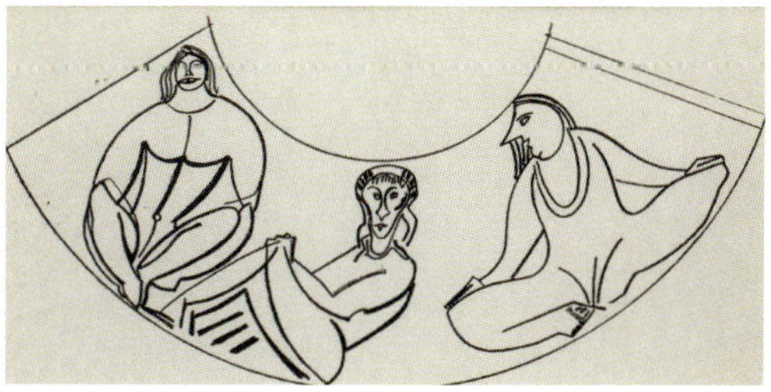
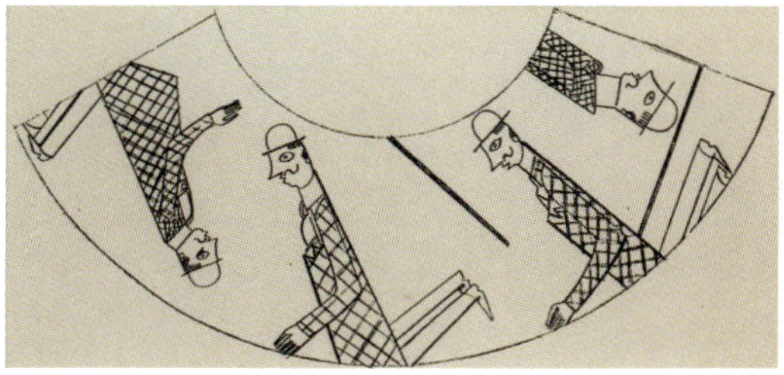
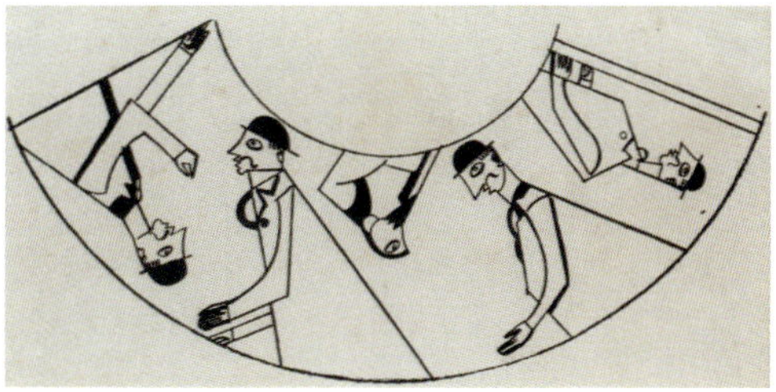
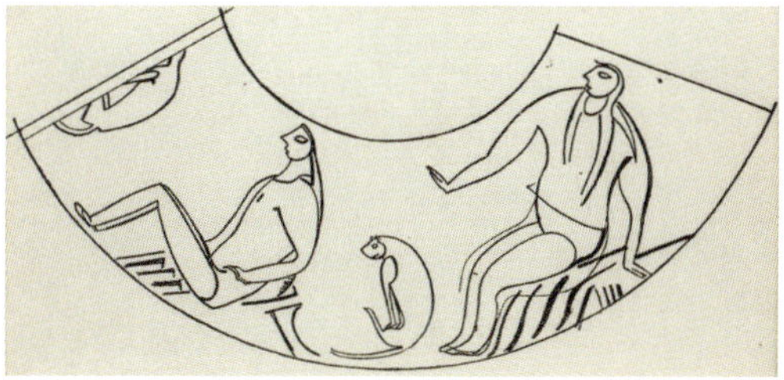

42

WYNDHAM LEWIS

Robe, 1913–14
Embroidered and block-printed silk robe
Height 132 cm | Height 52 in

Provenance

At Mallams, Oxford, 8 Dec. 2017, lot 620
Private Collection, London
Piano Nobile, London

Literature

Geoffrey Rayner, Richard Chamberlin and Annamarie Stapleton, *Artist's Textiles 1949–1976*, Antique Collectors' Club, 1999, pp. 14–15, pl. 4a and 4b (col. illus.) (similar example)

In July 1912 Lewis emerged as one of the leading English modernist artists, his work reflecting his interpretation of the Cubist experiments by Picasso and Braque that he had seen in Paris. Exhibited at the fifth salon of the Allied Artists' Association at the Royal Albert Hall in July 1912, his enormous painting *Kermesse* (now lost) depicted three festive Breton women in bright colours and Cubist style. Writing in *The Nation*, Roger Fry considered the design 'tense and compact' and the overall effect one of 'singular force and beauty of colour'.[120] Fry and Clive Bell included Lewis's work in a British section of the 'Second Post-Impressionist Exhibition' in 1912, which was notable for John's absence.

The Italian Futurists, who arrived in London with an exciting message promising a new approach to art and life worshipping speed, violence and modernity, would be an important influence on Lewis. His exit from the Omega Workshops led him to establish the Rebel Art Centre and then the Vorticist Group, a group of radical artists with a radical message. Like Omega, the RAC members produced works of interior design and items of dress, such as this robe. John would be unimpressed by Lewis's direction of travel, however.

In February 1914 John was invited to an open house to view Lady Drogheda's new dining room, which Lewis had redesigned. The ceiling and floor were jet black, the walls panelled in black velvet, and a frieze was painted in what *The Times* called 'the Cubist style', with vivid light reds and dark greens, panels with a chevron pattern in vermillion, and others of beveled and silvered plate glass. It was, John informed Dorelia, 'a perfectly bloody show.'[121]

In his lifetime, Lewis never achieved the fame he had once hoped for and expected. His flirtation with fascism in the 1930s did not help his cause, and in 1938 his portrait of T.S. Eliot was rejected for the Royal Academy Summer Exhibition; Augustus John showed his support by resigning from the Academy in protest. By 1948 Lewis was struggling. 'What I do is to eliminate every expenditure outside of food and cigarettes and the odd bottle of gin,' he wrote in a letter to John, 'and I shall wear the clothes I have until they drop off my back. —What an awful letter to have to write! But there it is.'[122] Three years later he was blind from the effects of a brain tumour. In 1956 the Tate Gallery held a large retrospective exhibition, 'Wyndham Lewis and Vorticism'. He died in London the following year, aged seventy-four. There are today at least two journals and a society dedicated to the study of Lewis's art and writings; there are none to Augustus John.

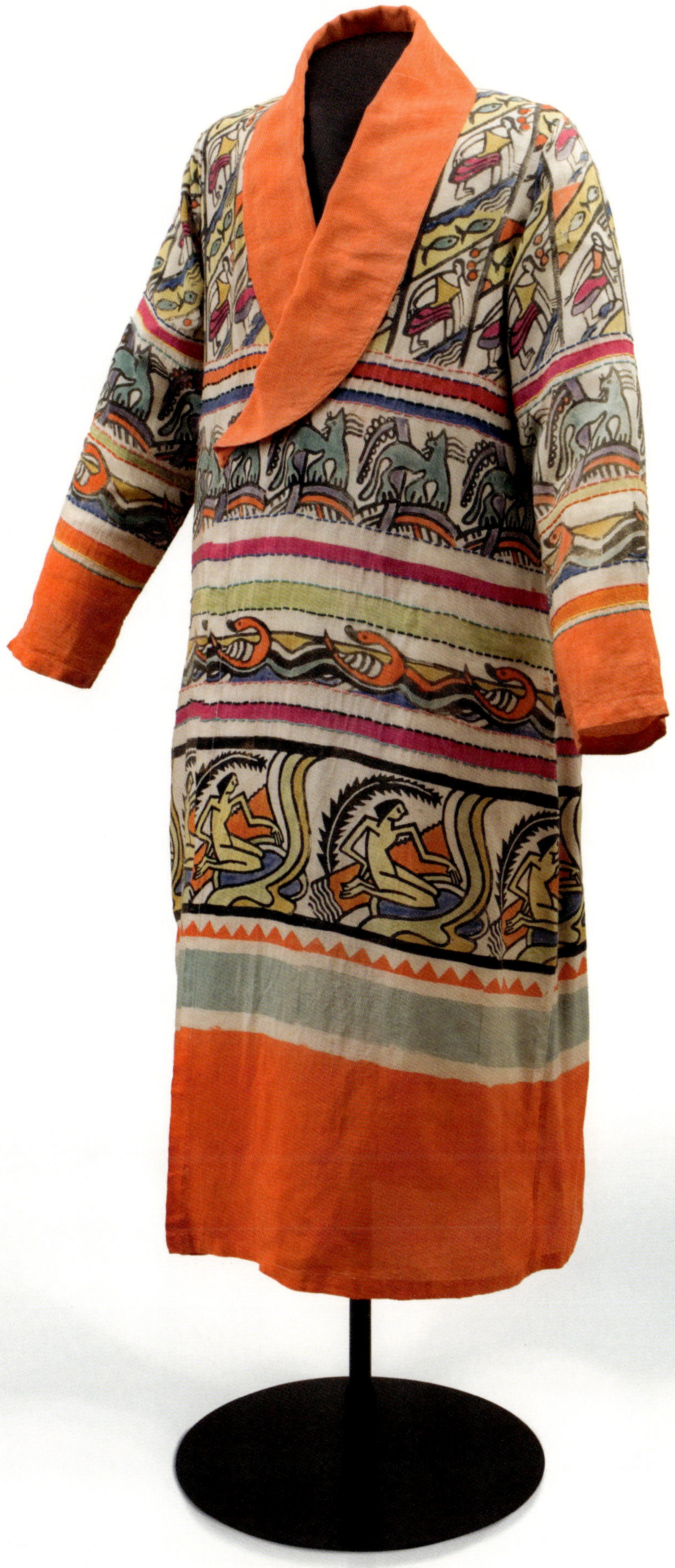

43

WILLIAM ROTHENSTEIN

Thomas Hardy, 1900
Signed and dated upper right 'R 1900'
Sanguine and pastel on paper
22.9 × 22.9 cm | 9 × 9 in

Provenance

Mrs Frances Cornford, given by the artist
Private Collection, by descent
Private Collection, 2021

Born in Bradford in January 1872, William Rothenstein was the son of a wealthy German-Jewish businessman who, a decade earlier, had moved with his wife to work in the Yorkshire textile industry. Exactly six years John's senior, Rothenstein had gone to the Slade in 1888, where a fellow student recalled him as 'brimful of vitality and formidable intelligence.'[123] He had been unimpressed by the school, however, which was then under the direction of the French artist Alphonse Legros, and he had gone to Paris to study at the Académie Julian instead.

In Paris Rothenstein met Walter Sickert, Roger Fry, Oscar Wilde, Paul Verlaine, Toulouse-Lautrec and Lucien Pissarro, and enjoyed early success as an artist with works such as *Parting at Morning* (1891), now in the Tate collection. In 1893 however, he returned to England, and his brother, Albert, who was then studying at the Slade, introduced him to John and Orpen. Of the two, Rothenstein preferred John's work, considering it to possess 'more magic'. Rothenstein would later write that John's talent and dynamism had helped 'raise the standard of drawing among Slade students in dazzling fashion'.[124]

Rothenstein would admit that John's brilliance intimidated him: 'I was shy, after seeing John's brilliant nudes, of drawing in his company [...]. John drew nudes as no one, I thought, had drawn them in England, and his drawings of heads were remarkably fine.'[125] Yet as Rothenstein's portraits from this period reveal, he was a talented draughtsman in his own right, and his portrait of Thomas Hardy is particularly impressive. It is reproduced (in black and white) in the first volume of Rothenstein's fascinating autobiography, *Men and Memories* (1931).

In 1923 John would be introduced to Hardy, and painted his own portrait of the famous Dorset author. Hardy was eighty-three by then, and would remark of John's picture, 'I don't know whether that is how I look or not, but that is how I *feel*.'[126]

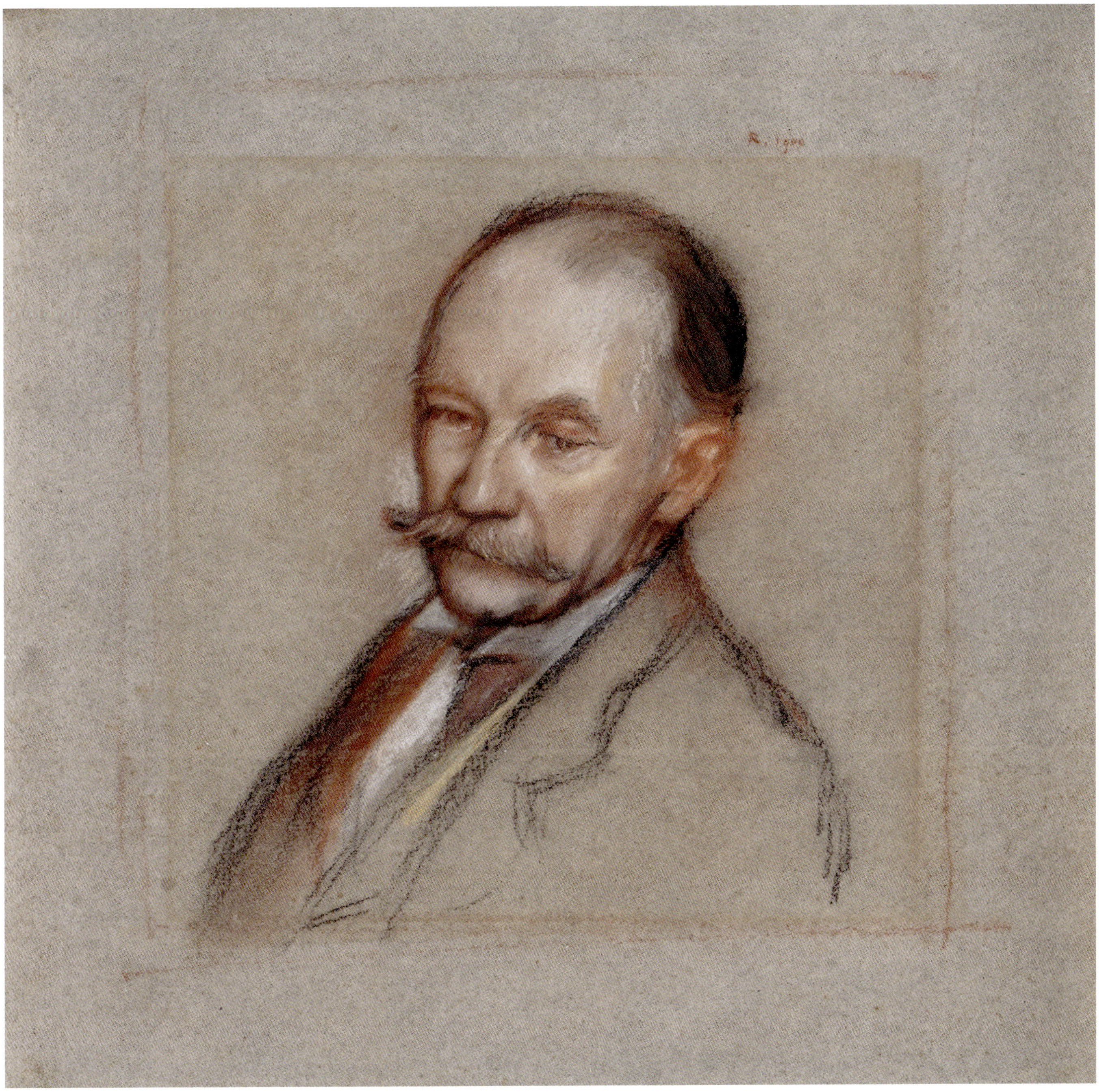

44

WILLIAM ROTHENSTEIN

Arthur Wing Pinero, Playwright, c. 1920
Black chalk and sanguine on paper
22.9 × 17.8 cm | 9 × 7 in

Provenance

John Drinkwater, London
Private Collection

Literature

John Rothenstein, *The Portrait Drawings of William Rothenstein 1889–1925*, Chapman & Hall, 1925, cat. no. 536, p. 62

As an avid writer, it was no surprise that novelists and playwrights were among the many friendships William Rothenstein courted, and whose portraits he took. His own volumes of autobiography would be filled with anecdotes and insights into British cultural life in the late nineteenth and early twentieth centuries. Best known today for his 1898 comic play, *Trelawny of the "Wells"*, Pinero's dramas were very successful in the late Victorian period.

Rothenstein's life and career was appraised by his son, John, in his fascinating collection of short biographies, *Modern English Painters*. It was John Rothenstein's opinion that, at the start of the twentieth century, 'a radical change' had begun to manifest itself in his father's work, 'involving both loss and gain [...]. It was a change due perhaps mainly to intellectual conviction, but it may be in part the consequence of some psychic disturbance possibly unconnected with painting.' My suggestion, laid out in my introduction to this catalogue, was that this 'psychic disturbance' was to do with Rothenstein's encounter with the brilliant early work of Augustus John and William Orpen.

But as John Rothenstein continued, prior to this change, his father's work had been 'distinguished by an eager curious insight into character, whether of face, or figure, or of locality, which expressed itself, notwithstanding his obvious high spirits and irrepressible humour, with a grave, disciplined detachment. His drawing, elegant and tenuous though it was, showed a surprisingly sure grasp of form.'[127]

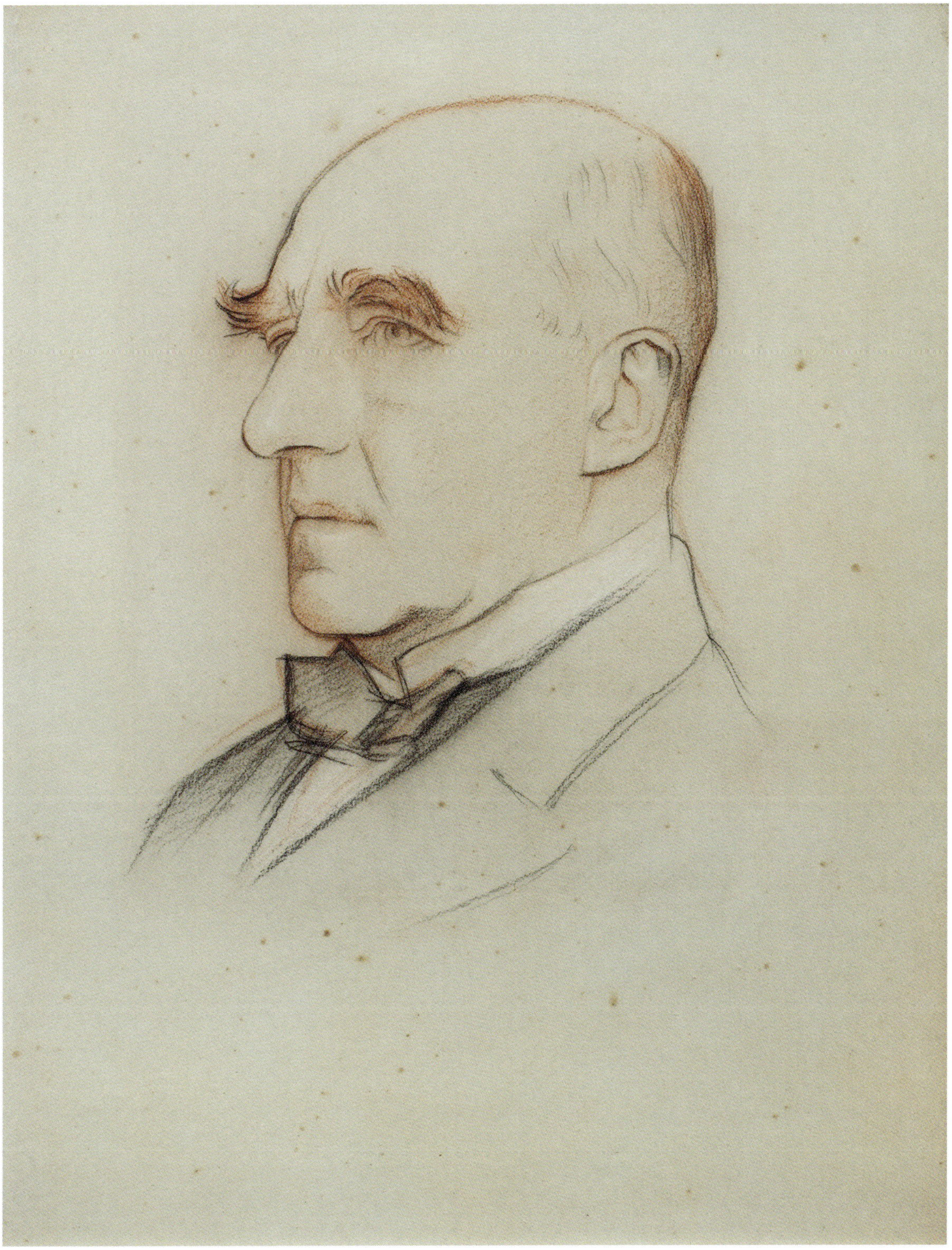

45

WILLIAM ROTHENSTEIN

Portrait of E. M. Forster, 1923

Inscribed and initialled lower right '1st sketch - W.R.'
Sanguine with white heightening on grey paper
19 × 12.5 cm | 7½ × 4⅞ in

Provenance

The Artist
Sir John Rothenstein, by descent
World Wildlife Fund
At Christie's, South Kensington, 11 Nov. 1985, lot 23
Private Collection
Piano Nobile, London

Literature

John Rothenstein, *The Portrait Drawings of William Rothenstein 1889–1925*, Chapman & Hall, 1925, cat. no. 664, p. 76

Rothenstein's most enduring influence was as a supporter and encourager of youthful talent. As well as helping Augustus John, other promising students he assisted early in their careers included Mark Gertler, Paul Nash and Eric Ravilious. 'A walking intelligence of a distinctly uncommon sort', the artist Muirhead Bone described him in around 1902. 'He's a sort of sizer-up of all the art work being done everywhere. He never flatters, is quite sincere, and so has (consciously or unconsciously) acquired a great influence.'[128] Yet Rothenstein is now overlooked, even if he divided opinions in his day. As the scholar Samuel Shaw has suggested, '[h]e was, in one sense, a born leader with an innate distrust of leadership. Uncommon vitality kept pace with "awful doubts" throughout Rothenstein's career: neither would ever seize absolute control.'[129] He certainly did not enjoy the same influence as Roger Fry, who became something of a rival force, nor has his named resonated as fully.

Rothenstein played an important role in aiding the early career of Augustus John, but his patience for the brilliant young man and his equally talented sister eventually wore thin. In September 1908 John would once again be facing a shortage of money, and he wrote to Rothenstein from Normandy, telling him that he wanted to go to the Pyrenees, 'instead of lingering in the chilly north, but I lack the necessary millions. So back again to the horrors of a Cockney winter. Are there no millionaires of spirit?'[130] His letter (or another one much like it) was not well received. 'I had a letter from John,' Rothenstein complained to his brother: 'not one I cared for much, for there was a hint to further pecuniary needs—he writes as though he were entirely neglected, but this is scarcely the case—one sees his drawings about everywhere, doesn't one?'[131] A few months later John would be telling Ottoline Morrell that he felt a history of his old friend's career 'would be the most ludicrous, abject and scurrilous psychological document ever penned.' He thought the best man to write it would be Wyndham Lewis.[132]

Having served as an official war artist, in 1920 Rothenstein was appointed Principal at the Royal College of Art. 'After eight years largely devoted to landscape painting,' he later wrote, 'I was grateful for the stream of sitters who consented to be drawn or painted.' The novelist E.M. Forster was not a close acquaintance, but Rothenstein made this drawing as a preliminary study for one acquired by King's College, Cambridge.[133] Rothenstein remained at the RCA until 1935, during which time his students included Edward Bawden, Evelyn Dunbar, Henry Moore and Eric Ravilious. He was knighted in 1931.

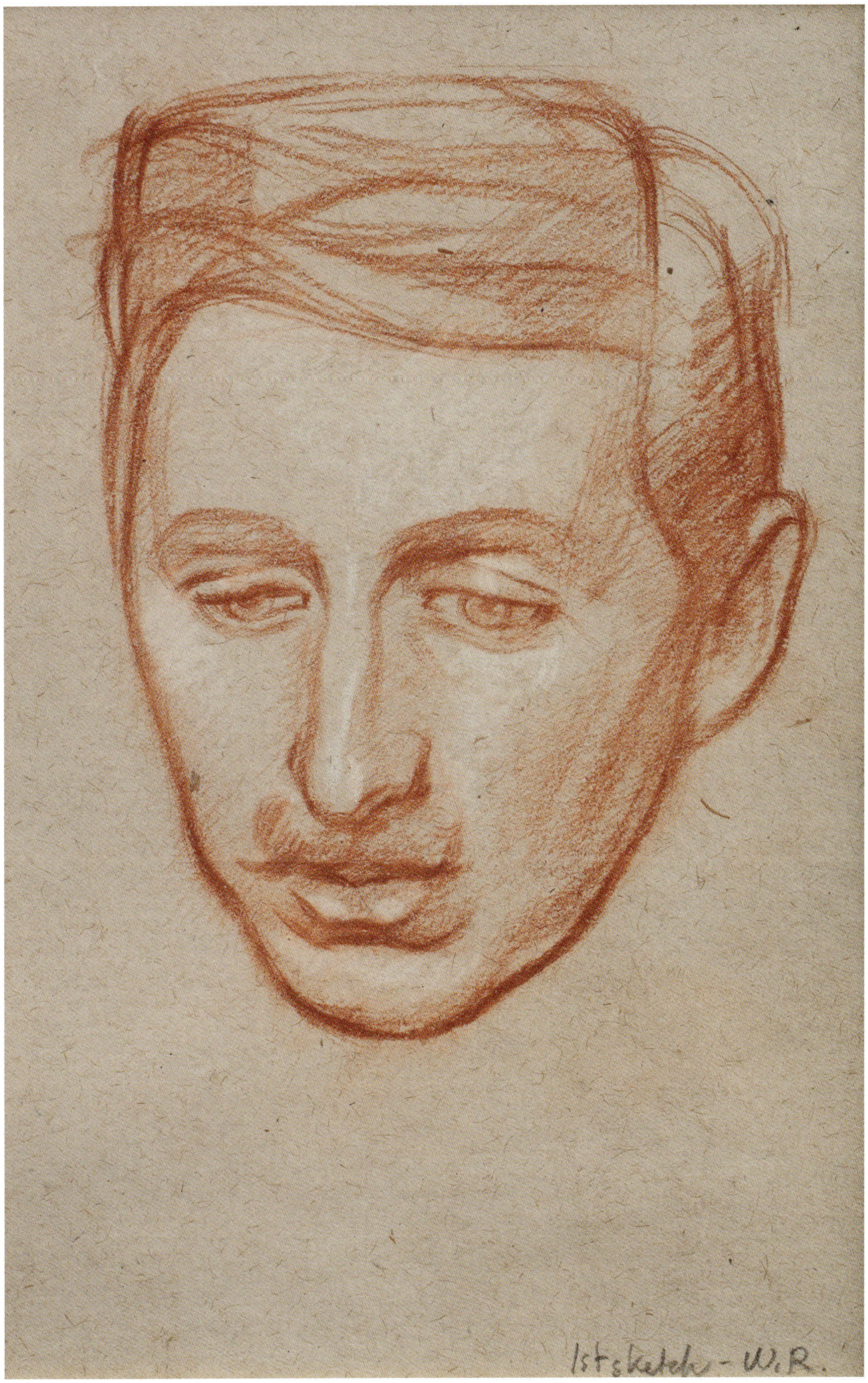
1st sketch - W.R.

ENDNOTES

'THE PROMISE OF ASTONISHING GENIUS'

1 'Sketches Life & Manners' in *Tait's Edinburgh Magazine*, cited under 'genius, II.9' in *The Oxford English Dictionary*, digital edition.
2 Augustus John, 'Fragment of an Autobiography – II,' *Horizon* (June 1941), pp. 395–6.
3 Claude Phillips, 'Twentieth century exhibition', *The Daily Telegraph*, 12 May 1914.
4 Lewis (1915), p. 80.
5 Marriott (1917), p. 4.
6 John (1964), p. 45.
7 *The Times*, obituary, 1 November 1961.
8 Rothenstein (1931), p. 334.
9 Ibid., pp. 333, 340, 346.
10 'The New English Art Club,' *The Athenaeum*, 15 Nov. 1902.
11 Anthony Blunt, 'Art: Augustus John', *The Spectator*, 27 May 1938.
12 'Genius, II.9' in *The Oxford English Dictionary*, digital edition.
13 James Creed Meredith, ed., *Kant's Critique of Aesthetic Judgement*, Clarendon Press, 1911, p. 168.
14 Jefferson (2015), pp. 81–2, 137.
15 Ibid., pp. 1–8; see also Christine Battersby, *Gender and Genius: Towards a Feminist Aesthetics*, The Women's Press, 1989.
16 Auguste Rodin to Camille Claudel, 1897, in Anne Rivière and Bruno Gaudichon, eds., *Camille Claudel: Correspondence*, Gaudichon, 2003, letter 121, p. 138.
17 'Why have there been no great women artists?' in Linda Nochlin, *Women, Art, and Power and Other Essays*, Harper & Row, 1988, p. 158.
18 *Guerrilla Girl's Code of Ethics for Art Museums* (1990, Tate).
19 Ruth Millington, 'The artist "genius": Are museums finally rethinking the myth?', 4 Nov. 2022, https://artuk.org/discover/stories/the-artist-genius-are-museums-finally-rethinking-the-myth.
20 Cody Delistraty, 'The myth of the artistic genius', *The Paris Review*, 8 January 2020.
21 Holroyd (1997), p. 49.
22 Virginia Woolf, 'Old Bloomsbury' (1921–2) in Jeanne Schulkind, ed., *Moments of Being: Autobiographical Writings*, Pimlico, 2002, p. 56; Lewis (1915), p. 80.
23 Gathorne-Hardy (1963), p. 157.
24 Letter from Lytton Strachey to Virginia Woolf, 1 Dec. 1912, quoted in Levy (2005), p. 217.
25 'The New English Art Club', *The Observer*, 24 Nov. 1912.
26 Walter Sickert, 'Whitechapel', *The New Age*, 28 May 1914, in Robins (ed.) (2000), pp. 372–373.
27 Letter from Wyndham Lewis to his mother, 1905, quoted in Rose (1963), p. 11.
28 Letter from Wyndham Lewis to his mother, July/Aug. 1906, quoted in Rose (1963), p. 38. See Richard Humphreys, 'Wyndham Lewis and Picasso', in James Beechey and Chris Stephens, eds., *Picasso and Modern British Art*, exh. cat., Tate Britain, 2012, pp. 73–75.
29 Lewis (1915), p. 80.
30 Draft letter from Wyndham Lewis to Malcolm MacDonald, Aug. 1943, quoted in Rose (1963), p. 359n.
31 Rothenstein (1931), p. 333.
32 Ibid., p. 353.
33 Rothenstein (1932), p. 130.
34 William Rothenstein, *Twenty-Four Portraits*, Chatto & Windus, 1923, n.p.
35 Letter from Gwen John to Auguste Rodin, c. 1906, Musée Rodin, MGJ/B.j5: 'J'était pensant avant de dormer de mon frère et comment il m'a fait misérable en Angleterre et comment j'étais miserable en Angleterre.' Author's translation from French original. See also Chitty (1981), p. 80.
36 'A Futurist Manifesto: Vita English Art', reproduced in Walsh (2002), pp. 76–77.
37 Lewis (1915), p. 80; letter from Wyndham Lewis to Augustus John, August(?) 1915, quoted in Rose (1963), pp. 70–2.
38 Hone (1939), p. 44; Duncan Grant, 'Memoir of the Year 1906–7', Tate Archive. TGA 8010/9/3, p. 18. For a recent study of this subject, see Mengting Yu, *London's Women Artists, 1900 – 1914: A Talented and Decorative Group*, Springer, 2020.

WORKS

1 Edna Clarke-Hall, 'The Heritage of Ages', Tate Archive. TGA 8226/2/1, f. 15.
2 Katherine Everett, *Bricks and Flowers: Memoirs of Katherine Everett*, The Reprint Society, 1951, p. 73.
3 John Piper, 'Art: Drawings by Augustus John', *The Spectator*, 13 Dec. 1940.
4 Letter from Spencer Gore to John Doman Turner, 25 Jan. 1909, quoted in Rothenstein (1957), p. 177; letter from Wyndham Lewis to his mother, 1905, quoted in Rose (1963), p. 11.
5 John (1964), p. 32; Holroyd (1997), p. 81.
6 Letter from Ida Nettleship to Edna Waugh, 30 Dec. 1895, quoted in Holroyd and John (2017), p. 31.
7 D.S. MacColl, 'Augustus John', in Fothergill (ed.) (1907), p. 9.
8 Letter from Ida Nettleship to Edna Waugh, 1 Jan. 1896, quoted in Holroyd and John (2017), p. 33.
9 Augustus John, 'Fragment of an Autobiography VII', *Horizon*, vol. VI, no. 32 (Aug. 1942), p. 129; Gathorne-Hardy (1963), p. 141.
10 *The Artist: An Illustrated Monthly Record of Arts, Crafts and Industries* (American Edition), Feb. 1901, p. 28; *The Athenaeum*, 12 April 1902.
11 Rutter (1933), pp. 77–84.
12 'Mr. John's Drawings', *The Manchester Guardian*, 19 March 1903; Rothenstein (1931), p. 2.
13 O'Keeffe (2000), pp. 69–70.
14 Lewis (1915), p. 80.
15 Letter from Wyndham Lewis to Augustus John, Aug. 1915(?), quoted in Rose (1963), pp. 70–72.
16 Letter from Dora Carrington to Lt. Noel Carrington, undated (March 1917), Harry Ransom Center, University of Texas at Austin.
17 Laurence Binyon, 'Preface', in *The Society of Twelve*, exh. cat., Obach & Co., 1904, n.p. D.S. MacColl, 'Augustus John', in Fothergill

Cat. 22 (detail)

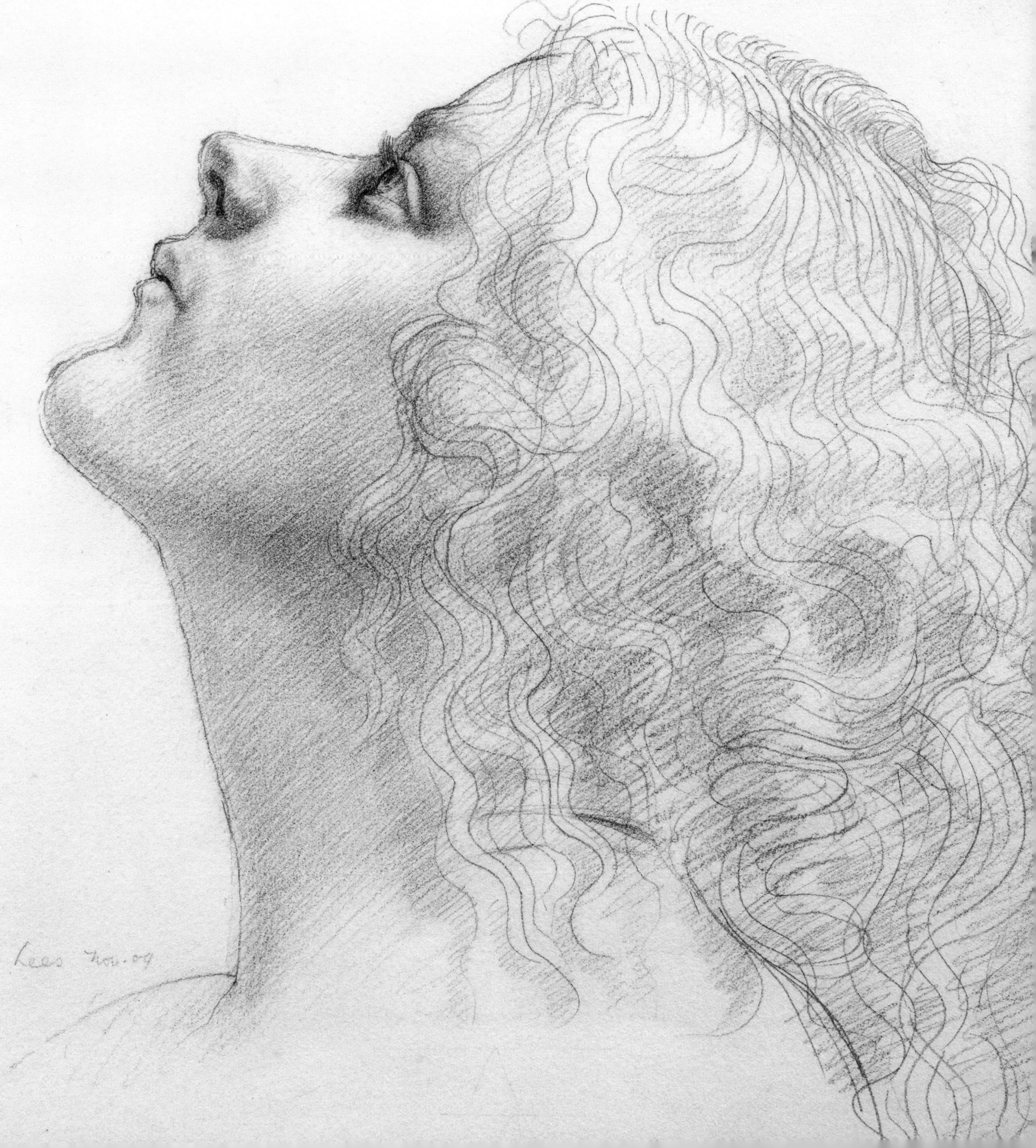
Lees Nov-09

(ed.) (1907), pp. 7–8.
18 Holroyd (1974), p. 44.
19 Edna Clarke-Hall, 'The Heritage of Ages', Tate Archive. TGA 8226/2/1, f. 60.
20 'The New English Art Club', *The Athenaeum*, 20 April 1901.
21 Rothenstein (1931), pp. 332–325.
22 Ibid., p. 333.
23 Ibid., p. 340.
24 Lewis (1951), p. 119.
25 Letter from Lucien Pissarro to Spencer Gore, undated, quoted in O'Keeffe (2000), p. 110. See also Richard Cork, *Vorticism and Abstract Art in the First Machine Age: Volume 1. Origin and Development*, Gordon Fraser, 1976, p. 15.
26 Michel and Fox (eds.) (1971), p. 457.
27 O'Keeffe (2000), pp. 160, 207.
28 Epstein (1955), p. 89.
29 T.E. Hulme, 'Mr. Epstein and the critics', *The New Age*, 25 Dec. 1913, quoted in Hynes (ed.) (1955), p. 104.
30 Arnold Haskell, *The Sculptor Speaks: Jacob Epstein to Arnold Haskell*, Heinemann, 1931, pp. 111–112.
31 Letter from Augustus John to Dorelia McNeill, c. Sept. 1911, NLW 22776, ff. 155–156, 158.
32 John (1952), p. 24.
33 John (1932), p. 8.
34 Jed Perl, 'The Armory Show made modern art something you love to Hate: Against the cult of novelty', *The New Republic*, 16 Feb. 2014.
35 Holroyd (1997), Appendix 3, p. 607.
36 John (1932), pp. 2, 3, 45.
37 Clements (1985), p. 48.
38 Letter from Lytton Strachey to Leonard Woolf, 7 Dec. 1905, quoted in Levy (2005), p. 86.
39 Letter from Virginia Woolf to Violet Dickinson, April 1906, quoted in Nicolson (ed.) (1975), p. 215; Virginia Woolf's diary, 2 Aug. 1920, quoted in Bell (1978), p. 54.
40 Clements (1985), p. 45.
41 Charles Maresco Pearce Memoir, Tate Archive. TGA 200724, f. 117.
42 Letter from Virginia Woolf to Violet Dickinson, May 1906, quoted in Nicolson (ed.) (1975), letter 1.219.
43 Clements (1985), p. 34.
44 Letter from Augustus John to Dorelia McNeill, probably spring 1906, NLW 22776D, ff. 60–61.
45 Letter from Augustus John to Henry Lamb, c. 1906, Tate Archive. TAM 15B.
46 Letter from Augustus John to Henry Lamb, undated (1908), Tate Archive. TAM 15B.
47 Clements (1985), p. 49.
48 Fothergill (1946), pp. 6–7, 12.
49 Jacob Epstein, *Let There Be Sculpture: An Autobiography*, Michael Joseph, 1940, p. 56.
50 Letter from Jacob Epstein to John Quinn, 1 May 1924, quoted in Gardiner (1993), p. 128; letter from Augustus John to John Quinn, 3 April 1915, quoted in Reid (1968), p. 203.
51 Letter from Jacob Epstein to John Quinn, 20 July 1917, quoted in Rose (2002), p. 108.
52 John (1952), p. 93.
53 Nicolette Devas, *Two Flamboyant Fathers*, Collins, 1966, pp. 39–40.
54 Letter from Henry Lamb to Lytton Strachey, 18 Aug. 1911, quoted in Moore-Gwyn (2019), p. 40.
55 'The New English Art Club', *The Times*, 22 May 1911; *The Glasgow Herald*, 4 Dec. 1911, quoted in Moore-Gwyn (2019), p. 17.
56 P.G. Konody, 'New English Art Club', *The Observer*, 18 Nov. 1906.
57 P.G. Konody, 'Art Notes: The New English Art Club', *The Observer*, 30 May 1909.
58 Moore-Gwyn (2019), p. 40.
59 Letter from Augustus John to Ottoline Morrell, summer 1908, Harry Ransom Center, University of Texas at Austin.
60 Lewis (1951), pp. 116–117.
61 Clements (1985), p. 90.
62 Ibid., p. 90.
63 Clements (1985), pp. 116–117.
64 Schwabe (1943), p. 9.
65 'Derwent Lees', *The Times*, 13 April 1934.
66 Edna Clarke-Hall, 'The Heritage of Ages', Tate Archive. TGA 8226/2/1, ff. 1.60–61.
67 Lawrence Hendra, ed., *Divine People: The Art & Life of Ambrose McEvoy 1877—1927*, exh. cat., Philip Mould & Co., 2019, p. 48.
68 Letter from Lytton Strachey to Leonard Woolf, 7 Dec. 1905, quoted in Levy (2005), p. 86.
69 Letter from W.B. Yeats to John Quinn, 4 Oct. 1907, quoted in Kelly (2005), 4.738–9.
70 Ibid.
71 Letter from John Quinn to Agnes Tobin, 21 Dec. 1909, quoted in Holroyd (1974), p. 318; letter from John Quinn to Townsend Walsh, 3 Sept. 1909, quoted in Reid (1968), p. 73.
72 D.S. MacColl, 'Augustus John', in Fothergill (ed.) (1907).
73 *The Athenaeum*, 15 Nov. 1902. Both paintings are now in Manchester Art Gallery.
74 Roger Fry, 'The Exhibition of Fair Women', *The Burlington Magazine*, vol. 15, no. 73 (April 1909), p. 17.
75 Laurence Binyon, 'The New English Art Club', *The Saturday Review*, 29 May 1909.
76 McConkey (2006), p. 105.
77 Lewis (1915), p. 81.
78 C.J. Holmes, 'Two modern pictures', *The Burlington Magazine*, vol. 15, no. 74 (May 1909), p. 81.
79 Rothenstein (1931), p. 3.
80 P.G. Konody, 'Art Notes: The New English Art Club', *The Observer*, 30 May 1909.
81 Hoole and Simons (2013), pp. 64, 81.
82 Letter from Augustus John to John Quinn, 10 Feb. 1911, quoted in Holroyd (1997), p. 354.
83 Letter from James Dickson Innes to Augustus John, undated, quoted in Hoole and Simons (2013), p. 76.
84 Letter from John Fothergill to Albert Rothenstein, quoted in Holroyd (1997), p. 353.
85 Fothergill (1946), p. 8.
86 Letter from Wyndham Lewis to Thomas Sturge Moore, undated, quoted in O'Keefe (2000), pp. 93–94. O'Keefe suggested the 'sickening bitch' was Euphemia Lamb, but it seems more likely that Lewis meant Dorelia.

87 John (1952), p. 206.
88 Rowan (1982), p. 19.
89 Frank Rutter, 'A contrast in methods', *The Sunday Times*, 15 April 1934.
90 Letter from Augustus John to Dorelia McNeill, March 1911, NLW 22776D, ff. 137–138.
91 Augustus John, Tate Archive. TAM 21F, 12/67.
92 Letter from Augustus John to John Rothenstein, 14 May 1952, quoted in Rothenstein (1970), p. 23.
93 Ibid., p. 23.
94 Augustus John, Tate Archive. TAM 21F, 12/67.
95 Letter from Augustus John to Dorelia McNeill, 3 Jan. 1913, NLW 22777D, ff. 17–18.
96 John (1952), pp. 202–203.
97 Ibid., p. 225.
98 Letter from Katherine Mansfield to Ottoline Morrell, 13 July 1917, quoted in Vincent O'Sullivan and Margaret Scott, eds., *The Collected Letters of Katherine Mansfield, Volume One*, Clarendon Press, 1984, pp. 316–317.
99 Clements (1985), p. 116.
100 Claude Phillips, 'Twentieth century exhibition', *The Daily Telegraph*, 12 May 1914.
101 John Turpin, 'The education of Irish artists, 1877 – 1975,' *Irish Arts Review Yearbook*, vol. 13 (1997), pp. 188–193.
102 Orpen (1924), pp. 4–5.
103 John Turpin, 'William Orpen as student and teacher', *An Irish Quarterly Review*, vol. 68 (Autumn 1979), pp. 173–192.
104 Arnold (1981), pp. 51–52, 284, 298, 303.
105 Michael Holroyd, 'Introduction', *Gwen John 1876–1939*, exh. cat., Anthony d'Offay, 1982, p. 2.
106 Draft letter from Gwen John to Véra Oumançoff, 1928, NLW 22288A, f. 13; Lloyd-Morgan (1995), p. 7. Translated from French.
107 Edna Clarke-Hall, 'The Heritage of Ages', Tate Archive. TGA 8226/2/1, ff. 1.23–24.
108 Letter from Gwen John to Michel Salaman, March 1902(?), NLW 14930C, ff. 22–23.
109 Tamboukou (2010), p. 105.
110 Roe (2001), p. 75.
111 Letter from Ida John to John Rothenstein, 25 Dec. 1906. Quoted in Holroyd and John (2017), p. 280.
112 Tamboukou (2010), pp. 56–57.
113 Hone (1939), p. 44.
114 Tamboukou (2010), p. 65.
115 Letter from Augustus John to John Rothenstein, 14 May 1952, quoted in Rothenstein (1970), pp. 21–22.
116 Augustus John, 'Fragment of an Autobiography VII', *Horizon*, vol. VI, no. 32 (Aug. 1942), p. 238. John actually wrote 'stick at nothing', rather than 'stop at nothing', but his meaning has subtly changed since the 1940s, and 'stop' conveys his meaning better.
117 Letter from Augustus John to John Rothenstein, 14 May 1952, quoted in Rothenstein (1970), p. 21. John's comments were in response to Rothenstein's essay about Gwen John in *Modern English Painters*.
118 Paul O'Keeffe, *Some Sort of Genius: A Life of Wyndham Lewis*, Pimlico, 2001, p. 127.
119 Lewis (1971), pp. 176–177.
120 O'Keeffe (2000), p. 114.
121 'A Cubist Room', *The Times*, 28 Feb. 1914. Letter from Augustus John to Dorelia McNeill, Feb. 1914, NLW 22777D, f. 40.
122 Letter from Wyndham Lewis to Augustus John, 17 Aug. 1948, quoted in Rose (1963), p. 456.
123 Thornton (1938), p. 5.
124 Rothenstein (1931), p. 26.
125 Ibid., p. 334.
126 Quoted in Holroyd (1997), p. 464.
127 Rothenstein (1957), pp. 126–7.
128 Samuel Shaw, 'Equivocal Positions: The Influence of Sir William Rothenstein, c. 1890–1910', PhD thesis, University of York, 2010, p. 9.
129 Ibid., p. 12.
130 Letter from Augustus John to William Rothenstein, undated (Sept. 1908), quoted in Holroyd (1997), p. 277.
131 Letter from William Rothenstein to Albert Rothenstein, 10 Sept. 1908, quoted in Holroyd (1974), pp. 187–188.
132 Letter from Augustus John to Ottoline Morrell, March 1909, Harry Ransom Center, University of Austin at Texas.
133 Rothenstein (1931), p. 368.

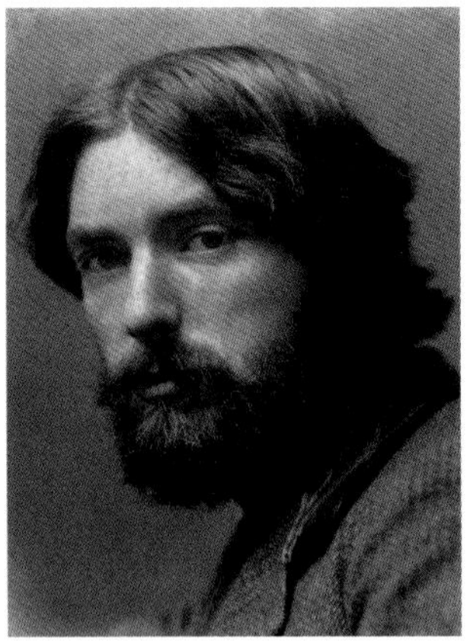

Augustus John

1878–1961

Referring to his prodigious natural talent, William Rothenstein wrote that Augustus John was born 'with a whole series of silver spoons between his gums'. He studied at the Slade School of Art between 1894 and 1898. In the summer holidays of 1897 he went to practise his diving from Giltar Point—a rocky promontory south of Tenby, Wales, where he grew up—and dashed his scalp open on the rock. A legend spread that he thereafter grew in confidence, bombast and talent. He lived in London at the turn of the century, mixing with the likes of McEvoy, Orpen and the brothers Will Rothenstein and Albert Rutherston, but he was often away from the city and lived variously in Liverpool, Matching Green in Essex, Paris, Dorset and finally Fordingbridge, Hampshire, where he settled in 1927. He and Orpen established the Chelsea Art School, which operated between 1903 and 1907. At the Café Royal in Regent's Street, John held court and attracted a wide following. Many admired his striking physical presence and Osbert Sitwell once described him as being 'like some kind of Rasputin-Jehovah'. He won acclaim for his informal, vividly characterised figure paintings and portraits including those of his wife Ida, whom he married in 1901, his mistress and later common law wife Dorothy ('Dorelia') McNeill, whom he met in 1903, and his children. Beyond his immediate circle he painted definitive portraits of William Nicholson (1909), George Bernard Shaw (1915) and Thomas Hardy (1923). He was elected a Royal Academician in 1928 and received the Order of Merit in 1942.

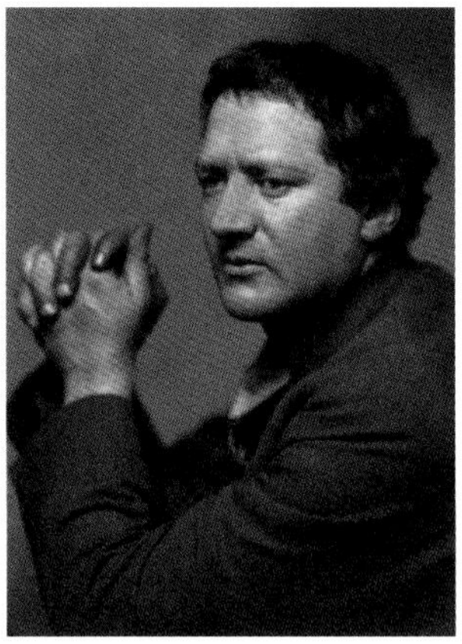

Jacob Epstein

1880–1959

In 1913, Wyndham Lewis described Jacob Epstein as 'the only great sculptor at present working in England.' Taking offence at Lewis and Epstein's *avant-garde* 'Pornometric gospel', Walter Sickert resigned in protest from the London Group shortly after its establishment in 1914. (Ironically, Sickert later resigned as a Royal Academician because the Academy's President failed to protest the mutilation of Epstein's carved sculptures on the British Medical Association building.) Epstein was born in New York, studied in Paris from 1902, first at the École des Beaux-Arts then the Académie Julian, and moved to London in 1905. He became a British citizen in 1907. Nina Hamnett remembered how 'Epstein lived in Cheyne Walk and I would stand outside hoping to get a glimpse of him. I saw him through the window one day.' Such was Epstein's fame. Among his most original works are the monument to Oscar Wilde in Père Lachaise cemetery, completed in 1912; *The Rock Drill*, documented in photographs and subsequently destroyed; and four carvings of mating doves. After the First World War, his output was predominantly bronze busts and figures modelled in clay. His subjects in this later style ranged widely and included Albert Einstein, William Blake and St Michael and the Devil, the latter made for the ruined shell of old Coventry Cathedral. Owing to the reputation he established early on, even in later life his very name could provoke 'general uneasiness' amongst the public. He was knighted in 1954.

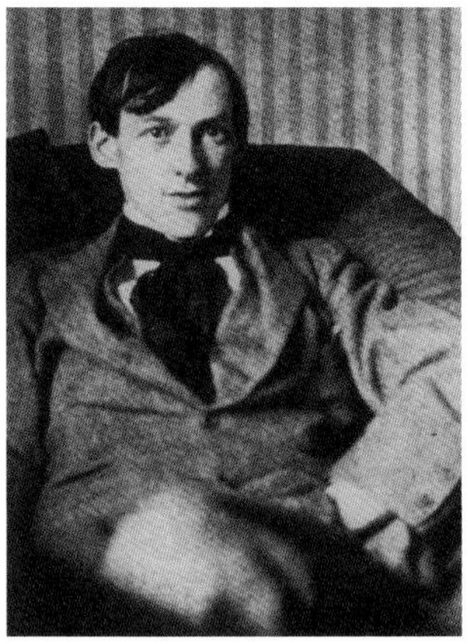

James Dickson Innes

1887–1914

Dick Innes, as his friends knew him, was born in Llanelli, Wales, but spoke with an English accent. His mother was said to be of Catalan descent. He studied at the Slade between 1905 and 1908 where he took inspiration from the painting tutor Philip Wilson Steer. Augustus John gave this striking description of his appearance: 'a Quaker hat, a coloured silk scarf, and a long black overcoat, set off features of a slightly cadaverous cast, with glittering black eyes, a wide sardonic mouth, a prominent nose and a large bony forehead, invaded by streaks of thin black hair.' He and John became close friends, probably meeting in the Café Royal, a favourite haunt of artists and bohemians, and they passed 'a considerable time together in Wales and elsewhere'. They established there a cottage overlooking the mountain Arenig Fawr, which Innes regarded, 'with good reason,' John wrote, 'as his spiritual property'. They spent the spring and summer of 1911 and 1912 painting there. Innes also painted in the south of France and Spain with Derwent Lees. He died young from tuberculosis yet he worked quickly, in Wales especially his 'activity was prodigious', and he produced a small but personally distinctive oeuvre of landscape paintings. He exhibited at the New English Art Club from 1907, had seven paintings and watercolours included in the Armory show in 1913 and was remembered in commemorative exhibitions at the Tate Gallery and the Chenil Galleries in the early 1920s.

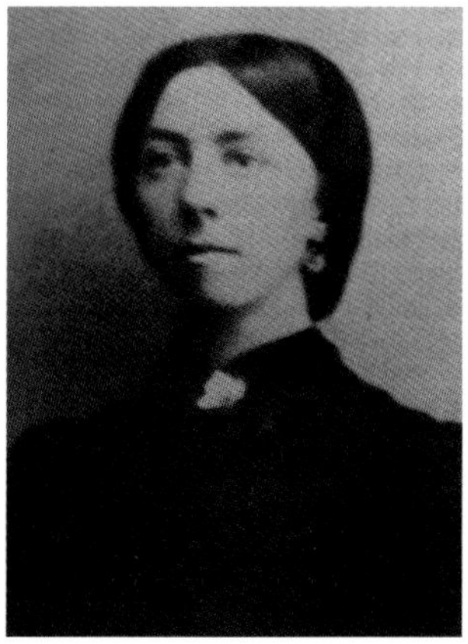

Gwen John

1876–1939

Borrowing Charlotte Brontë's description of her sister Emily, Kenneth Clark once took Gwen John to be 'stronger than a man, simpler than a child'. Her brother Augustus thought her a romantic and once wrote, 'Nobody suffered from frustrated love as she did.' She herself wrote that 'a beautiful life is one led, perhaps, in the shadow, but ordered, regular, harmonious.' As a student at the Slade between 1895 and 1898, she and her brother 'lived solely on fruit and nuts'. She then studied at Whistler's school in Paris and later modelled for the *Monument to Whistler* by Rodin, with whom she had a decade-long relationship from 1904. In 1903 she sailed for Bordeaux with her brother's lover, Dorelia McNeill, from where they embarked on a pilgrimage to Rome. They made it only as far as Toulouse, where they remained in the boarding house of a 'very very wicked' woman before moving the following year to Paris. She settled there permanently, only seldom returning to England and then not even when war broke out in 1914. She met the American lawyer and collector John Quinn in the summer of 1910, and his financial support permitted her to forsake modelling and pay more attention to painting. At Quinn's instigation, two of her paintings were included in the Armory show in 1913. Her subjects mostly consisted of still interiors and contemplative female figures, and her oeuvre is widely regarded as one of the most singular produced by any British artist in the first half of the twentieth century.

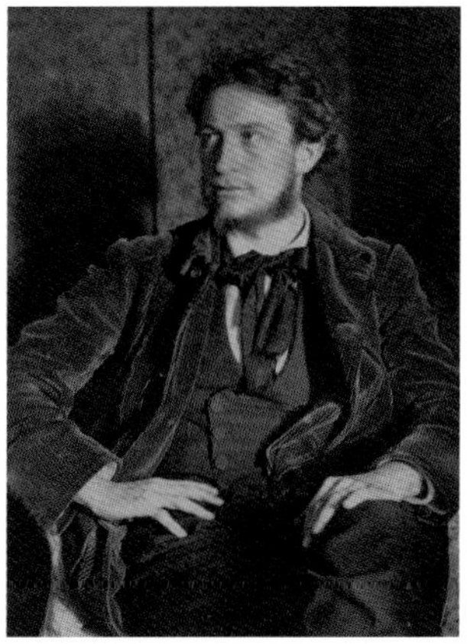

Henry Lamb

1883–1960

Born in Adelaide, Australia, raised in Manchester, and trained in medicine, Lamb only gradually resolved to become a painter. He fled Manchester for London in July 1905, absconding with his wife-to-be Nina Forrest (better known to all as Euphemia), and shortly afterwards encountered Augustus John with whom he frequented the taverns of Chelsea. In 1906 he studied with John and Orpen at the Chelsea Art School. He spent long periods in Paris and Brittany until 1911, and often saw John in Paris where they spent hours in the Rue de la Gaîté 'under the spell of an unusually efficient mechanical orchestra.' 'As a musician himself,' John recalled, 'Lamb, better than I, was able to disentangle the obscure symbolism of the infernal din.' Lamb's magnum opus was the large portrait of the author Lytton Strachey (1914), measuring eight feet by six and painted in the Vale of Health Hotel. He made a career from portraiture, later being elected as a Royal Academician in 1949, and painted persuasively life-like portrayals of the Behrend family (1927), Evelyn Waugh (1930) and Cecil Beaton (1935) among others. In 1928, Lamb and his second wife Pansy Pakenham settled at Coombe Bissett, Wiltshire. The architectural historian Mark Girouard, Lamb's one-time sitter, remembered that 'the most powerful object in [their house] was Stanley Spencer's great painting of the Centurion's servant', which the Tate Gallery acquired after Lamb's death. He was awarded the Military Cross in 1918 while serving with the Royal Army Medical Corps in Palestine.

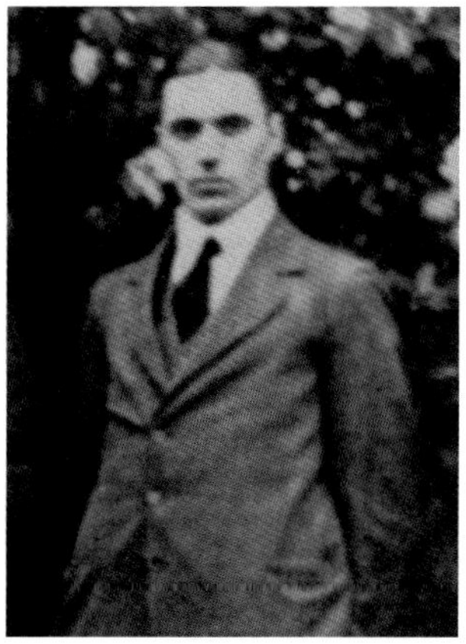

Derwent Lees

1884–1931

Lees travelled to Europe from Australia in 1905. Before this a riding accident had cost him a foot, in place of which he wore a prosthetic limb. He studied first at Melbourne University and then in Paris before attending the Slade, where he met Dick Innes whose approach to Nature he assimilated and practised with similar vitality and freshness. He remained at the Slade after completing his studies and served as Assistant Drawing Master between 1908 and 1918. Randolph Schwabe later recalled that '[h]is teaching was highly thought of by his colleagues and by those who came under him.' Schwabe also remarked that his technical facility enabled him, 'chameleon-like,' to adapt the styles of Innes, Augustus John and Ambrose McEvoy, all of whom he admired. (The biographer Michael Holroyd described him less sympathetically as a 'copycat of genius'.) Three landscapes by Lees were included in the International Exhibition of Modern Art at the Armory, New York, in 1913. The same year he married Edith Price, known as Lyndra, an artist's model who had sat for Augustus John. His career was curtailed by a severe mental illness, which saw him confined to asylums in Epsom, Surrey—later described as 'Europe's largest psychiatric hospital complex'—from 1919 until his death.

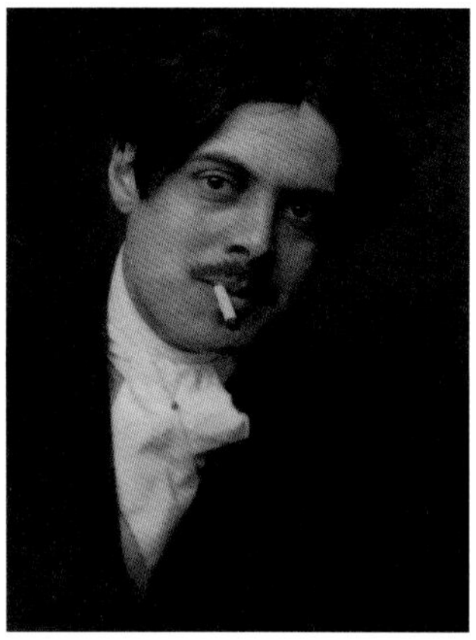

Wyndham Lewis

1882–1957

Lewis's father was American and he was reputedly born on the family yacht at Amherst, Nova Scotia. He attended Rugby School before winning a scholarship, aged sixteen, to train at the Slade, which he did between 1898 and 1901. According to Mary Chamot he became known as 'the best draughtsman at the Slade since John', with whom he established a tempestuous friendship. Remembering his first impressions of John, Lewis described him as 'one who had gigantic ear-rings, a ferocious red beard, a large angry eye, and who barked beautifully at you from his proud six foot, and, marvellously, was a great artist too.' John in turn thought that Lewis 'played the part of an incarnate Loki, bearing the news and sowing discord with it. He conceived the world as an arena, where various insurrectionary forces struggled to outwit each other in the game of artistic power politics.' After the Slade, Lewis travelled in Europe, variously studying and working in Munich, Paris, Holland and Spain until his return to England in 1909. Before the First World War he established a reputation as a precocious, sharp-penned member of the *avant-garde*. Absconding from the Omega Workshops, he publicly accused Roger Fry of lying and referred to it as a 'family party of strayed and Dissenting Aesthetes'. He became a proponent of Vorticism, established the Rebel Art Centre, edited the journal *BLAST* (1913/14), and joined the London Group at its formation in 1914. He latterly achieved fame as an author of modernist fiction including the novel *Tarr*.

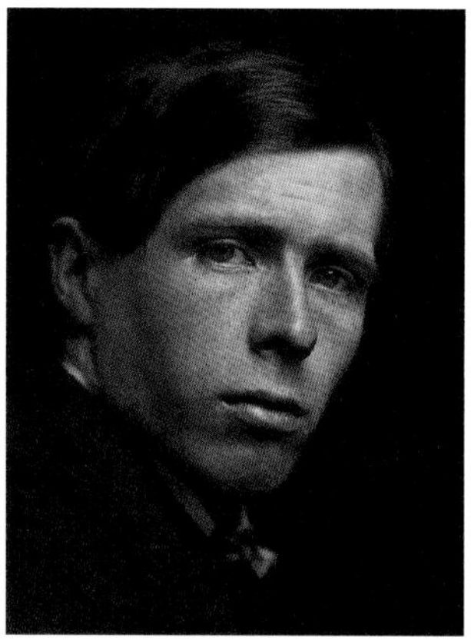

William Orpen

1878–1931

William Orpen first studied at the Metropolitan School of Art, Dublin, between 1890 and 1897. He then moved to London and attended the Slade between 1897 and 1899. His composition prize winner in 1899, *The Play Scene from 'Hamlet'*, was described by John Rothenstein as a masterpiece marked by the artist's 'exuberant whimsicality'. Rothenstein was Orpen's nephew and described him as 'a small man with a pale, high-cheekboned face, light grey eyes that observed much and revealed little and a figure without a trace of the atrophied staidness that marks most adults, being slim and active as a boy's.' With Augustus John, who admired his 'industry' and 'native drollery', he established the Chelsea Art School. The venture wound down as the principals 'began to waste too much time in conversation at the Cooper's Arms opposite.' Orpen later won financial rewards for his portraiture, but his artistic capabilities—sincere emotion, mordant satire, steeply-pitched drama, a biblical sense of characterisation—are richly apparent from three large-scale allegorical paintings, the 'Irish' trilogy, executed between 1913 and 1916: *Sowing New Seed, The Western Wedding* and *The Holy Well*. He mastered a wide range of genres, among them the nude, the self-portrait, and the group portrait. Of landscape, he depicted blasted haunts of the Western Front with devastating clarity. He was an Academician of the Royal Hibernian Academy between 1908 and 1915, received a knighthood in 1918 and was elected Royal Academician in 1919.

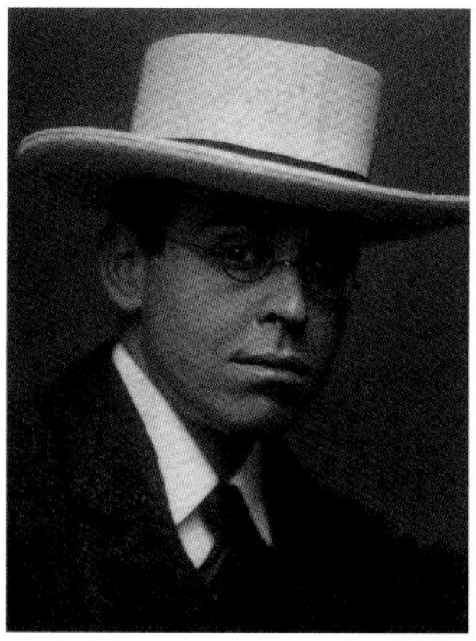

William Rothenstein

1872–1945

Referring to Balzac's *La Comédie humaine*, Will Rothenstein once said he wished 'to play the part of Vautrin to [Augustus John's] Lucien de Rubempré'. John once quipped that Rothenstein could 'turn wine into water'. They were close for a time despite John's ribbing, Rothenstein being the older man who had studied at the Slade under Alphonse Legros in 1888–89 and then in Paris at the Académie Julian in 1889–93. He gradually moved back to London in 1894 and made stylish and vivid pastel portraits of literary figures including George Moore, Arthur Symons and Oscar Wilde. He helped to establish the Carfax Gallery in 1899 and facilitated several early exhibitions of Augustus and Gwen John's work there. Between 1903 and 1908 Rothenstein painted scenes of Jewish ritual, one of which his friend Sickert described as being 'of National Gallery quality'. But it was his informal portrait drawings that secured him the greatest public recognition and many eminent figures sat to him. He was one of the best-connected nodes in the art world of his generation, as attested by his three volumes of memoir *Men and Memories*, and early in the 1900s his home in Hampstead hosted an impressive salon of artists and writers, Max Beerbohm, Jacob Epstein and W.B. Yeats amongst them. He latterly became an effective administrator and committee member as Principal of the Royal College of Art between 1920 and 1935 and a trustee of the Tate Gallery between 1927 and 1933. He was knighted in 1931.

Cat.35 (detail)

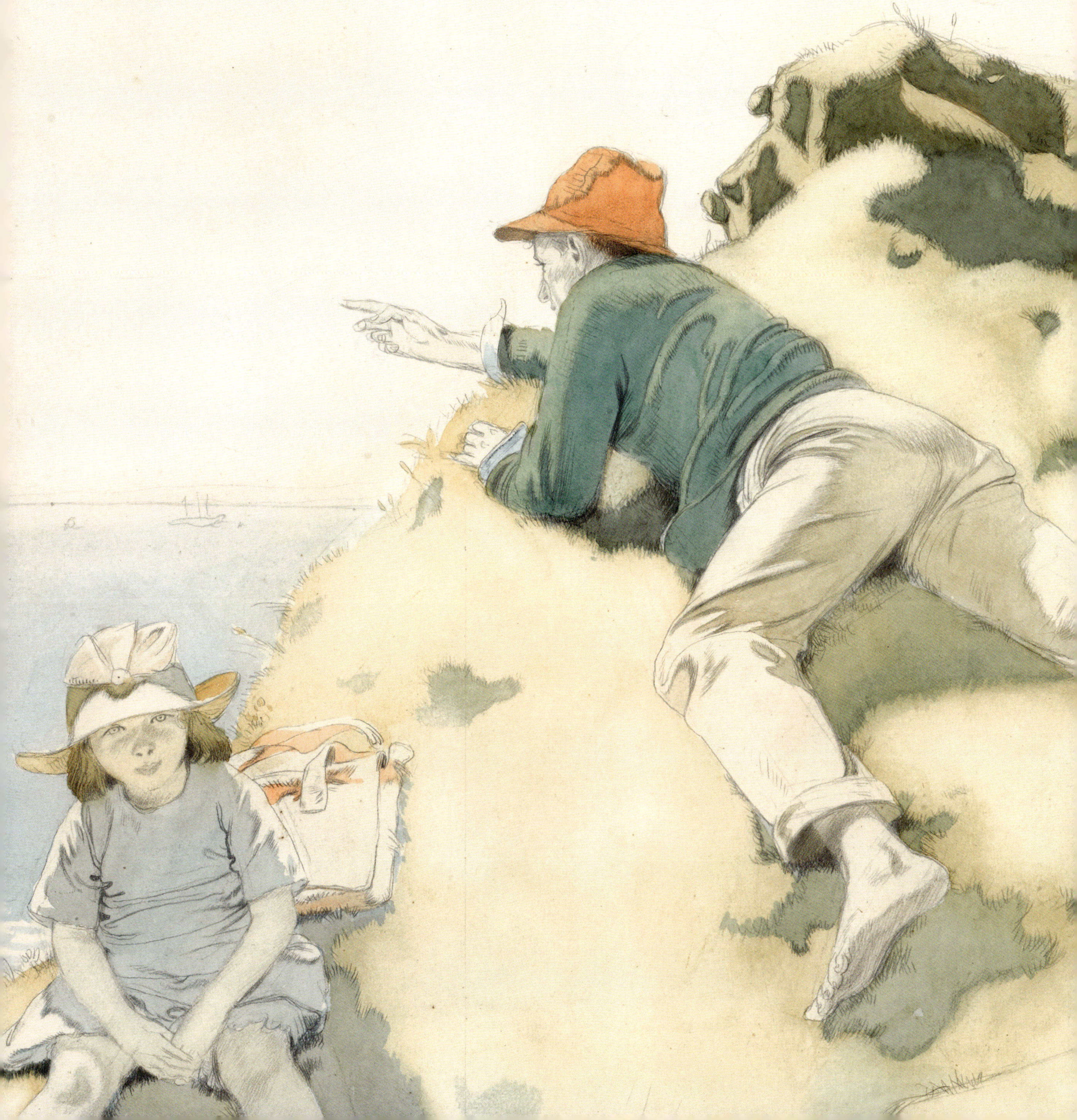

1894
Augustus John begins studying at the Slade School of Art, where he remains until 1898. He befriends many fellow students including Ambrose McEvoy, Benjamin Evans, Spencer Gore, his future wife Ida Nettleship, Michel Salaman, Gwen Salmond and Edna Waugh.

1895
Gwen John begins studying at the Slade, where she remains until 1898.

1897
William Orpen begins studying at the Slade, where he remains until 1899. In the summer, John, McEvoy and Evans go camping in Wales with a donkey.

1898
Wyndham Lewis begins studying at the Slade, where he remains until 1901. He first sees Augustus John on a visit to work in the life room.

1899
In summer, the newly married William and Alice Rothenstein stay in Vattetot, Normandy, where they are joined by William's brother Albert, Alice's sister Grace Knewstub, Charles Conder, Augustus John and Orpen.

1901
In January, Augustus John and Ida Nettleship marry at St Pancras Register Office in London. In August, Orpen and Grace Knewstub marry at All Saints Church, Highgate.

1902
McEvoy marries a fellow Slade alumnus Mary Edwards.

1902/3
Gwen John meets Dorothy ('Dorelia') McNeill and introduces her to Augustus, who quickly becomes infatuated and develops an unconventional living arrangement with her.

1903
Augustus John and Orpen establish the Chelsea Art School in Flood Street; it closes in 1907. Gwen John and Dorelia McNeill sail to Bordeaux and walk from there to Toulouse, where they live for a few months.

1904
Gwen John and McNeill go to Paris; John remains in the city and its suburbs for the rest of her life, only making occasional visits back to England.

1905
Jacob Epstein moves from Paris to London and meets Augustus John and other *eminences grises* of the New English Art Club. Derwent Lees moves from Australia to Paris and then London, and begins studying at the Slade, where he remains as a student until 1907 and then as an Assistant Drawing Master until 1918. James Dickson Innes also joins the Slade, where he remains until 1908. In July, Henry Lamb and Nina Forrest elope from Manchester to London; later in the year Lamb meets Augustus John in Chelsea and in 1906 joins the Chelsea Art School.

1907
Ida John dies in Paris following the birth of her fifth child.

1911
Lamb spends time in Brittany where he paints Dorelia's sister Edie McNeill. Innes, Augustus John, Lamb and Lewis become founder members of the Camden Town Group.

1911–13
John, Innes and Lees paint landscapes together in Snowdonia, Dorset and the south of France.

1913
The International Exhibition of Modern Art at the Armory, New York, includes work by James Dickson Innes, Augustus John, Gwen John and Derwent Lees.

1914
Augustus John and Euphemia Lamb visit Dick Innes in hospital shortly before his death. The First World War begins.

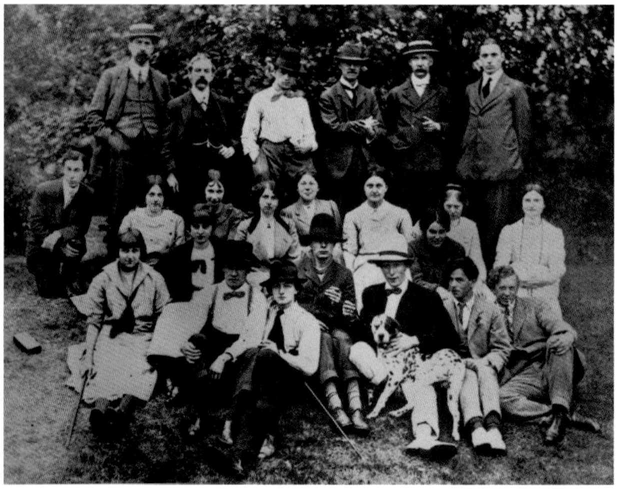

Fig. 14. Staff and students including Derwent Lees (top right) at the Slade School of Art annual summer picnic, c. 1912, Tate Archive Photograph Collection

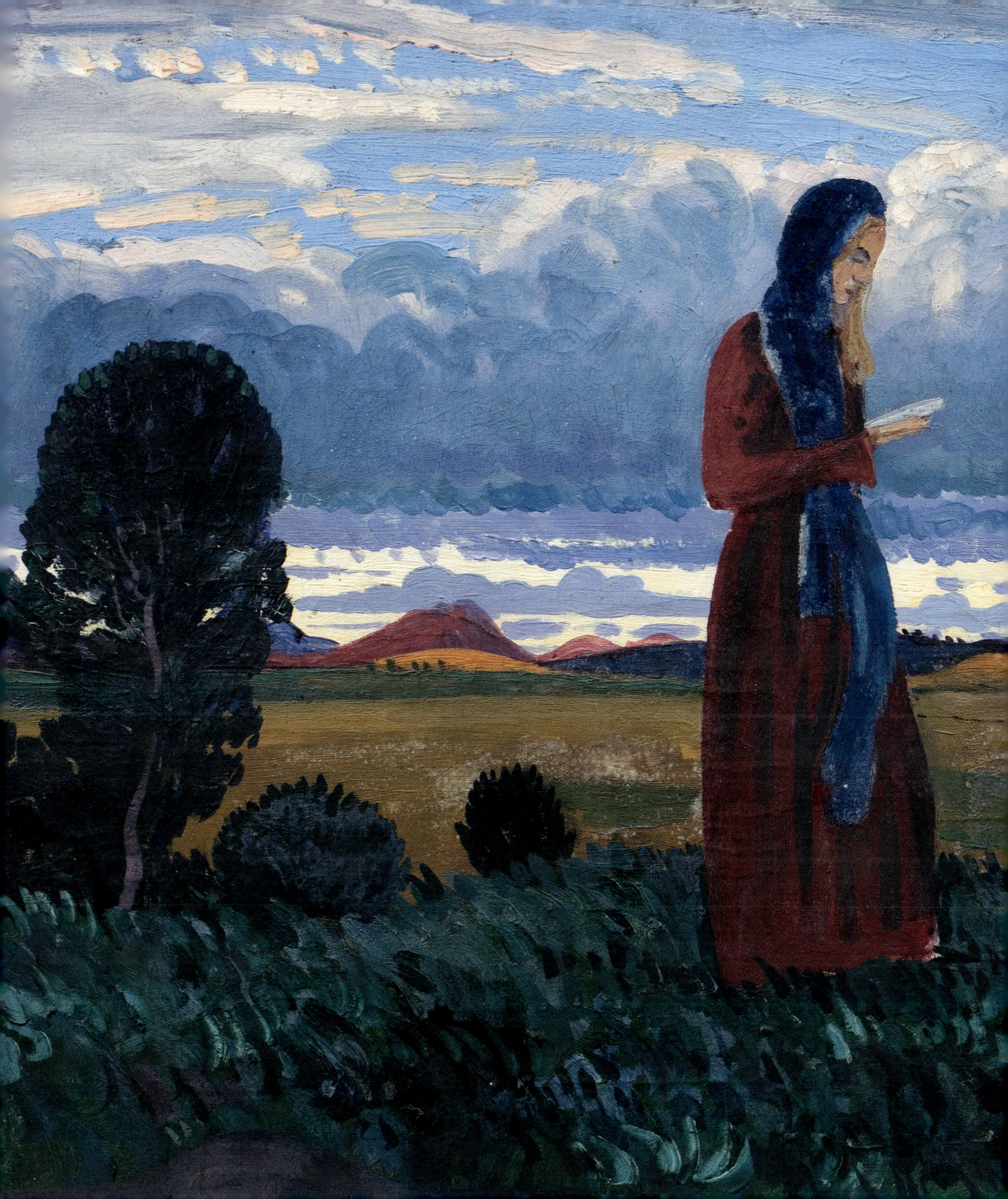

BIBLIOGRAPHY

Bruce Arnold, *Orpen: Mirror to an Age*, Jonathan Cape, 1981

Anne Olivier Bell, ed., *The Diary of Virginia Woolf, Volumes 1–2,* The Hogarth Press, 1977–1978

Lillian Browse, ed., *Augustus John: Drawings*, Faber & Faber, 1941

Keith Clements, *Henry Lamb: The Artist and his Friends*, The Redcliffe Press, 1985

Susan Chitty, *Gwen John 1876–1939*, Hodder & Stoughton, 1981

Jacob Epstein, *Epstein: An Autobiography*, E.P. Dutton, 1955

John Fothergill, ed., *The Slade: A Collection of Drawings and some Pictures Done by Past and Present Students of the London Slade School of Art, 1893–1907*, Richard Clay & Sons, 1907

John Fothergill, *James Dickson Innes*, Faber & Faber, 1946

David Fraser Jenkins and Chris Stephens, eds., *Gwen John and Augustus John*, exh. cat., Tate Britain, 2004

Stephen Gardiner, *Epstein: Artist Against the Establishment*, Flamingo, 1993

Robert Gathorne-Hardy, ed., *Ottoline: The Early Memoirs of Lady Ottoline Morrell*, Faber & Faber, 1963

David Boyd Haycock, *Augustus John: Drawn from Nature*, exh. cat., Paul Holberton Publishing, 2018

David Boyd Haycock, *Brilliant Destiny: The Age of Augustus John*, Lund Humphries, 2023

Michael Holroyd, *Augustus John: A Biography, Volume 1*, William Heinemann, 1974

Michael Holroyd, *Augustus John: The New Biography*, Vintage, 1997

Michael Holroyd and Rebecca John, *The Good Bohemian: The Letters of Ida John*, Yale University Press, 2017

Joseph Hone, *The Life of Henry Tonks*, William Heinemann, 1939

John Hoole and Margaret Simons, *James Dickson Innes 1887--1914*, Lund Humphries, 2013

Sam Hynes, ed., *Further Speculations by T.E. Hulme*, University of Minnesota Press, 1955

Ann Jefferson, *Genius in France: An Idea and its Uses*, Princeton University Press, 2015

Augustus John, *Chiaroscuro: Fragments of Autobiography*, Jonathan Cape, 1952

Augustus John, *Finishing Touches*, Jonathan Cape, 1964

Romilly John, *The Seventh Child: A Retrospect*, William Heinemann, 1932

John Kelly, ed., *The Collected Letters of W.B. Yeats*, Oxford University Press, 2005

P.G. Konody and Sidney Dark, *Sir William Orpen: Artist and Man*, Seeley Service & Co., 1932

Cecily Langdale, *Gwen John: With a Catalogue Raisonné of the Paintings and a Selection of the Drawings*, Yale University Press, 1987

Paul Levy, ed., *The Letters of Lytton Strachey*, Viking, 2005

Wyndham Lewis, 'History of the Largest Independent Society in England', *BLAST*, vol. 2 (July 1915), pp. 80–81

Wyndham Lewis, *Rude Assignment: A Narrative of my Career up to Date*, Hutchinson & Co., 1951

Ceridwen Lloyd-Morgan, *Gwen John Papers at the National Library of Wales*, The National Library of Wales, 1995

Charles Marriott, *Masters of Modern Art: Augustus John*, Colour Ltd., 1917

Kenneth McConkey, *The New English: A History of the New English Art Club*, Royal Academy of Arts, 2006

Walter Michel and C.J. Fox, eds., *Wyndham Lewis on Art: Collected Writings 1913–1956*, Thames & Hudson, 1971

Harry Moore-Gwyn, *Henry Lamb: Out of the Shadows*, exh. cat., Paul Holberton Publishing, 2019

Nigel Nicolson and Joanne Trautmann, eds., *The Letters of Virginia Woolf, Volumes I–IV*, The Hogarth Press, 1975–1978

Paul O'Keeffe, *Some Sort of Genius: A Life of Wyndham Lewis*, Jonathan Cape, 2000

William Orpen, *Stories of Old Ireland and Myself*, Williams & Northgate, 1924

B.L. Reid, *The Man from New York: John Quinn and his Friends*, Oxford University Press, 1968

Anna Gruetzner Robins, ed., *Walter Sickert: The Complete Writings on Art*, Oxford University Press, 2000

Sue Roe, *Gwen John: A Life*, Chatto & Windus, 2001

June Rose, *Demons and Angels: A Life of Jacob Epstein*, Carroll & Graf Publishers, 2002

W.K. Rose, ed., *The Letters of Wyndham Lewis*, Methuen & Co., 1963

John Rothenstein, *The Portrait Drawings of William Rothenstein 1889–1925*, Chapman & Hall, 1925

John Rothenstein, *Modern English Painters: Sickert to Moore*, Eyre & Spottiswoode, 1957

John Rothenstein, *Time's Thievish Progress: Autobiography III*, Cassell, 1970

William Rothenstein, *Men and Memories: Recollections of William Rothenstein, 1872–1900*, Faber & Faber, 1931

William Rothenstein, *Men and Memories: Recollections of William Rothenstein, 1900–1922*, Faber & Faber, 1932

Eric Rowan, *Some Miraculous Promised Land: J.D. Innes, Augustus John and Derwent Lees in North Wales, 1910–13*, exh. cat., Mostyn Art Gallery, 1982

Albert Rutherston, ed., *Ambrose McEvoy*, Ernest Benn, 1924

Frank Rutter, *Art in My Time*, Rich & Cowan, 1933

Randolph Schwabe, 'Reminiscences of Fellow Student', *The Burlington Magazine*, vol. 82, no. 478 (Jan. 1943), pp. 6–9

Evelyn Silber, *The Sculpture of Epstein*, Bucknell University Press, 1986

Maria Tamboukou, *In the Fold Between Power and Desire: Women Artists' Narratives*, Cambridge Scholars Publishing, 2010

Mary Taubman, *Gwen John: A Retrospective Exhibition*, exh. cat., Arts Council, 1968

Alfred Thornton, *The Diary of an Art Student of the Nineties*, Sir Isaac Pitman & Sons, 1938

Robert Upstone with R.F. Foster and David Fraser Jenkins, *William Orpen: Politics, Sex & Death*, exh. cat., Imperial War Museum, 2005

Michael Walsh, *C.R.W. Nevinson: This Cult of Violence*, Yale University Press, 2002

INDEX

ACKNOWLEDGEMENTS

Piano Nobile wishes to extend our sincere gratitude to all those who have been involved with facilitating this exhibition and publication. We are also grateful to all those who have kindly contributed content or lent works, many of whom wish to remain anonymous. We would especially like to acknowledge with profound thanks Rebecca John, who has been generous with her advice and support.

Jonathan Anderson

Wendy Baron

Ben Uri Gallery & Museum, London

Arabella Bishop

Patrick and Cordelia Bourne

Mickey Charouneau

The Most Hon. The Marquess of Cholmondeley

Charles Cholmondeley

Duncan Clark

Jonathan and Adam Clark

Nikki Coleman

Jemma Craig

Joshua Darby

Lynn and Peter Davies

Anthony d'Offay

Robert Enserro and Vanessa Colomar

Nigel Farrow

Edmund Fetherston-Dilke

Olivia Fetherston-Dilke

Natalia Fetherston-Dilke

Victor James

David Fraser Jenkins

Rebecca John

Christopher Kingzett

Kasia Kolendarska

Lady Amabel Lindsay

Ludovic Lindsay

Sarah MacDougall

Kenneth McConkey

Rupert Maas

Clare Matthews

Charlie Minter

Rebecca Moisan

Philip Mould

Andrea Obholzer

Stephen Ongpin

Gillian and Piers Recordon

Stuart and Jenny Sanderson

Ruth Seager

Richard Shone

Southampton City Art Gallery

Dan and Henrietta Thornton

Isidor Travers

Romilly Turton

Gordon Vint

Jack Wakefield

Francesca Whitham

Cat. 39 (detail)

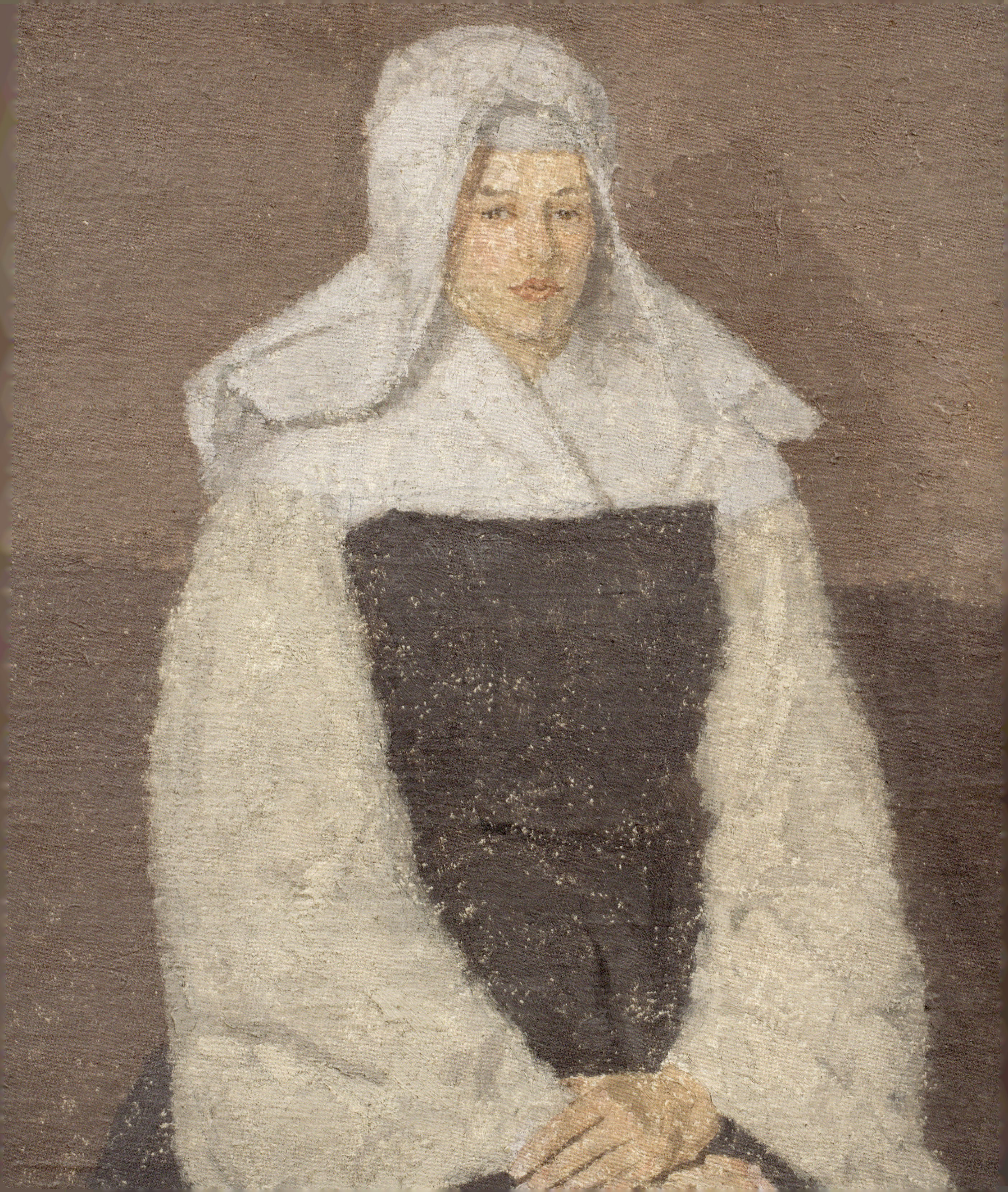

COLOPHON

Published on the occasion of

AUGUSTUS JOHN
& the First Crisis of Brilliance

26 April – 13 July 2024

Piano Nobile Publications No. LXI
978-1-901192-65-0

Editorial Director
Matthew Travers

Essay and catalogue entries
David Boyd Haycock

Cataloguing and artist biographies
Luke Farey

Logistics
Selina Fischer

Image Research and Editorial
Polly Pentreath

Press and Digital
Hannah Bestley Burt

Design
Graham Rees Design

Print and Binding
Gomer Press

Photography
Colin Mills

Proof-reader
Katharine Ridler

Index
Emma Caddy

Author

Distributed by Casemate Group
The Old Music Hall
106–109 Cowley Road
Oxford, OX4 1JE
casemategroup.com

Piano Nobile was established by Dr Robert Travers in 1985. The gallery plays an active role in the market for twentieth-century British and international modern and contemporary art. With curatorial flair, a refined aesthetic and rigorous scholarship, we seek to source and present exceptional works of art. Whether our clients are buying or selling, we place the utmost importance on discretion and tailoring to the specific needs of each individual. The gallery also acts as an agent for private, corporate and museum collections, dealing with appraisals, acquisitions and dispersals.

Front cover:
Cat. 33 (detail)

Frontispiece:
Augustus John, c. 1907, photographed by Jacob Hilsdorf

Page 4:
Cat. 18

Page 14:
Cat. 13 (detail)

Page 116:
Augustus John, 1902, photographed by George Charles Beresford; Jacob Epstein, 1916, photographed by George Charles Beresford; James Dickson Innes, n.d., unknown photographer

Page 117:
Gwen John, c. 1902, unknown photographer; Henry Lamb, n.d., unknown photographer; Derwent Lees at the Slade School of Art annual summer picnic, c. 1912, Tate Archive Photograph Collection (detail)

Page 118:
Wyndham Lewis, 1913, photographed by George Charles Beresford; William Orpen, 1903, photographed by George Charles Beresford; William Rothenstein, 1902, photographed by George Charles Beresford

Back cover:
Cat. 42 (detail)

PIANO NOBILE

Piano Nobile | Robert Travers (Works of Art) Ltd
96 / 129 Portland Road | London W11 4LW | +44 (0)20 7229 1099
info@piano-nobile.com | piano-nobile.com

9 781901 192650